Globalisation and Equality

Is globalisation creating a more unequal world? Is it creating new forms of inequality? Does it make certain pre-existing forms of inequality more morally or politically significant than they would otherwise have been?

Globalisation and Equality examines these and related questions, exploring the way increasing globalisation is challenging our conceptions of equality.

The contributors explore these themes from both theoretical and empirical perspectives. Some adopt a more abstract approach, exploring foundational questions concerning the meaning of equality, its social and political dimensions, and more specifically its moral implications in a global context. Others engage the general themes of globalisation and equality by focusing on specific topics, such as welfare, citizenship, gender, culture and the environment.

Original in the questions it poses, and interdisciplinary in its approach, this collection of essays will appeal to all those with an interest in globalisation and equality.

Keith Horton is a Research Fellow at the Centre for Applied Philosophy and Public Ethics, Charles Sturt University, Australia.

Haig Patapan is Senior Lecturer in the School of Politics and Public Policy, Griffith University, Australia.

Routledge/Challenges of Globalisation
Edited by Charles Sampford and Haig Patapan
Griffith University, Australia

1 Globalisation and Equality
Edited by Keith Horton and Haig Patapan

Globalisation and Equality

Edited by Keith Horton and
Haig Patapan

Routledge
Taylor & Francis Group

LONDON AND NEW YORK

First published 2004
by Routledge
2 Park Square, Milton Park, Abingdon, Oxon, OX14 4RN

Simultaneously published in the USA and Canada
by Routledge
270 Madison Ave, New York NY 10016

Routledge is an imprint of the Taylor & Francis Group

Transferred to Digital Printing 2006

© 2004 Keith Horton and Haig Patapan for selection and editorial
matter; individual contributors for their chapters

Typeset in Baskerville MT by
Newgen Imaging Systems (P) Ltd, Chennai, India

British Library Cataloguing in Publication Data
A catalogue record for this book is available from the British Library

Library of Congress Cataloging in Publication Data
    Globalisation and equality/edited by Keith Horton and Haig Patapan.
        p. cm.
    Includes bibliographical references and index.
        1. Equality. 2. Globalization. I. Horton, Keith, 1961–
    II. Patapan, Haig, 1959–

    JC575.G633 2004
    323.42–dc22   2003020757

ISBN10: 0–415–32539–0 (hbk)
ISBN10: 0–415–42973–0 (pbk)

ISBN13: 978–0–415–32539–4 (hbk)
ISBN13: 978–0–415–42973–3 (pbk)

Contents

Notes on contributors   vi
Acknowledgements   ix

1 **Introduction**   1
   KEITH HORTON AND HAIG PATAPAN

2 **Equality and globalization**   6
   GARRETT CULLITY

3 **Globalising equality: the Equal Worth Project**   23
   TOM CAMPBELL

4 **Moral universalism and global economic justice**   49
   THOMAS W. POGGE

5 **Reclaiming equality in a globalised world**   77
   DUNCAN KERR

6 **Welfare, equality and globalisation: reconceiving
   social citizenship**   95
   SHEILA SHAVER

7 **Gender, equality and globalization**   114
   GILLIAN YOUNGS

8 **Globalisation for a multicultural world**   129
   BHIKHU PAREKH

9 **Environment, equality and globalisation**   146
   GIOREL CURRAN

10 **Legacy of danger: the *Kyoto Protocol* and
   future generations**   164
   HENRY SHUE

References   179
Index   191

Contributors

Tom Campbell is Professorial Fellow in the Centre for Applied Philosophy and Public Ethics (CAPPE), Charles Sturt University, Canberra. He was formerly Professor of Law at the Australian National University and Professor of Jurisprudence at the University of Glasgow. He is Visiting Professor at the School of Law, King's College, London. Professor Campbell is the author of *The Left and Rights* (1985), *The Legal Theory of Ethical Positivism* (1996) and *Justice* (2nd edn 2001).

Garrett Cullity is a Senior Lecturer in the Philosophy Department at the University of Adelaide. He previously taught in the Department of Moral Philosophy at the University of St Andrews. He writes and teaches in the areas of applied, theoretical and meta-ethics. His book, *The Moral Demands of Affluence*, will be published by Oxford University Press.

Giorel Curran is a Lecturer in the School of Politics and Public Policy, Griffith University. Her main research interests include environmental political theory, environmental policy, democratic theory and practice and neo-populism. She has published regularly in the areas of environmental political theory and environmental policy for both national and international journals and has recently co-edited *Business, Government and Globalisation* (Pearson, 2002).

Keith Horton is a Research Fellow at the Centre for Applied Philosophy and Public Ethics, Charles Sturt University, Australia. His main research interests are in moral philosophy. He is the author of *Should We Give to Aid Agencies?* (Edinburgh University Press (forthcoming)).

Duncan Kerr MP is a member of the Australian Parliament representing the electorate of Denison for the Australian Labor Party and a barrister. He was formerly Attorney General and then Minister for Justice in the Keating government (1993–96). Before his election to parliament he was Crown Counsel for the state of Tasmania and Dean of the Faculty of Law, University of Papua New Guinea. He has written several legal texts and articles (as Duncan Colquhoun-Kerr) and two books for the general public. His most recent book is *Elect the Ambassador: Building Democracy in a Globalised World* (Pluto Press, 2001).

Bhikhu Parekh is Centennial Professor at the London School of Economics and Professor of Political Philosophy at the University of Westminster. He is a Fellow of the British Academy, President of the Academy of the Learned Societies in Social Sciences and a Labour Member of the House of Lords. He has written extensively in the fields of political philosophy, history of political thought and Indian political ideas. His latest book, *Rethinking Multiculturalism*, was published by Macmillan, London and Harvard University Press, in 2000. He is currently completing a book on the nature and logic of the politics of identity. He is also active in British public life and chaired the Commission on the Future of Multi-Ethnic Britain whose report was published in 2000. He has frequently broadcast on British radio and television on race relations and international politics.

Haig Patapan is Senior Lecturer in the School of Politics and Public Policy, Griffith University. His main research interests are in political theory, constitutionalism and jurisprudence. His book, *Judging Democracy* (Cambridge University Press, 2000), examines the way the judiciary is shaping democracy in Australia.

Thomas W. Pogge teaches moral and political philosophy at Columbia University. He is the author of *Realizing Rawls* (Cornell University Press, 1989), and *World Poverty and Human Rights* (Polity Press, 2002) and the editor of *Global Justice* (Blackwell, 2001). He has also published a number of essays on the work of Immanuel Kant. He is editor for social and political philosophy for the Stanford Encyclopedia of Philosophy and a member of the Norwegian Academy of Science. His work was supported, most recently, by the John D. and Catherine T. MacArthur Foundation, the Princeton Institute for Advanced Study and All Souls College, Oxford.

Sheila Shaver is Pro Vice-Chancellor Research at the University of Western Sydney. She was formerly Professor of Sociology and Social Policy at the University of New South Wales, and Deputy Director of the Social Policy Research Centre, where she conducted the research reported here. Her main research interests are in the sociology of social policy, gender and the welfare state. In recent years she has pursued these through comparative international study of welfare states and social policies. Her most recent book is *States, Markets, Families, Gender, Liberalism and Social Policy in Australia, Canada, Great Britain and the United States* (Cambridge University Press, 1999), written jointly with Julia S. O'Connor and Ann Shola Orloff.

Henry Shue is a Senior Research Fellow of Merton College and Professor of Politics and International Relations, Oxford University. He was a founding member of the Institute for Philosophy and Public Policy at the University of Maryland and the inaugural Hutchinson Professor of Ethics and Public Life at Cornell University. Best known for *Basic Rights* (Princeton, 1980; 2nd edn 1996), he has written a series of eight previous articles on issues of justice raised by attempts to slow climate change, beginning with 'The Unavoidability of Justice' (1992) and 'Subsistence Emissions and Luxury Emissions' (1993). The other focus of his current research is limits on war, especially constraints on acceptable targets for bombing.

Gillian Youngs is Senior Lecturer in the Department of Politics and the Centre for Mass Communication Research, University of Leicester. She conducts research and policy-related work on globalization, gender and global restructuring, feminism and women and information and communications technologies. She is author of *International Relations in a Global Age: A Conceptual Challenge* (Polity, 1999), editor of *Political Economy, Power and the Body: Global Perspectives* (Macmillan, 2000) and co-editor of *Globalization: Theory and Practice* 2nd edn (Continuum, 2003). She is co-editor of *International Feminist Journal of Politics*, associate editor of *Development* and serves on the editorial board of *Political Geography*.

Acknowledgements

This book had its origins in a Workshop held in Canberra, Australia in July 2001. We would like to thank the Centre for Applied Philosophy and Public Ethics (CAPPE), Charles Sturt University, and the Key Centre for Ethics, Law, Justice and Governance (KCELJAG), Griffith University, for their assistance both in organising that Workshop, and in producing this book. We would also like to thank all those who attended the Workshop: Tom Campbell, David Coady, Margaret Coady, Tony Coady, Garrett Cullity, Robert Fullinwider, Duncan Kerr, Brendan Mackey, Jeremy Moss, Tim Mulgan, Thomas Pogge, Emma Rooksby, Charles Sampford, Sheila Shaver and Henry Shue.

The editors and publishers would like to thank Sage Publications for allowing us to reprint 'Moral Universalism and Global Economic Justice' by Thomas W. Pogge, which originally appeared in *Politics, Philosophy and Economics*, Vol. 1 (1), 2002.

1 Introduction

Keith Horton and Haig Patapan

It has become increasingly common, in recent years, to raise concerns linking the two main themes of this volume, globalisation and equality. It is often claimed, for example, that globalisation is exacerbating social and economic inequalities both within and between countries. Another claim is that, as well as exacerbating pre-existing inequalities, globalisation is creating new forms of inequality, such as inequalities in power to shape the rules which regulate the emerging global order. And a third is that, whether or not it is exacerbating pre-existing inequalities, or creating new forms of inequality, globalisation makes certain inequalities more morally or politically significant than they would otherwise have been. According to those who make this third claim, there is more reason to be concerned about certain inequalities in a more globalised world than there would be in a less globalised world.

Claims like these raise a great variety of questions. Some of those questions are conceptual or semantic. Thus one needs to ask, for example, what precisely those who make such claims are referring to when they talk about 'globalisation', and what the 'metric' or 'currency' of the relevant comparisons are. Equality or inequality of *what*, exactly? And then there are a variety of empirical questions. Does the available data actually support the claim that economic inequalities within countries have increased during the period of globalisation, for example? And if so, does it also support the claim that globalisation – on one or another specification of that term – is a major causal factor in such change?

But perhaps the deepest questions raised by the kinds of claims sketched earlier are normative questions concerning exactly why such inequalities might be taken to matter, morally or politically speaking. For example, take the case of inequalities in income between people living in the world's richer and poorer countries. These inequalities are extreme, and growing. To quote from the 1999 United Nations Development Report, 'The income gap between the fifth of the world's people living in the richest countries and the fifth in the poorest was 74 to 1 in 1997, up from 60 to 1 in 1990 and 30 to 1 in 1960' (UNDP 1999: 3).

Just about everyone finds these statistics disturbing. But what exactly is it that is so troubling about them? A variety of different answers might be given to this question. And each of those answers raises further questions. Thus one might find the statistics in question troubling, for example, because one thinks that everyone in the world should have roughly equal life chances, and that rough equality of income is necessary in order to assure this. But if that is the source of one's concern, then the next question to ask is why one thinks that everyone should have roughly equal life chances. Does one think that such an equal distribution of life chances would be good in itself? And if so, again, why does one think this? Or does one think that such a distribution, rather than being good in itself, would be good in virtue of its consequences? But if so, what consequences?

Alternatively, instead of stemming from the thought that an equal distribution of something or other would be good, one's concern about such statistics might stem from the thought that we should not let anyone slip below some minimum standard. Whether or not equality of income would be good, surely extreme poverty is bad. But if that is the source of one's concern, then why should the *inequality* in particular between the rich and the poor matter? Because one takes it as a rough measure of how little it would cost the rich to bring the poor up to the minimum standard, and thus of how callous the rich are? Or does the extreme inequality matter because it exposes the poor to the risk of exploitation by the rich?

Talk of exploitation raises yet another reason why one might be concerned about the statistics cited earlier. One's concern might stem not so much from the thought that such inequalities offer great scope for exploitation, as from the thought that they have *arisen*, in large part, through exploitation or other forms of injustice. And this thought too, of course, would raise many further questions. What instances of injustice does one have in mind? Is one thinking primarily of colonial history and its consequences, for example? Or is one thinking of phenomena that took place in the more recent past and continue into the present, such as certain of the processes that tend to be associated with the term 'globalisation'? If so, which of those processes in particular warrant the label 'exploitation', and why?

Of course, these are only a few of the reasons why one might be concerned about the kinds of statistics cited above. And equally clearly, similar questions might be asked about many other global inequalities. These include inequalities affecting many different subjects, apart from individuals – subjects such as states, classes and genders. And they also include inequalities measured in terms of many different metrics, apart from income – metrics such as power, security, well-being and so on. In each case, one needs to ask why the inequality in question might be taken to matter. And in each case, a variety of answers to that question might be available.

Even the little we have said so far is enough to indicate the number and variety of issues which arise when one starts to think about the connections between globalisation and equality. It will also be clear that these issues do not respect traditional inter-disciplinary divisions in academia. Specialists in a number of different disciplines can be expected to have something to say about them, and what such specialists say is likely to be all the more enlightening if they are brought together with specialists in other relevant disciplines. With this in mind, we thought that it would be helpful to bring together individuals from many different disciplines and backgrounds – both academics and active politicians, and from different disciplines within academia – to discuss some of these issues. The first result of this enterprise was the Workshop referred to in the acknowledgements. The second result is this book.

Our contributors approach the issues concerning globalisation and equality from many different perspectives. This diversity we consider to be one of the strengths of this book. Some of the contributors adopt a more abstract approach, exploring foundational questions concerning the meaning of equality, its social and political dimensions and more specifically its moral implications in a global context. Others engage the general themes of globalisation and equality by focusing on specific topics, such as welfare, citizenship, gender, culture and the environment. This distinction between the theoretical and the specific informs the overall structure of the book. The book starts with the broader, more theoretical contributions that introduce and examine the major issues and arguments before moving on to those that take up specific topics. Each chapter, however, stands alone, advancing its own argument. This can be seen clearly when we turn to the details of each contribution.

To what extent should our concern for social equality be politically bounded? And what difference does globalisation make to these boundaries? Garrett Cullity's contribution, 'Equality and globalization', is focused on these two questions. He begins by arguing that certain kinds of social inequality are bad in themselves, as opposed to being bad merely because of the deprivation they involve. He then surveys arguments for the claim that the scope of proper concern for such inequalities, and of distributive justice in general, should be politically bounded. Most of these arguments, he argues, are undermined by the 'globalist challenge': given that our significant social relationships now extend globally, so too does the scope of distributive justice. He then focuses on what he takes to be the strongest reply to the globalist challenge, based on the argument from self-determination developed recently by John Rawls. Cullity finishes, however, by arguing that, even if such a Rawlsian view is correct, the scope of proper concern about the forms of social inequality referred to above is still importantly affected by globalisation.

Tom Campbell begins his contribution, 'Globalising equality: the Equal Worth Project', by making a number of distinctions between what he calls the 'descriptive', 'evaluative' and 'prescriptive' aspects of equality discourse. He then goes on to discuss the relation between these three aspects, with particular reference to the claim that all humans have equal worth. He points out that it is common to assume this claim without specifying exactly what the properties are in virtue of which it holds. Doing so, however, leaves us unable to resolve many important issues. Indeed, he suggests that establishing some kind of 'foundational descriptive equality' among all humans – equality, that is, in the properties that give them worth – may be a necessary basis for transnational obligations.

In 'Moral universalism and global economic justice,' Thomas Pogge draws attention to an asymmetry in the way national and global economics orders are commonly assessed. We tend to think that any national economic order, in order to be just, must meet the following two standards: its rules must be under democratic control, and it must preclude life-threatening poverty as far as is reasonably possible. But we do not tend to think that our global economic order must meet these standards. Can this asymmetry be justified? Can it be justified, in particular, in the light of 'moral universalism' – the idea, roughly speaking, that moral assessment must be based on fundamental principles that do not discriminate arbitrarily against particular persons or groups? If it cannot, Pogge argues, then we are guilty of a form of covert and arbitrary discrimination against the global poor.

In 'Reclaiming equality in a globalised world', Duncan Kerr argues that the 'golden straitjacket' of social, economic and political measures imposed on nation-states is leading to increasing inequality within and between states. As a consequence the state's ability to provide a foundation for common provision is being eroded, resulting in 'post-welfare' states. Kerr suggests that the conventional responses to such inequality – attempts to strengthen local communities and the private sector – are not sufficient to meet this challenge. What is needed to address these concerns is to shift the focus of democratic debates to the international sphere. Accordingly he advocates a global social democracy, with greater strengthened transnational representative institutions to resolve the twin issues of growth and fairness, allowing alternative conceptions of citizenship and equality to be reasserted into our increasingly globalised world.

Contending notions of equality are at the foundations of modern welfare systems. This starting point allows Sheila Shaver in 'Welfare, equality and globalisation: reconceiving social citizenship', to examine the restructuring of modern welfare systems to reveal the way globalisation is shaping equality. Because of the significance of globalisation in Australia, Shaver's case study of Australian welfare reform allows her to discern a shift in the conception of equality. Employing T. H. Marshall's concept of 'social citizenship', Shaver sees the transformation of welfare from a limited social right to support provided on condition as a redefinition of social citizenship that challenges its conception of equality as equal citizenship.

Gillian Youngs, in 'Gender, equality and globalisation', argues that feminism provides a distinctive and valuable perspective in addressing questions of equality and the differences in social relations of power. Globalisation, understood as a masculinised phenomenon of capital and finance and a feminised phenomenon of supporting services defines and accounts for women's differentiated experience of globalisation. In seeking to understand the inequalities among women, as well as between men and women, the chapter confronts both the new inequalities and opportunities created by globalisation.

In his contribution, 'Globalisation for a multicultural world', Bhikhu Parekh focuses on the cultural dimensions of globalisation. He discusses, among other things, the different ways in which multiculturalism impacts on Western and non-Western societies, the conditions under which it may be appropriate for a society to take steps to defend its culture against global forces, and the reasons why each society needs other cultures. He finishes by arguing that, since the culture of a society cannot be dissociated from its economic and political life, each country needs to be able to choose its own path to economic and political development. Under the set of policies embodied within the Washington Consensus, however, it is impossible for countries to do this. Thus cultural considerations provide a further reason for instituting a programme of global justice.

The influence of globalisation on the environment and its implications for equality is the theme of Giorel Curran's chapter, 'Environment, equality and globalisation'. Curran notes that globalisation has exacerbated environmental risks by increasing levels of pollution and toxic waste, as well as reducing biological diversity. Significantly, this increasing risk has been distributed unequally, both domestically and internationally. In addition to the increasing risk, however, globalisation has come to challenge, and perhaps transform, conventional notions of equality, principally in its conceptions of intra-generational, inter-generational and inter-species equality. In light of these developments Curran suggests cosmopolitan democracy, planetary citizenship and ecological democracy as useful models for thinking about, and addressing, environmental equality and justice.

Henry Shue also focuses on the environment in his contribution, 'Legacy of danger', with particular reference to the problem of climate change. He points out that the greatest inequality of power of all is that between current and future generations. And he shows how two connected tendencies shift burdens greatly from the former to the latter. The first is the tendency to pursue least-cost-first policies. And the second is the tendency to continue using fossil-fuel technologies until doing so is no longer cost-effective for the then-current generation, while failing to invest much in research or development of alternative energy technologies. These tendencies, Shue argues, function so as to postpone the 'date of technological transition' – the date at which the transition from a predominant reliance on fossil-fuel-driven technologies to a reliance on alternative energy technologies will occur. But the later the date of technological transition, the more dangerous the world is likely to be. In pursuing the tendencies referred to earlier, then, we are imposing risks of great harm on future generations. Shue finishes by showing how a particular aspect of the Kyoto Protocol – the 'Clean Development Mechanism' – is likely to exacerbate both of those tendencies, and thus to increase further the risks to future generations.

Clearly each of these contributions raises a range of complex, subtle and difficult questions. It is our hope that this volume encourages such further deliberation and debate, allowing a more profound engagement with the important themes of globalisation and equality.

2 Equality and globalization

Garrett Cullity

When we ask what kind of equality we should be morally concerned about, it is natural to look for answers in three different directions. First, we can cite the fundamental moral equality of each individual person. The second direction to look in concerns equality of political and legal status – equality of political representation, equality of opportunity to occupy political office and equality before the law. And the third concerns what we might broadly call equality with respect to how well off each person is.

In the current philosophical debate about equality, equality of the first of these kinds is not at issue. Taking our fundamental moral equality as given, the debate concerns its proper social expression: how we ought to take account of it in structuring our social institutions.[1] The thought that our moral equality should be reflected in equality of political status is itself largely uncontroversial – although that still leaves room for debate over whether modern Western forms of democracy succeed in embodying the ideal of equality of political representation, and just what should be taken to count as satisfying the ideal of equality of opportunity to occupy political office. It also leaves open the question of whether the moral equality of persons can be respected by endorsing manifestly undemocratic forms of political organization as intended staging posts on the way to realizing the democratic ideal later. The main focus of recent discussion, however, has been equality of the third kind: 'equality with respect to how well off each person is'. What is the good to be equalized in this category? Is it the resources that each person has at his or her disposal (Dworkin 1981a,b)? Is it personal welfare – how well a person's life goes for her? Is it rather *opportunity* for welfare (allowing that inequalities in welfare are not objectionable insofar as they result from different uses and misuses of the same opportunities) (Arneson 1989)? Or is it instead what Cohen calls 'access to advantage' – 'access', not opportunity, in order to cover shortfalls in personal capacity that do not diminish opportunity (Cohen's examples: weakness and stupidity); and 'advantage', not welfare, in order to span *both* resource deficiencies (such as poverty and physical weakness) and welfare deficiencies (such as despondency and failure to achieve one's aims)?[2] Perhaps all these options should be rejected: the other view to be considered is that there is no sense in which it is morally desirable to equalize how well off everyone is (Nozick 1974). Notice, however, that even this last view does not depart from the assumption of the fundamental justificational importance of moral equality. Rather, the thought is that our fundamental equality is appropriately reflected in the attribution to us of equal liberty-rights, the free exercise of which leads to some people being much better off than others.

Taking this debate as its background, the aim of this chapter is to examine a question about the scope of equality. To what extent should our concern for equality be politically bounded, and what difference do contemporary facts about globalization make to those boundaries?

An answer to this question needs to start by giving a fuller account of the kinds of equality that do have moral significance. The first section does this, identifying four morally important kinds of social equality. Defending this account fully is beyond the scope of this chapter; but I shall at least give a preliminary argument in its support. In the second section, I survey arguments that our concern to eliminate social inequality should be politically bounded. The third section introduces what I shall call the 'globalist' challenge to these arguments, and shows the reply to this challenge that can be developed along lines recently set out by John Rawls. The fourth section then asks what difference the facts of globalization make to the scope of each of the four different kinds of morally significant social equality identified in the first section. Globalization makes an important difference, I shall argue, in relation to all of them.

Four kinds of social equality

Is social inequality of *any* kind ever a bad thing in itself? The alternative is to think that what is bad is deprivation, not inequality. If one person is deprived of something important, then that is bad, and we have a reason to provide him with it if we can. But it is not as if the existence of a second, better off person makes the situation any worse. After all, the first person is made no worse off by the existence of the second. And reducing the second person to the same level of deprivation as the first, although it removes the inequality, surely makes the situation no better. It does not benefit anyone, and it harms someone. So since there is no one for whom it is better in any way, it is not better in any way. Therefore equality cannot in itself be good, nor inequality bad. This is the 'levelling down' objection.[3]

The levelling down objection focuses on the case where there is deprivation without inequality. The other way to emphasize the distinction is to look at the case of inequality without deprivation. Suppose everyone in the world enjoyed the purchasing power of today's richest billionaires – except for a few, who were even better off. Would this be bad? If not, this again suggests that it is deprivation, and not inequality itself, that is morally important.[4]

Someone who presses these objections can still endorse egalitarian distributive practices. For there will still be a clear case for thinking that if a given unit of resources which is available for distribution will do more good to someone who is badly off than to a person who is already better off, then it ought to be given to the person to whom it does more good.[5] The only way to justify giving it to the person who would benefit less would be by holding either that she had a greater claim to it, or that benefits to her were more important. In this way, it can be argued that we ought to produce more equal social distributions of goods not because social inequality is in itself a bad thing, but because of the badness of deprivation.

However, it seems to me that we should reject this view. For at least four main forms of social inequality, there is a simple and plausible case, grounded in our fundamental moral equality, for thinking that they are bad in themselves. Taking each in turn, let me briefly outline that case. Without attempting a full defence here, it will be possible at least to indicate the force of the argument for attaching moral significance to these forms of inequality, and to survey the different ways in which the levelling down and inequality-of-the-rich objections can be met.

Inequality-as-domination. A first form of objectionable inequality involves gaining or sustaining privileges for one group by imposing hardships or restrictions on others. A concern with this is at the heart of egalitarian complaints about aristocratic forms of social organization, in which the privileges of a ruling class are sustained by means of the deprivations of wealth and status of those producing the goods and services they enjoy. It is easy to see how accepting the fundamental moral equality of persons should lead us to oppose this. If the welfare of the dominant group were more important than that of the subordinate group, then that would explain why we ought to sustain a social structure of this kind. But if that is not true, there is no good explanation of why some people ought to be made to undergo hardships for the benefit of others.

If we hold that inequality-as-domination is itself bad, how do we defend this against the levelling down and inequality-of-the-rich objections? The answer is that there is something else that is bad about standing in a relationship of inequality-as-domination to other people, beyond the deprivation that may be involved: namely, being forced to undergo hardship for another person's benefit. To undergo hardship is bad, but to be forced to do so in the service of someone else's interests is bad in a further way, since it violates your standing as a person of equal moral importance − it forces you to stand in a relationship to that other person which would only be appropriate if his welfare were more important than yours. If so, we can answer the levelling down objection. Levelling down is rarely the best way of eliminating inequality.[6] But if it eliminates inequality-as-domination, that is something good about it. There is one way in which it *is* good for the badly off − it removes them from a relationship of domination − and although it is bad for the better off, the importance of this is undermined if their advantages rely on forcing others to be subordinate to them. The objection from the inequality of the rich can also be answered. If the advantages of the super-rich are produced by forcing disadvantages on the rich, then that is objectionable, not because of facts about deprivation, but because of the way in which domination violates moral equality.

Inequality of political and legal status. The case for thinking that inequalities in this second category are bad in themselves is closely related to the first. Where such inequalities exist, one group is governing another. But amongst persons who are fundamentally morally equal, it should be the case that each person has an equal say in how he or she is to be governed.[7] Again, the two earlier objections provide no obstacle to thinking this. The levelling down objection is met by noticing that the political power possessed by any one member of a polity is essentially relative to the amount possessed by others. Short of dissolving a polity altogether, there is no way of reducing the amount of political power possessed by the more power-ful without increasing the amount possessed by the less powerful. To reduce polit-ical inequality is to improve the situation of the worse off. And turning to the other objection, the only way to make sense of a society in which everyone is 'rich' in political power but some have more than others is as a society which is close to realizing the democratic ideal, but in which some members have a marginal enhancement of power. This is obviously less objectionable than more pro-nounced forms of political domination; but it is objectionable none the less, in ignoring the way in which our moral equality gives us an equal entitlement to determine how we are governed.

The kind of political inequality that this argument relates to is inequality amongst members of a polity. But notice that there is another kind: the inequal-ity that exists between members of a polity which it is desirable to belong to and those to whom membership is denied. Let us call these 'internal' and 'external' political inequality, respectively. Later, we shall need to address the question on what grounds external political inequality might be defensible, given that internal political inequality is not.

Inequality-as-callousness. For a third way in which the badness of inequality goes beyond that of deprivation, we can return to deprivations of welfare. It may be bad that some people do not have enough resources to meet their basic needs; but it is also, additionally, bad that others have superfluous resources and do not use them to help – bad because it is callous.[8] Of course, against the suggestion that all inequalities of resources or welfare are bad in this way, the inequality of the rich objection would be decisive: in a society containing only the rich and the super-rich, the latter cannot be accused of callousness towards the former. Inequality-as-callousness only occurs where there is deprivation. But that does not mean that the badness of inequality-as-callousness reduces to the badness of dep-rivation. The fact that there are people who do nothing to help the badly off although it would cost them little to do so is a further bad feature of a social arrangement, beyond the fact that it contains people who are badly off. It is also easy to see why levelling down is a poor response to inequality-as-callousness: it involves taking away the resources of the well-to-do rather than doing anything about the plight of the badly off. If you criticize the well off for callousness in not helping the badly off, it can hardly make sense to recommend levelling down to remove the inequality: that does nothing to help the badly off either, and does nothing to undo the callousness.[9]

Brute inequality. The last of the four kinds of inequality for us to consider is brute undeserved inequality of welfare: differences in how well people's lives go that do not reflect what they deserve or are responsible for. (I use this disjunctive phrase to cover cases of risk-taking in which it sounds wrong to say that someone *deserves* to lose a gamble, but in which he is responsible for the outcome nonetheless.)[10] Is brute inequality bad? The alternative is to hold that there is no amount of resources that a person deserves independently of the relationships of acquisition and exchange into which he enters with other agents. If a person has acquired a set of resources in a procedurally just way, then he is the person who deserves to have them, and if he uses those resources in a way that results in a certain level of welfare for himself, there is no other level of welfare that he deserves instead. Beyond this, it does not make sense to ask whether he deserved to have the genetic and material inheritances that have enabled him to acquire what he has: desert does not go 'all the way down' (Nozick 1974: 225). The reply to this takes the same form as before: we can ground the concern to eliminate brute inequality in a respect for fundamental moral equality. Whenever someone is less well off than he might be, this matters; and it matters for everyone equally, because we are all equally important. There is always a reason to help someone who is less well off than he might be to be better off; and this reason is stronger the worse off he is. In some respects, your being less well off than you might have been is your own responsibility; but in others, it is not. And some of *those* respects – the welfare deficiencies for which you are not responsible – may be ones in which you could have been better off had we collectively structured our social institutions and relationships differently. Thus, if there are ways in which we could collectively structure our social institutions and relationships to stop people being less well off than they deserve to be, then equal respect for each person suggests that this would be good.

Again, this gives us a case for the badness of inequality that goes beyond the badness of deprivation. It is bad if people are worse off than they might be – bad for those people – but it is also, additionally, bad that we are collectively failing to address this by structuring our society differently. The badness of brute inequality must be distinct from the badness of deprivation, because it can be present where there is no deprivation. Certainly, welfare deficiencies matter less, the better off a person is – the reasons to remedy them are weaker. But they still matter. So if a society of the well off and super-well off fails to structure itself in a way that eliminates eliminable brute inequalities of welfare, that is still a bad feature of that society. It might seem that the levelling down objection poses more of a problem. After all, if the badness of brute inequality is additional to that of deprivation, then it would seem that removing the inequality must count as good. And yet surely there is *nothing* good about responding to a situation in which some people have less than they deserve by ensuring that everyone else has less than they deserve too. However, the reply is this. What is bad about brute inequality, over and above any deprivation it may involve, is that it also involves a failure collectively to rectify that deprivation. But if we responded to deprivation by adopting a policy of levelling down, that would involve the same failure. So levelling down would be just as bad as retaining the status quo of brute inequality: however, saying this is compatible with thinking that the badness of brute inequality goes beyond that of deprivation.

So: for four kinds of social inequality we have, at least in outline, arguments for thinking that they are themselves morally bad. Rather than developing and defending those arguments more fully, however, what I want to concentrate on here is the question of their scope. If we find these arguments plausible, to what extent should our concern for the kinds of social equality they recommend be politically bounded, and to what extent is the significance of political boundaries affected by the facts of globalization?

Arguments for boundedness

The four kinds of social inequality just identified all depend on the existence of social relationships between the people whose inequality of status is held to be morally bad. No case has been made for thinking that, if two people are living in complete isolation from each other and one enjoys advantages which the other lacks, there is anything bad about that. In situations exhibiting the kinds of inequality we have identified, either one person is benefiting from the imposition of hardship on another, or one stands in a relationship of political privilege to another, or one stands in the relationship of potential benefactor to the other, or they both belong to a society that ought to be reformed to remove remediable welfare deficiencies.

The question we need to examine is how far the relevant social relationships extend. For a variety of reasons, it is often maintained that these relationships are politically bounded: requirements of distributive justice extend to, but not beyond, the boundaries of political states. In this section, I offer a fourfold taxonomy of these arguments.[11] With this taxonomy in place, we shall then be able to go on to assess to what extent their plausibility is affected by the facts of globalization.

The nature of distributive justice. A first category comprises arguments that derive the boundedness of distributive justice from claims about its nature. One argument of this general kind is Michael Walzer's argument from the nature of the goods that are candidates for distribution (Walzer 1983, ch. 1). Such goods are social goods: they get what Walzer calls their 'meanings' – their values – from the roles they are given within a history and culture of social transactions. Thus bread, to use Walzer's own example, can have a sacramental value or a value as an expression of hospitality, as well as a merely nutritional value (Walzer 1983: 8). And the social meaning of any good will determine the appropriate principles to govern its distribution: 'All distributions are just or unjust relative to the social meanings of the goods at stake' (Walzer 1983: 9). What the world gives us as the boundaries of the social settings that confer these meanings are political communities.[12] So distributive justice is politically bounded, and not global in its application.

Other arguments in this category seek to draw conclusions about the boundedness of justice from an account of its essential subject. In this spirit, it is claimed that the subject of justice is the basic structure of a society – political states being the entities that do constitute themselves publicly as a society with an institutional structure.[13] Or it is claimed that the subject of justice is the distribution of the fruits of social cooperation; or, in a broader Hobbesian spirit, the regulation of arrangements for mutual advantage.[14]

More ambitiously, it has sometimes been argued that the nature of morality itself confines it within political boundaries. One finds this way of thinking in nineteenth-century romantic nationalists, according to whom there is no moral community beyond the nation-state. There are ways of arguing for the community-anchored character of moral agency which deserve to be taken seriously. One avenue to consider here is a neo-Aristotelianism according to which moral norms are only intelligible in relation to the roles occupied by individuals in virtue of their membership of a specific moral community (MacIntyre 1985, esp. ch. 15). And another – to sketch the Hegelian line of thought suggested by the British idealists – is the view that the capacity for moral agency is not presocial, but is possible only given a specific normative social structure into which a person is educated, which furnishes that person with externally defined choices (choices the nature of which is determined by something other than one's own choice itself). Self-realizing ethical decision is only possible against such a background, and this background is a particular normative system of publicly recognized rights and obligations. If you are an ethical being at all, therefore, you are a being whose ethical life and world is *given* by the specific normative structure which your society provides.[15]

The other main argument in this first category is an argument from the nature of political obligation. Given the obligations we owe to members of our own political community in virtue of our relations of mutual political dependence, any case for distributing goods beyond our shared polity will be overridden by the obligation to distribute them to our compatriots.

Respect for self-determination. A second category of arguments for the political boundedness of distributive justice emphasizes the value or rightness of political self-determination.[16] One way in which this view is often developed is to embrace a strong doctrine of state sovereignty, maintaining that it is wrong for any state or its citizens to intervene in the internal affairs of another, as a policy of cross-border redistribution would seem to require. However, notice that arguments from self-determination for the political boundedness of distributive justice need not embrace a strong sovereignty doctrine. It is possible to hold that one state is entitled to intervene to resist political oppression within another, but to maintain that the value of allowing political communities to determine their own goals and priorities means that we should resist the idea that one state that has pursued a particular course of economic development is required to distribute its resulting wealth for the benefit of another which has taken a different course. (As we shall see in the next section, Rawls's *Law of Peoples* presents such a view.) Broadly speaking, defences of the value or rightness of political self-determination can draw on two main sources, emphasizing the importance of liberties of association, and the way in which personal autonomy ought therefore to be reflected in political autonomy; or stressing the value of international pluralism and cultural diversity.[17]

Further bad consequences. A third category contains a number of more obvious arguments, according to which principles of distributive justice ought not to be applied globally because of the further bad consequences this would have, beyond simply infringing self-determination. Thus, one line of complaint is that global redistribution would require a global distributor, that this would amount to a world government, and that that would be unfeasible, would threaten a world tyranny or would be destructive of the kinds of communities that enrich their members' identities.[18]

Another objection in this category emphasizes the way in which the root causes of poverty and severe deprivation lie in political injustice.[19] If so, it is often argued, these evils cannot be rectified by international resource-redistribution. On the contrary, pouring resources into an unsound political structure will usually merely exacerbate the problems, stimulating corruption and providing an incentive for the usurping of political power.[20]

Political liberalism. A fourth, distinct kind of argument should also be considered.[21] Perhaps you are convinced that we ought to be following egalitarian principles of social organization. But others disagree; and in doing so, they are not exhibiting unreasonableness of the kind that disqualifies someone from making a serious contribution to political discourse. There is reasonable disagreement about how egalitarian we should be. Accordingly, each community will need to resolve this question, by the use of public reason – that is, without importing moral convictions that other parties to serious political discussion cannot reasonably be expected to share – for itself. There is no question of settling on egalitarian principles that are global in scope, since the reasonable resolution of competition between diverging political convictions is for each polity to bind itself to its own public resolution of the distributive principles by which it is to guide its own institutions.

The globalist challenge

We have surveyed four kinds of arguments for the political boundedness of a proper concern for social equality. Now we need to assess whether these arguments are undermined by the facts of contemporary globalization. The case for thinking so is easily summarized. The kinds of social relationships we live in have now become global in scope. The facts of global economic interdependence, along with mass communications and the global travel industry, mean that no part of the world can any longer pretend to live in isolation from the rest. Our economic interrelationships bring political and cultural interdependence in their wake. Our political decisions are now taken in a global context – one increasingly influenced by powerful transnational corporations and bureaucracies – and the capacity for us to participate in forms of agency that produce global effects brings with it the need to discuss, deliberate about and coordinate our activities on a global scale. We all now participate in activities of global significance: we cannot escape the fact that we stand in global social relationships. And given this, the boundaries of justice have widened: they can no longer be identified with the boundaries of individual states.

Against arguments in the first of our four categories – arguments from the nature of distributive justice – this 'globalist' challenge is a powerful objection. The awkward question it raises for Walzer's view is, Why identify the boundaries of shared social 'meanings' with political boundaries? Surely, there are (and always have been) some goods – goods of health, freedom from coercion and economic security – that are of universal importance as preconditions for a flourishing life, even if the dimensions of human flourishing are themselves diverse, embedded in the evaluative lives of different communities. But as globalization progresses and we become increasingly economically and socially connected to others across political boundaries, the more plausible it becomes to think that, even if the appropriate distribution of a good is determined by its social 'meanings', the community across which many of those 'meanings' are shared is now global. Likewise, the view that the subject of justice is the basic structure of a society invites the reply that we do now inhabit a global society with an institutional structure, and that this raises collective questions about how it should justly be constituted. And when it is claimed that the subject of justice is the distribution of the fruits of social cooperation, or the regulation of arrangements for mutual advantage, then the reply is that we need to distribute the fruits of global cooperative interaction and to regulate global relationships to our mutual advantage. The facts of global agency force these decisions upon us, and there is no good case for denying that they are the kinds of decisions to which norms of justice apply.

What about the more drastic view that there is no moral community beyond the nation-state? Even if we were to go along with the idea that the demands of morality for any agent are dictated by his specific normative social environment, that still leaves us without a convincing case for denying that morally significant social relations can be global. A plausible Aristotelianism will acknowledge that some moral norms arise from roles which we occupy as members of the entire human community; and the follower of the idealists' train of thought should accept that the norms which make ethical agency possible are not exclusively positive ones, but include the moral norm of regarding the needs of other people (simply as such) as justifications for helping them.[22]

Our first category of arguments for boundedness also included arguments from the nature of political obligation. Someone endorsing the globalist challenge need not deny that there are political obligations that are exclusively owed to compatriots. But what is implausible is the claim that these completely override moral reasons of other kinds. It is hard to see why that should be any more plausible than the claim that obligations to fellow family members have such importance that there are no all-things-considered obligations to non-family-members. The globalist's claim is that we stand in global relationships to non-compatriots that generate obligations. What we lack is a convincing argument for thinking that accepting the existence of special obligations to compatriots is incompatible with this, as one of a variety of significant moral relationships in which we stand to other people.

Thus, the arguments in the first of our four categories do seem to be directly undermined by the facts of globalization. Turn next to arguments in the third category – from the bad consequences of having a world government or of distributing resources into an unjustly structured state. These are clearly important considerations to be taken into account in devising a satisfactory policy of global redistribution. However, can they succeed in supporting the claim that requirements of distributive justice are politically bounded? There are two ways to read this claim. Interpreted strongly, it amounts to the claim that inequalities spanning political boundaries are not unjust. But notice that arguments of this kind cannot deliver that strong conclusion. For there is a clear distinction to be made between the questions of whether an injustice exists and what action it is right to take in addressing it. If an indigenous people has had its lands forcibly taken by colonizers, there will be a straightforward case for saying that they have been treated unjustly, but it will be a further, difficult question what it is right now to do in response, given the injustice of simply dispossessing current owners. To argue from the problems with a redistributive policy to the absence of distributive injustice seems fallacious. The claim that the requirements of justice are politically bounded can be read a second way: as the claim that the redistributive practices we ought to engage in are politically bounded. If there were reasons for thinking that *all* schemes for global redistribution would be likely to produce more harm than good, then this second claim would need to be taken seriously. However, the work being done to describe alternative distributive practices that avoid these problems makes that conclusion premature (Pogge 1994, 1998).

The fourth kind of argument, from political liberalism, makes the point that the question which distributive practice it is right for us to adopt cannot be settled by simply asking which distribution is just and what is the most effective means of achieving it. For if there is reasonable disagreement about which distribution is just, then it may not be reasonable to impose your own preferred distribution, in spite of the justifications you are able to give for preferring it. The question what distributive practice should be adopted is a political question, and it is right to settle it by means of public discourse, in contributing to justly structured methods of public deliberation. This does seem an important point. However, notice that what it bears on is the question which distributive practice is the right one to adopt, and not whether a certain distribution is good or bad. If there is actually reasonable disagreement about the injustice of inequality, that affects the reasonableness of implementing egalitarian policies, but it does not itself speak to the question whether inequality *is* unjust. It is at most an argument for the boundedness of political debate concerning distributive practice, and not for the boundedness of distributive justice itself. Moreover, it does nothing to oppose the globalist thought that one of the important subjects of debate within a polity concerns the distributive policies its members should adopt towards those outside it.

This leaves arguments from self-determination: the second of our four categories. These are the strongest of the arguments for the political boundedness of distributive justice. The most prominent view of this kind is the one Rawls sets out in *The Law of Peoples* (Rawls 1999b). In this book, Rawls explicitly rejects egalitarian global principles of distributive justice, arguing that although what he calls 'well-ordered peoples' have a duty of assistance towards societies burdened by unfavourable political, cultural and material conditions, that duty extends only to helping other societies to achieve a just internal structure. Beyond that, inequalities of welfare that exist between different peoples do not generate duties of distributive justice on the well off to benefit the badly off (§§ 15–16).

This has seemed to some prominent writers in the field to invite a criticism of inconsistency when it is set alongside Rawls's 'difference principle' in relation to domestic justice, which requires that material inequalities internal to a society only be tolerated when they are to the advantage of the worst off. One target for this objection is his derivation of principles of international justice from the agreement that would be reached behind a veil of ignorance by parties representing *peoples*, rather than global individuals. But the second is that, even if the parties to such an agreement are representing peoples, each such representative ought to be concerned to further his people's interest in well-being. Thus, there remains the same case for the generation of a global difference principle as there was for the adoption of a difference principle in the domestic case (Pogge 1994).

However, these objections can be answered. The view articulated in *The Law of Peoples* is that the just internal ordering of a people furnishes that people with the conditions for its own self-determination. We are already politically constituted as peoples. Within a people, none of us should be penalized for his or her undeserved natural disadvantages. And we should have an equal chance to participate in the decision-making process whereby we set our collective priorities. However, as a people, our welfare is not determined by the level of material resources at our disposal, but by our political and moral culture. Other peoples may owe us a duty of assistance in securing the conditions of justice that do make us self-determining; but once they have done so, the responsibility for our collective material welfare in relation to that of other peoples lies with us (Rawls 1999b: 16).

This presents a much stronger form of resistance to the globalist challenge than arguments of the other kinds we have examined. Notice that it is not an adequate objection to complain that the ability of burdened societies to achieve true self-determination is severely restricted by the operation of global markets and financial institutions. Rawls can agree that globalization importantly complicates and extends the duties of assistance between peoples. But his view is that the target of such duties is self-determination, not equality.

What we find, then, is that the globalist challenge to arguments for the political boundedness of social equality does make arguments in the first category implausible. Arguments in the third and fourth categories can only properly be presented as arguments for limiting the scope of redistributive practice, rather than of injustice itself, and even when restricted in this way they look difficult to sustain. However, a Rawlsian argument from self-determination – an argument in the second category – offers a more powerful reply to the globalist challenge. What we need to assess now is the extent to which that powerful reply is actually successful.

Global inequalities

If Rawls is right, there are important limits to the extent to which inequalities between self-determining peoples are morally significant. However, even if he is right, that would not mean that there are no forms of morally significant inequality that are global in scope. On the contrary: this is true of all four of the morally significant forms of social inequality discussed in the first main section of this paper. As I shall now argue, the scope of a proper concern about these forms of inequality is crucially affected by facts about globalization, even if the Rawlsian view is right.

The first form of inequality we identified was 'inequality-as-domination', which occurs when the privileges of one group are gained or sustained by imposing hardships or restrictions on others. Opposing this does not require you to condemn all voluntary transactions that produce winners and losers. The question is whether the transaction has been forced upon the loser. If not, then there is no violation of your moral equality with me in insisting that you, as a free agent entitled to commit yourself to agreements with others, should bear the loss to which the transaction commits you, even though this involves deprivation to you for the sake of benefiting me. You are not being made to benefit me because I am more important than you, but because we are both equally entitled to commit ourselves to such agreements.

However, this does not mean that all voluntary market transactions are free from imposition. A weak enough bargaining position can make it the case that you are being forced to harm yourself for someone else's benefit. This is most obvious in the case where the person you are benefiting is responsible for the weakness of your bargaining position: having monopolized the supply chain for your product, I offer to buy your business cheaply rather than driving it to the wall. But notice that it also applies when the weakness of your bargaining position is not itself caused by me. If I find you after a shipwreck, and offer to rescue you on condition that you give me 90 per cent of what you earn thereafter, then I am taking advantage of the threat to your life to force you to subordinate yourself to me. Notice that it remains true, however, that I have benefited you. You would have been worse off had you not been rescued at all. If so, I have actually lessened the inequality of welfare between us by helping you. But in forcing you to make sacrifices for my benefit, I have created a new kind of inequality – inequality-as-domination – which is morally objectionable because it is incompatible with our fundamental moral equality. An interesting question is what are the necessary and sufficient conditions for the existence of a relationship in which one party is *forcing* another to undergo hardship for his benefit. I do not offer such an account here. However, any plausible account of these conditions will need to be one on which, in the shipwreck example, I am taking advantage of your weak bargaining position to force you to benefit me.

In this example, I am to blame for creating a relationship of inequality-as-domination. More commonly, the responsibility for creating inequality of this kind is collective.[23] And that is what we should say about one prominent aspect of globalization: the globalization of manufacturing industry, generating ever-cheaper prices for consumer goods through employing low cost labour in countries with poor populations.[24] It is said that such workers would be worse off without the employment opportunities that such global business brings; but notice the reply. No doubt that is often true – and not only true, but good. But that was also true in the shipwreck example. The important question, that example shows us, is not whether the terms of a proposed bargain are better for the other party than complete non-cooperation would have been, but whether people are being forced to undergo hardship for our benefit. Voluntary, mutually advantageous economic exchange can provide examples of this; and the globalization of manufacturing industry implicates us all in one such example.

This is not an argument for simply withdrawing such industries from countries where cheap labour is used. It is an argument for thinking that we collectively stand in a morally significant relationship to those on whose labour we rely for cheap consumer goods – one that is unjust. We should not think that we can discharge the duties created by that relationship simply by terminating it, any more than I can properly rectify my injustice to the shipwrecked person by abandoning him on the next island.

Next, let us turn to inequality-as-callousness: the inequality that exists when there is deprivation together with superfluity which could be used to address it. Globalization has extended the scope of this kind of inequality too, in two main ways. The globalization of information means that the well off have swift and reliable information about the severe deprivation of people who are physically remote, and the global reach of aid agencies means that it is a simple matter to make a material contribution towards addressing it. Given this, there is a strong case for thinking that the failure of the well off to help the world's poor amounts both individually and collectively to callousness.[25] Saying this does not involve the economically and politically naïve view that private or collective philanthropy is itself a long-term solution to the problems of world poverty. This will only be eradicated by addressing its causes in political and economic structures. But the point is that the failure to use superfluous resources to contribute both to immediate relief and longer-term structural change does invite moral criticism.

Thus, there are straightforward reasons for thinking that, thanks to facts of increasing globalization, we stand in relationships of inequality-as-domination and inequality-as-callousness towards the world's poor. Moreover, the claim that there are morally significant global inequalities of these kinds is not blocked by the Rawlsian position described in the previous section. Rawls himself partly accommodates this claim; for his Law of Peoples includes the requirement that interactions between peoples be governed by standards of fair trade, and the duty of assistance that well-ordered peoples have to burdened societies (Rawls 1999b: 42–3, §15). However, the accommodation is only partial. Rawls's discussion concerns moral relationships between peoples – self-identified groupings sharing a history, culture and traditions. But the conclusion of our discussion is just as naturally put in terms of a relationship in which *the well off* collectively stand towards the badly off, or a relationship in which each well-off person stands towards those she could help.[26]

Consider next 'brute inequality': inequality in respect of how well people's lives go that does not reflect what they deserve or are responsible for. In the first section, I outlined an argument for thinking that brute eliminable inequality is a bad feature of a society that contains it: if we could collectively structure our society to stop people being less well off than they deserve, the importance of equal respect for each person makes that a good thing. This defence of the significance of brute inequality does make it socially bounded: brute inequality is bad when it is a feature of a society to which the unequal people belong, and whose members could collectively reform its structure. But here again, we find that there is force in the globalist's challenge. The global social, economic and political structures now connecting us to each other mean that there is now a global society to which we collectively belong, which has a structure we could collectively (if not individually) reform. Our global society is a society characterized by brute inequality; and that is a bad feature of it.

If global brute inequality is bad, what should we do about it? The Rawlsian position is that international justice requires us to assist other societies to achieve a well-ordered, self-determining status, but not to seek to implement a global egalitarian redistribution of resources beyond that point. This view is compatible with thinking that brute inequality beyond that point would be a bad feature of global society: it simply adds that, in a world of self-determining peoples, responsibility for the lower level of welfare of one people would lie with that people itself. However, notice an important point. Rawls's view opposes the ideal of an egalitarian global redistribution of resources. But it offers no resistance to the ideal of global *access* to life-enriching goods. Some people with an outstanding talent for opera singing grow up in countries where there are no opera houses. The Rawlsian view tells us to reject the thought that resources should be globally redistributed to construct opera houses wherever there are those whose lives would be enriched by it. The decision whether to generate and spend resources on such projects is one that we should be concerned to help other peoples to take for themselves. However, it is important to see that it is a separate question whether we ought to provide individuals whose compatriots have collectively chosen not to produce such goods with opportunities for access to them. And the argument for the badness of brute inequality remains in force as a justification for requiring us to do so. Given that we could collectively structure our institutions so that other members of our global society can possess opportunities for self-enrichment that would otherwise be denied to them, it would be bad for us not to do so. In the absence of any strong countervailing reasons, we ought to do so.

Finally, we need to consider political inequality. Obviously, what I called 'internal' political inequalities are themselves clearly bounded – these are the inequalities of political status that exist between the members of a given polity. However, there may be duties that we have to help secure internal political equality in other polities. Rawls suggests one source of such duties – as duties of assistance that well-ordered peoples have to help other peoples to become well-ordered. Our discussion has supplied a second. Others' severe needs create a requirement on us to help them – a requirement that applies to us both individually and collectively, without regard to political boundaries – and effective long-term help needs to take the form of political restructuring.[27] As we have already seen, globalization does affect the extent to which we can be criticized for failing to do this.

'External' political inequality is the inequality of political status between those enjoying the privileges of membership of a polity it is desirable to belong to, and those who do not. Perhaps this is defensible: but notice that defending it would require going beyond the argument we focused on from Rawls earlier – the argument that once polities are self-determining, there is no further moral requirement of equality between peoples. An additional argument would be needed to show that we are morally entitled to constitute ourselves politically as peoples – an entitlement it is natural to seek to ground in individual liberty-rights.

A successful argument of this kind for the legitimacy and value of distinct self-determining polities would amount to a defence of political exclusion.[28] What form can that exclusion legitimately take? That is a large question, spanning complicated issues about asylum, refugee status and immigration policy. However, while leaving several of these issues open, our discussion has supplied at least one substantial part of the answer. If distinct self-determining polities are legitimate, then we are entitled to exclude others from political co-membership. But that is not an argument for barring others from access to goods which provide opportunities for self-enrichment. There is an argument from the badness of brute inequality for thinking that borders ought to be open, if not in relation to political membership, at least in relation to such opportunities.

Review

This chapter has examined the relevance of globalization to four kinds of social equality which it is plausible to think of as morally significant. In each case, we have found a strong argument for thinking that the facts of growing global interrelationship and interdependence that characterize the contemporary world do importantly extend the moral requirements that these forms of equality generate.

This leaves us with a moral challenge. I have emphasized that the question how we should go about addressing that challenge is a separate one, and it is one to which I have given only a partial answer here. The complexities of a fuller answer to that question I shall have to leave for discussion elsewhere. But it is surely hard to see how we could simply reconcile ourselves to living in a world of great injustice, and doing nothing about it.[29]

Notes

1 Highlights in this debate include Williams 1962, Nagel 1979, 1991, Sen 1980, 1992, Dworkin 1981a,b, Arneson 1989, Cohen 1989 and 1993, Scanlon 1975, 1986, 1996, Raz 1986 and Parfit 1991. Useful short survey articles of this literature are Arneson 1993, Barry 1992, and Weale 1998; see also McKerlie 1996.
2 See Cohen 1989: esp. 916–21. Cohen follows Dworkin in thinking of welfare either in hedonic terms or as preference-satisfaction.
3 See Parfit 1991: 17. The objection is that levelling down does not improve a social arrangement in *any* way. After all, few of those who think that social equality is morally important think that its importance overrides that of every other social good. Their claim is that if one social arrangement is more equal than another, then it is in one way better, although it may be in other ways worse – for example, if it is Pareto inferior. It is *this* claim that the levelling down objection denies.

Notice that the argument in the text relies on the 'person-affecting principle' that a situation cannot be better unless there is a person for whom it is better. For this label (applied to related but different claims), see Parfit 1984: 370, 1991: 32.

4 See the discussion of the difference between Egalitarianism and the Priority View in Parfit 1991: 19–28.

5 Of course, the important and controversial question this raises is just when a unit of resources is 'available for distribution'.

6 It might seem at first glance that levelling down is never an option in relation to inequality-as-domination: when advantages to the better off are produced by imposing hardships on the worse off, then removing the advantages will remove the hardships and improve the situation of the worse off. But this needn't be true. There can be situations in which a relationship of inequality-as-domination, although it involves hardships for the dominated person, still leaves her better off than she would be without it. Removing the hardships created by the relationship of domination would leave her with even greater ones.

7 This does not mean that inequality of this second kind is simply a subclass of the first: it need not involve imposing hardship on some for the benefit of others.

8 Compare Pogge (Chapter 4): 49.

9 Levelling down might prevent future callousness, however. And although – for the reasons given in the text – that will rarely be enough to make it the best response to this sort of inequality, that is at least one good thing to be said about it. Notice that saying this involves rejecting the 'person-affecting principle' identified in note 3.

10 For this reason, it seems to me problematic to base the justification for egalitarianism on the desirability of eliminating the influence of luck on distributions, as Cohen does (Cohen 1989: 908).

11 For some useful survey articles offering other, simpler taxonomies of such arguments, see Beitz 1998, Barry and Matravers 1998, Brown 1993 and O'Neill 1992.

12 Walzer 1983: 28–30. See also Walzer 1985a,b.

13 See Rawls 1999a, section 2 for the claim about the subject of justice, although not the argument concerning its political boundedness.

14 For detailed description and criticism of this view, see Barry 1989.

15 See Green 1907, chs II and III; Bosanquet 1923, ch. XI; and Bradley 1927, Essays II and V. The latter writes memorably that 'to wish to be better than the world is to be already on the threshold of immorality', since 'the "world" in this sense … is the morality already existing ready to hand in laws, institutions, social usages, moral opinions and feelings' (199–200).

16 I write 'value or rightness' here in order to cover both teleological and deontological developments of this thought.

17 The second of these is prominent in Berlin 1969.

18 See Walzer 1985a,b, Bauer 1981, p. 19, and Rawls 1999b, p. 36, who cites Kant 1795, *Ak.* VIII: 367. For a response, see Nielsen 1988a.

19 The seminal work in making the case for this important empirical claim has been done by Amartya Sen. See especially Sen 1999a.

20 For a sustained defence of this claim, see Landes 1998. For a succinct discussion of the problems surrounding international aid see Calvert and Calvert 2001: 223–34. For a careful analysis of the relationship between corruption, development and inequality, see Ward 1989.

21 The form of this argument is suggested by the structure of Rawls's position in Rawls 1993. I am not claiming that Rawls himself applies this structure directly to the question of global distributive egalitarianism. His treatment of this question in Rawls 1999b is discussed in the section of this chapter titled 'The globalist challenge'.

22 Proponents of these ideas have typically been concerned to avoid the conclusion that our moral constituency is less than humanity as a whole – without needing to invoke any of the contemporary facts of globalization. See Green 1907: 206–17; Bosanquet 1923, ch. XI: 8; and Bradley 1927: 204–5. According to Green, 'There is no necessary

limit of numbers or space beyond which the spiritual principle of social relation becomes ineffective' (Green 1907: 250). Bosanquet and Bradley are concerned to insist that humanity does not itself furnish us with a *community* of the morality-constituting kind, but argue that the 'tissue of connection' (Bosanquet 1923: 330) between communities suffices to ground moral relations in respect of humanity as a whole.

23 It seems incorrect to say that any individual employer of a chimney sweep in Victorian Britain was personally forcing hardship upon a child by employing him. But members of Victorian society were collectively responsible for the economic structure that gave children no reasonable alternative to dangerous and life-stunting work.

24 For a forceful presentation of this case, see Brecher and Costello 1998.

25 An argument I develop at greater length in Cullity 1994.

26 Adopting the distinction proposed by Sen 1999b, we have a case not just for international equity, but for *global* equity.

27 For the most authoritative advocate of this view, see Sen 1999a.

28 Notice that a defence of the value of self-determination by itself would not be enough to vindicate political exclusion – there could be a single, self-determining world polity.

29 For helpful comments, I am grateful to David Archard, members of the CAPPE/KCELJAG Workshop on Reconceiving Equality in a Global World and, for especially helpful editorial advice, Keith Horton.

3 Globalising equality

The Equal Worth Project

Tom Campbell

It is obvious, again, that the word 'Equality' possesses more than one meaning, and that the controversies surrounding it arise partly, at least, because the same term is employed with different connotations. Thus it may either purport to state a fact, or convey the expression of an ethical judgment. On the one hand, it may affirm that men are, on the whole, very similar in their natural endowments of character and intelligence. On the other hand it may assert that, while they differ profoundly as individuals in capacity and character, they are equally entitled as human beings to consideration and respect, and that the well-being of a society is likely to increase if it so plans its organization that, whether their powers are great or small, all its members may be equally enabled to make the best of such powers as they possess.

(Tawney 1964: 46)

Several of the chapters in this book refer to the well known if in practice neglected paradox of the modern world that we live in a time of unsurpassed wealth and prosperity alongside astounding social and economic inequalities and widespread grave deprivation and suffering.[1] This paradox is traditionally assumed to break down into two distinct problems: how to address inequality within states (domestic justice), and how to deal with inequality between states (international justice). However, the picture of a dual problem of inequality is now complicated by the phenomenon of globalisation, involving, as it does, the declining significance of the nation state and the emergence of an integrated global economy, together with the beginnings of a global society based on shared trading interests and, to a limited extent, on a more or less shared ideology of human rights. If both the practical and the moral significance of national boundaries are in doubt then we have to confront the paradox of suffering amidst plenty with a global conception of equality that transcends the crumbling distinction between domestic and international spheres.

Globalisation, I take to be an economically led process whereby business and trade is increasingly interdependent worldwide and increasingly independent of geographical location and national boundaries. The twin faces of globalisation in this regard are the decline of the nation state (Sassen 1996) and the ever enlarging impact of global economic forces exerting pressure towards standardisation, particularly in economic spheres but also in moral and political practices and ideals (Braithwaite and Drahos 2000). Part of that standardisation involves a deliberate, or at least accepted, trend towards greater material inequalities within economic and political systems. The question of how far conceptions of equality that have been developed with a view to making political demands and policies within states have application beyond state boundaries is now partly overtaken by a retreat from substantive ideals of equality within nation states themselves. Thus, the idea of a universal welfare state, in which need is the dominant determinant of educational, health and housing allocation, has become vulnerable within nation states themselves (see Shaver, Chapter 6 this volume), as a result of those developments in the world economy and polity. The increasing inequality within nation states mirrors the even more drastic inequalities between developed and developing nations. The pervasiveness of inequality means that, quite apart from possible causal connections between the two spheres of inequality, questions may be raised as to the availability of *any* conception of human equality that is capable of addressing inequality in either domestic or transnational contexts. A major theoretical issue of our time is whether or not there is a conception of what may be called 'cosmopolitan equality' that expresses a common normative base for a transnational ideal of equality applicable in principle within and beyond the boundaries of nation states (see Shue 1996; Pogge 1998).

This chapter addresses the question of cosmopolitan equality through an analysis of our inherited conceptions of equality undertaken in preparation for identifying and assessing their possible transformation to meet the equality problems of the twenty-first century. My analysis starts off with the familiar distinction between the descriptive and the evaluative aspects of the discourse of equality identified by Tawney in his classic work on equality originally published over seventy years ago. Unlike Tawney's,[2] my analysis does not play down the idea that there are assumed factual equalities or similar natural endowments that underpin assumptions about the equal worth of all human beings. Indeed, I suggest that such foundational descriptive equalities may well be a prerequisite to establishing a cosmopolitan conception of human equality that applies within nation states and, at the same time, takes us beyond the reciprocal obligations of defined communities. I argue that some sort of basic descriptive equality is a sound, and perhaps necessary, ground for endorsing and giving substance to Tawney's ethical goal of creating social and economic equality as a core political ideal within, beyond and after the demise of, the boundaries of individual polities. I call this the 'Equal Worth Project'.[3]

Having distinguished the descriptive and evaluative aspects of equality discourse, and without disowning the importance of the ethical aspect of equality expressed by Tawney as an equal entitlement to consideration and respect, I distinguish between the evaluative and what I call the prescriptive aspects of equality discourse. This distinction draws attention to the very significant issues that arise in the transition from deploring inequality to recommending who and what should be involved in the implementation of remedial action. Distinguishing the evaluative and the prescriptive aspects of equality discourse may not be such an important matter when, like Tawney, we are considering issues of equality purely within societies, but it becomes central in the context of a world order in which a sense of mutual responsibility beyond national boundaries is still weak and patchy. The chapter goes on to explore the interrelationships between the three modes, the descriptive, evaluative and prescriptive aspects of equality discourse, giving particular attention to the equal worth thesis. The equal worth thesis is that a cosmopolitan conception of equality can, and perhaps must, be based on the assumption that there is a range of basic factual similarities between human beings that underpin the evaluations of social, economic and political (in)equality that are presupposed in any prescription for (re)distribution of benefits and burdens, including rights and duties, that can be classified as egalitarian.

Analytical markers

Equality is one of the most versatile of fundamental social and political concepts. There is scarcely any ideological position that cannot, with relatively little ingenuity, be presented as exemplifying equality of one sort or another. Even vast disparities of wealth and condition may be justified as being the consequence of equal liberty or equality before the law or equality of opportunity. We are therefore right to be sceptical of abstract commitments to 'equality'. No apology is therefore required for setting out a few basic analytical markers before tackling issues connected with the potential impact of globalisation on the ways in which we might conceptualise equality and inequality, and particularly which ideas of equality are sufficiently robust to qualify for the hopefully radical label 'egalitarian'.

The discourse of equality contains three analytically distinct dimensions which, for brevity, I call descriptive equality, evaluative equality and prescriptive equality. I consider each in turn and then discuss their relationships each to the other.

Descriptive equality

The descriptive aspect of equality discourse routinely concerns ways in which people are said to be equal or unequal with respect to properties or characteristics that are in principle identifiable and perhaps measurable without directly involving evaluations. These properties may be internal ones that relate to the body, person or character of persons (such as their height, intelligence or boldness), or they may be external ones that relate to their possessions, political power or situation (such as their income, social situation or employment). While evaluations standardly come into the selection of the properties that are considered worth describing and comparing, the actual describing, comparing and measuring are in themselves and in principle purely descriptive, hence the label 'descriptive equality'.

In fact the types of property that may be identified, described and compared vary considerably. The prototype statements of descriptive (in)equality are empirical propositions about the distribution of measurable benefits and burdens under various heads, principally properties external to the person conceived as a distinct entity, such as income, wealth or resources, but also including some internal properties, such as happiness or well-being, that are, as it were, part of what that person is. These properties, whether external or internal, may be called 'well-being (or benefit and burden) properties'. They have to do with whether or not a person may be considered 'well off'. The judgment as to what counts as well off, is of course, evaluative, but the properties identified as the criteria for being well off are such that their presence and degree can be determined in principle empirically. Well-being properties feature in statements of what may be called 'distributive descriptive (in)equality' in which people are compared with respect to the sort of desirable and undesirable possessions and characteristics (external or internal) that go into our assessment of what it is to be well or badly off in terms of the goods and ills of life.[4]

Statements of distributive descriptive (in)equality may take the simple form of comparing individuals or groups with respect to their well-being properties, or they may take the more complex, patterned, form of correlating such well-being properties with other properties that may either explain or justify the distribution of well-being properties. When the purpose of the description is one of justification or criticism, as when the distribution of wealth is correlated with the distribution of some admired or denigrated characteristic, such as effort or idleness, we may identify what may be called 'justificatory properties', which identify, for instance, what is considered meritorious or efficient. Justificatory properties are used to vindicate or criticise the distribution of well-being properties. Sometimes justificatory properties can be expressed in empirical terms (such as hours of work), in other cases (such as the quality of the work done) this seems difficult or impossible.[5] Usually the purpose of such patterned descriptions of (in)equality is to make critical or evaluative points about the rightness or wrongness of such patterns, with a certain proportionality of well-being to justificatory properties being preferred. However, where the properties in question are empirical or can be given empirical markers, statements of patterned (in)equality can be purely descriptive in meaning whatever the ulterior purposes of those who use them.

Returning to the more simple forms of descriptive equality, it is clear that the descriptive elements of equality discourse can range broadly or narrowly. At one extreme we have descriptive equality assertions that are tantamount to assertions of identity, covering all internal properties and total similarity of external properties. This may be called full equality or identicality.[6] At the opposite extreme, two people may be said to be descriptively equal if they are the same or identical in only one respect, such as their weight or wealth. In such cases it would be normal to make explicit, unless the context makes this clear already, the precise property in terms of which the persons are being compared. Nevertheless, it is perfectly meaningful to say that two people are equal, when comparing them with respect to only one property. I call this single-property equality.

In between the extremes of full equality (or identicality) and single-property equality, assertions of equality may be understood as indicating that persons are the same or similar with respect to any number and types of properties. It follows that if we wish to reach any degree of precision in equality statements it must be made clear which persons are being compared and with respect to which properties, qualities or features. In practice, all descriptive equality is equality with respect to particular properties, or some combination of properties, internal and external. This means that assertions of equality have to be made in terms of selected or relevant or agreed properties. Apparently context-free definitions of equality must therefore include an implicit reference to some as yet unstated context. In general terms, descriptive equality may be taken to mean broad similarity with respect to those properties that are considered to be relevant in a particular type of context. Where this is achieved it seems appropriate to say that the situation is, in that context, egalitarian.

This analysis may help in drawing attention to the all-important fact that assertions of descriptive equality in a social and political context make sense only in relation to some wider purpose or objective that prompts specific descriptive equality affirmations or denials. It is also helpful in drawing attention to the fact that, since equality is not the same as identity, there will always be properties with respect to which two or more persons are not similar or the same. Unless there is a tight identification of the relevant properties, equality affirmations are compatible with the existence of inequalities that may or may not be relevant to the context in question.[7] Unspecific equality affirmations may, therefore, always be challenged as matters of fact (are the persons similar or the same with respect to the relevant property?) and in terms of relevance (are the properties selected the appropriate ones?).[8]

Returning to those patterns of distribution that feature in justificatory assertions of (in)equality, I foreshadow here the particular importance that attaches to those statements that claim to identify the justificatory properties that underpin affirmations of what may be called equal 'human worth'. My thesis is that there are certain descriptive properties whose approximately equal distribution is the basis on which it may be claimed that all people are in some fundamental sense equal. This is traditionally expressed by saying that everyone is born equal or shares a common human nature. I call this 'foundational descriptive equality' because of its role in the justification of the ideal of the equal worth or importance of human beings that in turn features in the justification or critique of descriptive (in)equalities of well-being and ultimately in prescriptions as to what ought to be done to correct the current patterns of (in)equality. With important exceptions (Singer 1990; Pojman 1995; Arneson 1999), most contemporary analyses of equality take for granted the idea of equal worth but ignore the significance of foundational descriptive equalities. In so doing they make it more difficult to arrive at a genuinely cosmopolitan conception of equality or egalitarianism.

Evaluative equality

The evaluative element of equality discourse involves a variety of judgments as to the moral significance of descriptions with respect to distributive (in)equalities, patterns of (in)equalities and foundational equalities. Evaluative equality relates to decisions about the properties that are considered to be worth describing and comparing, either for the purpose of going on to affirm or deny the equality of human worth, or to formulate preferences as to the approved distribution of well-being properties. Thus, evaluation is involved in concluding that human beings are of equal worth, because they have, for instance, foundational descriptive equalities such as the capacity for choice, or self-awareness, or sentience. Evaluative judgment is also involved in assessing the relative value or importance of these and other internal properties and their normative relationship to the approved distribution of benefits and burdens. Thus, distributive descriptive (in)equalities of wealth are often presented in terms of an existing or non-existing pattern or proportionality or disproportionality between, say, the wealth of persons and their contribution to the economic well-being of a society. Such patterned distributive equalities are common ingredients of preferred social and political ideals.

The core of much social and economic equality discourse lies in the contested question as to the sort of distributive equality, patterned or otherwise, that is desirable or just. Initial questions have to do with what has come to be known as the 'currency' of equality (Cohen 1989: 914),[9] which may be something like well-being, or utility, or resources, or capabilities, or opportunities, or rights (see Sen 1980; Dworkin 2000: 285–303). This then enables us to raise questions about the preferred pattern of distribution of the chosen currency. I have signalled my view that equality discourse in its stronger forms is properly regarded as egalitarian in so far as it involves the desirability of actual equality of outcome in the distribution of a broad range of important well-being properties. A situation in which all human beings, or the members of the relevant group of human beings, are in a position of descriptive equality with respect to well-being properties is, on an egalitarian view, regarded as desirable, either for its own sake or for some ulterior reason associated with the idea of equality.

All evaluative positions that can be called egalitarian give high, but not necessarily overriding, priority to achieving descriptive equality of well-being properties. In this respect it is difficult to say how much weight must be given to descriptive equality for a theory to count as egalitarian. Indeed some philosophers are prepared to countenance as a form of egalitarianism theories that hold that there is no value in such equality for its own sake (Parfit 1996).[10] Weaker versions of egalitarianism permit significant justified inequalities as long as these arise out of some equality of initial situation, such as equality of opportunity. Inegalitarian theories are more concerned with the justification of patterns containing significant differences (or 'inequalities') between individuals and groups, perhaps mirroring inequalities of other properties, such as merit or status.[11]

It is sometimes argued or assumed that the strongest examples of egalitarianism make equality of well-being properties an end in itself, in that what is good about a situation of such equality is that no one has more or less than another person. This is something that is considered desirable in itself and is unrelated to the importance to the individual of the well-being properties themselves. On this view, it is not having well-being that matters, but having equal well-being. If equality is given priority over other values, it follows that a situation in which individuals have equality at a low level of well-being is better than a situation in which everyone is better off but some have more than others. This would mean disvaluing inequalities that are not otherwise detrimental to anyone (because they do not, for instance, involve the redistribution of a fixed quantum of benefits and burdens). This would provide a basis for policies that involve levelling down simply in order to achieve greater descriptive equality. However, while some theorists do not consider that equality is a distinct and separate ideal unless equality is valued for its own sake, it seems dogmatic not to include under equality ideals equality of well-being that is justified on the grounds that everyone's well-being is equally important, and not because it is bad in itself that one person's well-being is greater than another's. These issues are discussed in more detail by Garrett Cullity in Chapter 2 of this volume.

Egalitarianism need not, however, be identified with this 'equality for its own sake' ideal, at least in the strong form that requires levelling down (Temkin 2000: 126–61). While it may be that, within a community, there is value in such equality because of the nature of the social relationships that it brings with it, the core claim of evaluative egalitarianism may be expressed by saying that the maximisation of any one person's well-being is as important and desirable as the maximisation of any other person's well-being. The implications of such a view is that it is good that there be descriptive equality of well-being properties, but this is not because such equality is valued for its own sake rather than because it is the outcome of implementing the ideal of equal human worth (Campbell 2001: 27).

Prescriptive equality

The prescriptive aspect of equality discourse relates neither to the description of human conditions, properties or holdings, nor to judgments as to the worth of persons and the desirability of this or that pattern of distribution. Prescriptive equality concerns, rather, how we ought to react and respond to such matters as equal worth and to specific descriptive (in)equalities. Prescriptive equality involves commending, for instance, equality of treatment, or showing equal concern and respect, equal consideration, or equal treatment to bring about a descriptive equality of outcome. We are dealing here with the transition from evaluation to action, with issues of responsibility and efficacy, going beyond gladness and regret to maxims of obligation and policy.

Equality prescriptions are capable of widely divergent constructions. Thus, even the apparently homogenous conception of equal treatment, is capable of many different interpretations, some of which can be explicated in terms of the distinctions outlined earlier. Thus equal treatment can be construed as treating those involved identically, which is capable of being expressed in terms of the descriptive identity of what is done to or for them. Or it may be construed as treating people in ways that are equally valued or disvalued, which presupposes some prior evaluations as to the comparative desirability of the treatment involved. On the other hand, equality of treatment can be construed to mean treatment that results in the same outcomes for the persons treated, taking into account their prior properties and circumstances, such as their needs or desires. In other words, 'equal treatment' may mean identical or equivalent treatment, or it may mean treatment that produces a descriptively identical or equivalent outcome for those involved.[12] Further, equal treatment may be construed in an even weaker way as involving no more than equality of consideration, that is applying the same moral criteria to each case, with no presupposition that this is the result in anything resembling equal treatment in either sense defined earlier.

Prescriptive equality relates not only to the type of process to be used in bringing about a distribution of well-being properties, and the type of descriptive equality at which they are directed, but also deals with identifying whose duty it is to carry out these processes and achieve the desired equality situation. Prima facie, it may be assumed that once we have made the relevant evaluations as to what sort of descriptive equalities matter, then the prescriptions to do whatever is necessary to promote the most desirable pattern of equalities follows. But this is not the case. For a start, as we have seen, there may be other values at stake besides equality. Indeed, achieving a single property form of equality may thwart another single property form of equality. All this may be taken into account by accepting that there are justified inequalities, adjusting our overall objectives with this in mind, and formulating prescriptions to ensure only justified (in)equality. However, if redistribution is involved, this may require systematic takings from some people without their consent. This may limit any equality prescriptions to those that have the support of a democratic decision of those involved. Democracy itself is a matter of (political) equality that may result in other types of descriptive inequality. For these and many other reasons equality prescriptions merge into a general social and political programme that is quite removed from the equality evaluations on which they are grounded.

Some theories involve the assumption that prescriptive duties fall only on those who are responsible for bringing about the undesirable inequalities in question. Indeed it has been claimed that a particular form of equality theory – deontic egalitarianism – identifies egalitarianism with correcting inequalities that arise as a result of a wrong done and are, in this sense, unjust (Parfit 1996). While those responsible for harming others in ways that make them worse off are clearly prime candidates for being the subjects of prescriptive requirements to rectify such wrongs, it seems extraordinary to exclude the possibility that there are not other bases for ascribing the duties of prescriptive equality discourse, and certainly mistaken to hold that only such inequalities as arise from wrongdoing matter. Indeed, the righting of wrongs can be seen as an important moral transaction that can be identified and analysed without any reference to the idea of equality as we have been considering it. What seems to be going on here is a confusion of evaluative and prescriptive equality that makes the undesirability of inequality dependent on the existence of pre-existing duty of prescriptive equality deriving from some source prior to the act of wrongdoing. However, prior wrongdoing is neither necessary nor sufficient for the ascription of duties to bring about equality.

Nevertheless, a theory of equality does have to indicate how we are to move from evaluation to prescription. A core set of issues with respect to globalising equality, is how far these prescriptive forms of equality discourse and their associated institutions make practical and moral sense outside certain social and political settings. Equality of opportunity, for instance, may seem a prime example of an equality prescription that relates only to individuals within an existing social and political group. It is possible, therefore, that different objectives and prescriptions are appropriate in other spheres. It may indeed be that in the global dimension, evaluations of unequal situations do not give rise to prescriptions unless there has been a wrong done, or those ascribed the duties are in some way implicated in the system that produces such undesirable outcomes (Pogge 2001b), whereas in a specific community or nation prescriptions also arise through a combination of such phenomena as sympathy, identification and capacity to help. However, it seems reasonable to consider further whether some other criteria, such as comparative wealth and/or proximity might serve to bridge the gap between evaluation and prescription in transnational as well as national contexts.

Relating descriptive, evaluative and prescriptive equality

In practice, the descriptive, evaluative and prescriptive modes are often interconnected, and indeed, as we have just seen, they are often confused. The fact that people are the same with respect to a particular characteristic does not entail that this is a good or bad thing, and judgments as to the desirability of descriptive equalities or inequalities do not in themselves determine who if anyone ought to do anything to render the pattern of descriptive equalities more acceptable. Nevertheless, there is a recurrent tendency to connect the descriptive, evaluative and prescriptive element in the discourse of equality. One persistent paradigmatic equality model runs as follows. Because people are descriptively equal with respect to specified properties (foundational equality) they have equal worth (evaluative equality) and therefore ought to be treated equally or so as to being about equality (prescriptive equality). Basic descriptive equalities are postulated and positively evaluated as morally significant and appropriate prescriptions are then inferred in the light of the existing circumstances. One version of this is the Equal Worth Project.

In point of fact, there is no a priori need to relate the descriptive, evaluative and prescriptive elements of equality conceptions in this way. Each can stand on its own and be assessed in its own terms or justified in a variety of ways. Equality prescriptions need not be based on any equality evaluations and equality evaluations need not be based on equality descriptions. Thus, with respect to the connections between the constituent parts of this paradigm model of equality, not all judgments of equal worth are based on any assumed descriptive equalities, and assertions of equal worth do not necessarily entail any obligations, although they may entail a moral preference for persons enjoying some sort of descriptive equality. Similarly, prescriptions as to equality of treatment need not be based on the evaluation of alleged descriptive (in)equalities.

Nevertheless, I argue that there is need for a firm descriptive foundation for a working conception of equal worth that is strong enough to feed into a substantive evaluative ideal of equality that can serve as the basis for a variety of contextually dependent practical prescriptions. This provides a distinctive form of evaluative argument that moves, albeit non-deductively, from factual to evaluative equality, and, through complex empirical and evaluative connections, to prescriptive equality maxims and goals that together can serve as the basis for a theory of cosmopolitan equality that generates global obligations in relation to enhancing global descriptive equality. Currently, most theorists simply assume some form of evaluative equality, usually called moral equality,[13] and then concentrate on working out its practical implications, but neglect the deeper questions of justification.

Equal worth

Although the distinctions between descriptive, evaluative and prescriptive equality are of fundamental importance in the clarification of the discourse of equality, in themselves they are rather dry and abstract and need to be put to work in specific contexts. I move on, therefore, to a more direct approach to the Equal Worth Project that is grounded in the affirmation that all human beings are of equal worth, a moral insight that has profound implications for the way in which we evaluate and organise national and international society.

The idea of equal worth is sometimes assumed to be rooted in the belief that every person is as important as everyone else. My pleasure or pain matters as much as your pleasure or pain and indeed as much as any other human being's pleasure or pain. The mere fact that the interests of one person rather than that of another person are involved does not make any difference to the value or disvalue of these interests. This fundamental insight may be put in many different ways. We may say that morality, or at least public morality, is person-neutral (Fletcher 1996: 121),[14] or that people have the same 'individual worth' (Vlastos 1962: 43) or 'equal moral standing' (Nielsen 1988b), or the same 'basic moral status' (Arneson 1999: 103).

The scope and implications of equal worth interpreted as the evaluative affirmation of person-neutrality is unclear. Thus, in itself, equal worth in this sense does not tell us how much value attaches to persons and human lives, only that whatever value they have they have it equally. It may be that human life is of infinite value, or it may be that it is only of great value, or even quite minimal value, but such value it has attaches to each person equally.[15] While it is generally agreed that the mere fact of individual identity is in almost all cases morally irrelevant, it is not clear that anything of significance follows from person-neutrality by itself.

However, if human existence is deemed to have *some* positive value, which it would be hard for any human being to deny, then the affirmation of equal value does at least give a prima facie reason to applaud, in equal measure, the flourishing of human persons, and perhaps, in consequence, to act to protect and further the interests of such human beings on an equal basis. If all people are equally important it must be an equally good thing that each person enjoys any specified degree of well-being, hence, by aggregation, descriptive equality of well-being is a desirable state of affairs.

Further, equal importance does not by itself imply that the interests of one person should not be sacrificed to serve the interests of others, provided that this is not done because that person's interests are of lesser importance than those of others. Thus, Bentham's utilitarian dictum 'each to count for one and no more than one' appears to satisfy some conception of equal human worth without ruling out such sacrifices. We cannot assume that equal worth by itself takes us into the realm of the inviolable protection of the interests of the individual. Equal importance may require no more than that the interests of everyone be equally weighed in whatever distributive formula we use to determine distributive outcomes.[16]

Yet, 'equal worth', presuming some degree of value attaches to human existence, is an assertion of evaluative equality that has the potential to be truly universal. It seems to encompass the conviction that such matters as citizenship, nationality or geographical location are irrelevant to the assessment of the worth of the human individual. As such, equal worth can readily feature in a cosmopolitan ethic that has no regard for state boundaries and group differences. Moreover, equal worth could be culturally transcendent if it does not depend on any particular characterisation of what it is to be a human being, that is, it does not presuppose any agreement on the properties in virtue of which a person is deemed to be of equal worth. Such matters are inherently controversial and culture dependent. And so, even if nothing in particular follows from equal human worth outside a context of assumed values and a scheme of mutual obligations or established institutional arrangements, it does seem to have the potential to act as a common denominator from which the analysis of globalised equality might proceed.

Moreover, the idea of equal worth may be strengthened somewhat so that it becomes the basis for excluding certain practices that bear unevenly on human beings, such as dissimilar treatment based on grounds of race, gender or age. Perhaps the essence of equal worth is to exclude such discriminator classifications as evident denials of equal worth so that equality becomes at base a matter of non-discrimination, that is, the principle that no public act that embodies such proscribed criteria is compatible with equal worth.

Yet, even on this still relatively weak interpretation of equal worth there are problems when it comes to distinguishing between those criteria that are in this negative sense 'discriminatory' and those that are not. The idea of equal worth does not mean that we are never justified in treating people differently. On what basis can we determine what is discriminatory and what is not? The answer does not follow from the mere idea of equal worth on its own. Rather it requires us to identify the basis on which we ascribe equal worth and to use this basis to identify what is and what is not discriminatory and therefore compatible with equal worth.

This points to the inadequacy of a thin theory of equal worth that is unconnected with specific foundational descriptions and the value judgments as to what it is that grounds such an affirmation of equal worth. We must, therefore, go back to the foundational descriptive elements in equality discourse that assert or presuppose basic empirical or metaphysical sameness of some sort or another, those features of common human personhood or experience or existence that are judged to be of value and which give rise to the affirmation of equal worth or importance. The substantive impact of the idea of equal worth is dependent on the nature and extent of the value we ascribe to human life. This means that we must identify those features of human existence which render it valuable, albeit with an eye to the selection of properties in which human being share equally, in order to arrive at judgments of equal worth. And so, unavoidably, we come to that difficult task of ascertaining a normative theory of human nature that specifies those aspects of human life or person-hood that give people their worth, presumptively their equal worth, the issue that is routinely ignored in current equality debates.

The principal competing views as to the worth of human existence in Western culture are autonomy (the capacity to make rational choices, particularly moral choices, the views of Immanuel Kant), sentience, either, in a crude form, the capacity to feel pleasure and pain, or in a more sophisticated form, the capacity for a variety of self-conscious and complex experiences (according to Jeremy Bentham and John Stuart Mill respectively), and naturalism (the capacity to fulfil an essential nature by functioning in a variety of ways identifiable in terms of distinctively human activities, as per Aristotle, or perhaps Aquinas).

All these approaches can, in principle, fill out the idea of equal worth to make it a thicker and more powerful concept in so far as all human beings are held to be the loci of such values. They offer explanations as to why human life is valuable and, potentially, why that value applies in each and every case. Moreover, they may provide some insight into why certain types of unequal treatment are unacceptable in that they are irrelevant to the factors that give human life its value. All these foundational descriptive equalities, in putting forward a list of plausibly relevant fundamental properties, implicitly exclude other properties that are not listed, such as race, religion or gender, which are thereby deemed to be irrelevant to the affirmation of (equal) worth.[17] Further, foundational descriptive equality of some sort gives us an idea why it is that all human beings are deserving of the respect and consideration that are generally agreed to be appropriate responses to all human beings.

It is not my purpose here to choose between these normative paradigms of human nature.[18] Nevertheless, examining these alternatives from the point of view of descriptive equality, we can see that they are all vulnerable, in varying degrees, to the implication that the capacities they select as the basis of equal worth are not equally distributed throughout the human species (Fletcher 1996: 121; Arneson 1999: 105). The Kantian position is least exposed to this difficulty in so far as it depends on the postulation of an ineffable non-causal form of human autonomy which is presupposed by the experience of moral choice rather than observed as a phenomenon more or less present in each human life. The Aristotelian position is most exposed to the discovery of descriptive inequality on account of the broad range of capacities on which it draws to define human nature normatively conceived, and, of course, Aristotle was no believer in human equality. The sentience approach comes close to founding equality on an empirically observable similarity between human beings but becomes thereby the most vulnerable to empirical refutation.

Perhaps the prospect of empirical refutation of fundamental equality is one reason why philosophers usually seek to detach affirmations of equal human worth from any alleged descriptive equalities. Hence the attraction of the negative formulation with which I started this analysis of equal worth: the mere fact of whose interests are at stake is morally irrelevant. That my happiness is of equal value to your or anyone else's happiness does not presuppose that we have equal amounts of happiness or that we are equally capable of equal happiness.

As noted earlier, this would make equal worth compatible with one life having twice the value of another, not because it is the life of any particular person, but because the former is capable of experiencing twice as much happiness as the latter. This means that, while the thin or negative approach to human worth may enable us to provide a rationale for deploring discrimination on irrelevant grounds, such as race, it may introduce other forms of unacceptable preferences that are equally objectionable. More specifically, descriptive internal differences may be used to justify different distributional patterns. What we are then left with is the idea of proper proportionality of holdings in relation to the variable degree to which persons have particular external or internal properties. Such proportionality does not mandate equality in any strong descriptive distributional or egalitarian sense.

There are a number of ways that the retreat into an unhelpfully weak form of equal human worth may be resisted. One is to put forward the empirical claim that the differences between human beings in the relevant capacities, at least potentially, are relatively small. Rough fundamental descriptive equality is a fact that makes it reasonable to assume precise descriptive equality in practice. This is particularly plausible if the foundational characteristic is sentience. While it is hard to reject the view that a belief in equal human worth is not based on some such empirical assumptions about the potentially roughly equal capacities of human beings the world over, it does seem a defective approach if we want to be strongly committed to improving the welfare of those whose capacities or potential capacities are way below the average.

A more satisfactory line might be to argue that each capacity has a threshold that, once reached, is sufficient to ground the judgment of value on which the belief in equal worth is based. This is more plausible in the case of some capacities, such as self-awareness, than others, such as creativity. Few thresholds have that all-or-nothing quality that is necessary to vindicate a radically different evaluation of capacities that go beyond the proffered threshold. It may be that what is valued is the exercise of the capacity within the natural limits of the person concerned, so that what matters is an individual's 'personal best' assessed in relation to the extent of that person's capacities, as Tawney indicates in my opening quotation. However, to hold that people are descriptively equal because they have a potential, however small or large, remains a weak form of foundational equality.

There are other reasons why philosophers so often avoid the challenge of basing equal worth on a foundational descriptive equality. Foremost amongst these is the fear of falling foul of the naturalistic fallacy by assuming that because people are in some ways descriptively equal that they must have equal worth, a fallacious move from fact to value.[19] However, there is no need to assume that the relation-ship between the evaluation and the facts on which the judgment is supervenient is deductive or a matter of 'proof'. All that is required is that the judgment of equal worth is a judgment about something rather than about nothing.

Another reason behind the reluctance to seek out foundational descriptive equalities is that we may come away empty handed and have to withdraw our affirmation of equal human worth, extend it to include higher animals or narrow it to exclude very poorly endowed humans. These are, of course, implications that some philosophers are willing to take on board (Singer 1990). However, we may argue, along the lines outlined earlier, that, with a sufficiently full and varied description of the relevant human capacities, there is a rough equality of capaci-ties in the vast majority of persons that extend to few, if any, animals, that can serve as the basis for an evaluation of equal worth that is sufficiently accurate to justify radically egalitarian evaluations and prescriptions.

There is a danger in drawing the bounds of foundational equality too narrowly, encompassing, for instance, only a single property version of equality such as the capacity for moral choice or agency (Gewirth 1978), which greatly restricts the basis on which a reflective and sustainable commitment to equal worth is grounded. However, there are other reasons for regarding such criteria as too lim-ited to serve as the basis for our belief in foundational equality as they run counter to our firm intuitions about the independent significance of pleasure and pain.

Another reason for the general absence of attempts to justify equal worth by ref-erence to human properties, is anxiety about the demanding implications of a prop-erly grounded commitment to equality of worth that includes a judgment about the universal human capacity for specifically human forms of suffering and deprivation.

Whatever the reasons, it is normal for philosophers to argue that judgments of equal worth, and therefore judgments of the equal worth human life, are not based on any claims as to the capacities, variable or otherwise, of human beings. This is most effectively done by bringing in some alleged fact that is external to human nature, such as the proposition that human beings are all equally 'the chil-dren of God' or 'the product of Nature'. However, such claims do not distinguish human beings from other creations or products, such as animals or inanimate things and leave the affirmation of human worth either as a matter of religious faith or a naturalist dogma.

At this point most contemporary theorists argue or take for granted that the idea of equality of worth, or importance, is no more than an assumption, perhaps a rebuttable assumption, about how we ought to treat people, with no descriptive foundation whatsoever. On this common view, what we have in the affirmation of equal human worth is a shared intuition or supposition on the basis of which we can reach a consensus on certain matters irrespective of disagreement as to the basis of our practical agreement. We may agree that grave suffering arising from starvation and ill health are undesirable either for their own sake or for the reduced prospect of autonomous living and the attainment of personal well-being involved, whether or not there is any significant sameness in human beings beyond their membership of the species homo sapiens.

As I have indicated, such baseless conceptions of foundational equality may be considered a benefit when it comes to globalising the belief in equal human worth since it could be a shared evaluation associated with an increased variety of beliefs as to the relevant descriptive equalities. To the theories of Kant, Bentham and (perhaps) Aristotle, we may add those of Confucius, Buddha and Mohammed, excluding those elements of all these traditions that suggest that there might be a higher value placed on the lives and experiences of those humans who are born within the fold of a particular religion or civilisation.

Yet, the retreat from foundational descriptive equality leaves us with a philo-sophical void in theories that go straight to affirmations of equal worth of every human being. Any evaluations and prescriptions as to equality lack an adequate explanation as to why persons should be treated equally and what this involves. Moreover, an under-theorised prescriptive consensus generates a false confidence in our capacity to work out what this equality of worth implies in the harsh world of social and economic inequality. Only a thick conception of equal worth can generate any powerful imperatives beyond the boundaries of nation states.

This problem is compounded by the fact that those theorists who distance themselves from foundation descriptive equality tend to ground their recommen-dations about equal treatment within the nation-state to the idea of membership of a political community (Walzer 1983). A typical example is the thesis that equal concern is due to every citizen on the grounds that all citizens are expected to con-form to laws which require them to behave in ways that they may not themselves believe to be just or fair (Dworkin 2000). Such an analysis may have considerable force within a modern democratic state, indeed it could be regarded as constitu-tive of democracy as a form of government that is intended to serve equally the interests of all citizens. However, in the absence of a global state or society, this approach has little to offer those who seek to articulate a cosmopolitan ideal of human equality that has application beyond contingent political boundaries.

From equal worth to equality of lives

If equal worth is the philosophical core of the discourse of equality, it is the eval-uation of the distributive equalities that concern the pattern of benefits and bur-dens, external and internal, that is the focus of most intense political interest. Do we prefer or approve the equal distribution of material resources, or of the capac-ities to fulfil our nature, or of happiness, or of opportunities to realise variable life plans? And, whatever it is that we wish to see equalised, does the value we place on equality outweigh other considerations, particularly the maximisation or increase of those benefits and the minimisation and decrease of those burdens about whose equal distribution we are concerned? Precisely what is the content of the equality we value and what weight are we to give to that equality over other considerations?

I have suggested that a thick idea of equal worth provides a potential basis for working out answers to such questions. Indeed, I have suggested that it may pro-vide an essential ingredient for so doing. In this section I explore this stage in the

Equal Worth Project and consider the possibility that there might be alternative foundations for a strong, even an egalitarian, form of cosmopolitan equality.

We have seen that the hoped for gains in global consensus that might arise from a concentration on a thin or under-theorised conception equality of human worth wilt before the question of what sort of equality of life circumstances is or is not appropriate or desirable. This is why the foundational descriptive equalities on which, I suggest, we should we base our judgments of equal worth, are an obvious starting point in looking for those valued properties we might wish to see equally distributed. If the foundational descriptive equality we value in human life is everyone's capacity to makes choices, for instance, then a situation in which the opportunities for choice are equally distributed is likely to be preferred. If it is the capacity to make specific moral choices that makes for equal human worth then equality with respect to the sort of choices is appropriate. If it is the capacity not just to make choices but to carry out projects that are of value (or are valued by the individuals concerned) then a situation in which this is equally feasible for all is to be preferred over one where it is not. On the other hand, if it is the capacity to feel pleasure and pain that is the basis of equal worth, then it looks as if the existence of equal pleasure and pain for all is to be preferred.

Yet, even if the preferred foundational property points us in the direction of the preferred currency of the desired form of descriptive equality, does this really take us to the conclusion that it is to be preferred if that property is equally distributed between persons? The equalising aspect of the assumption of equal worth would appear to depend on calculations as to the most effective way of maximising the desired phenomena, such as choice or pleasure. For instance, if there are only so many choices or pleasures that any one individual can experience, arguably it makes sense, in the pursuit of maximising, to prefer an even distribution of desirable experiences, so that the best use may be made of them. Equal human worth does make for a preference for resources being where they most effectively promote the properties that give rise to an affirmation of human worth. But this only contingently makes it preferable to have the desired goods distributed to ensure their equal allocation, although that is not unlikely, given the law of diminishing returns which operates powerfully with respect to many of the values concerned.

Here we are entering the familiar territory of the critique of Benthamite utilitarianism from the point of view of equality. However, while utilitarianism may be seen as a form of equal worth theory that identifies the capacity for pleasure and pain as the foundational property on which equal worth is based, the idea of equal worth cannot be identified with the idea that what matters is the maximisation of a well-being property irrespective of its location, as if human beings were merely containers for pleasures and pains or a substratum to which well-being properties are attached. Rather the insight concerning equal worth is that we value equally the happiness (or whatever) of people, so that we have the same reason to welcome the fact that one person is happy as we do with respect to any other person. This is a more egalitarian proposition than at least some version of utilitarianism according to which it is the maximisation not the distribution of happiness that counts.

As to the prospect that utilitarianism might provide an alternative to equal worth as a basis for cosmopolitan equality or egalitarianism, this is true only in so far as utilitarianism approximates to one version of equal worth, a version in which the characteristic of human beings that matters is their capacity for experiencing pleasure and pain. In so far as this goes, and noting the problem of distribution encountered by most versions of utilitarianism, it does provide a basis for cosmopolitan equality, although not necessarily in its most convincing form. Equal worth theories that fix on the foundational property of hedonic sentience are distinctly utilitarian in flavour.

A variation on this theme that echoes the idea of 'negative utilitarianism', according to which the minimisation of pain takes priority over the maximisation of happiness, is the so-called 'priority' theory suggested in the article by Derek Parfit referred to earlier. On this approach, benefiting people matters more the worse off these people are (Parfit 1996: 213). As this is said not to be a matter of comparative advantage it avoids the criticism that it favours levelling down while still providing a basis for preferring a world that is in fact more egalitarian in terms of well-being properties. Again, this approach is not an alternative to equal worth as the foundation for the preference for morally approving of changes in distributive equality that favour the worse off. This is because, as an evaluative (and as a prescriptive) principle it lacks plausibility in the absence of a presupposition of foundational equality. Any effective justification for prioritism takes us back to affirmations of equal worth, in this case largely in terms of the capacity for suffering and with respect to person-neutrality.

There remain, however, considerable difficulties in charting the relationship between foundational (in)equalities, whether utilitarian or not, and evaluative distributive (in)equalities. One set of complexities arises from the fact that equality is not the only value relevant to actual social situations. This is evident not only because we have been considering equality in relation to the distribution of valued things, such as autonomy or pleasure, but also because other values, that may come into conflict with an egalitarian conception of equality, cannot be ignored once we come to evaluate actual situations.

Thus, even if we in principle prefer a situation where all people have equal well-being, this can be no more than a prima facie judgment that is revisable in the light of other factors, such as the comparative deserts of those involved. Introducing again the concept of justice, we may say that justice is satisfied if inequalities of properties and or holdings are such that they are justified in terms of the relative deserts of those involved. In this case, egalitarian equality is an element within a more complex set of preferences that may be expressed in terms of justice. In such cases it is not that the significance of comparative desert outweighs the significance of equality but that desert justifies or requires inequality.

Additionally, it may be argued, it is preferable that individuals be able to exercise their autonomy even if this results in an unequal distribution of valued properties or possessions. In such cases we have a trade off between values with different weights being given to one or the other according to the preferences of those making the evaluations. Some may think that in some circumstances the value of liberty makes a departure from equality desirable in those situations where it is not feasible to have both equal liberty and equal well-being. Others see this as a manifestation of another form of equality of opportunity.

From such complexities very different conceptions of evaluative equality emerge. At the extreme, egalitarian evaluative equality requires descriptive equality of valued properties, such as desert or autonomy, over all other considerations. This does not mean that descriptive equality is the only valued thing, for evaluations go into choosing which properties are to be equally distributed, only that whatever else is valued, equality is valued more, so that equality has lexical priority over other values.

Such extreme and complete egalitarianism is at one end of a number of different spectra in which the variables range over the extent to which maximisation takes precedence over equalisation, and the nature of the values to which preference may be given over egality (strict equality) where incompatibilities arise. The variety of alternative positions that are available make any sort of tabulation impossibly difficult although we can put together a variety of packages and consider how we might choose between them.

As we have seen, egalitarian positions vary not only in the degree and extent of their commitment to descriptive equality over all valued properties, but also in relation to what these valued properties might be. Single property egalitarianism is exemplified by the model of an equal distribution of wealth. In this case, distribution of other properties depends on how this affects the attainment of equality of wealth. This is tantamount to the distribution of such things as material resources, health care, personal attention and so forth in proportion to need, with need being identified by reference to any shortfall from the position of equality of wealth.

Other allegedly egalitarian models include the idea of equality of resources and equality of opportunity. Equality of resources is the model preferred (in Dworkin 2000) to counter that of equality of well-being which Ronald Dworkin considers unacceptable because it takes no account of individual responsibility and choices. He favours a situation in which people possess resources that are equal in the sense that they make it equally feasible for individuals to carry out their pursuit of their preferred version of the good life. This, due to the differential use that individuals make of their resources, leads to inequality of outcome when considered in terms of well-being or of success in the pursuit of the individual's favoured life style. But these differences are the responsibility of the individual and are therefore acceptable even in a society that is committed to equal concern for all individuals.

Dworkin's equality of resources can claim to be mildly egalitarian in so far as the calculation of what counts as equality of resources takes into account the internal properties of individuals rather than their social and economic circumstances alone. Thus talented individuals start with more resources than untalented ones and this is taken into account in the determination of what counts as an equal distribution, so that talented individuals receive proportionately less external resources than untalented persons.

This may be viewed as a version of equality of opportunity in which what counts as an opportunity is made more demanding than it is in more formal versions. Equality of opportunity is a complex concept that requires analysis in terms of whose opportunity is at stake, what the opportunity is to do and what counts as an opportunity. A meagre ideal of equality of opportunity is that, in the distribution of benefits and burdens all individuals (in a given society?) may compete for inclusion or exclusion on the basis of relevant criteria. This is taken to rule out preference on the basis of such prohibited properties as race and gender, but allows for discrimination on the basis of capacity and merit. However, it may be regarded as unfair and inegalitarian to distribute in accordance with capacity unless the person can claim credit for that capacity. Natural endowment makes a person better able to perform demanding tasks but it is not something for which he can take any credit and therefore it does not appear to be just to distribute many things on the basis of such criteria. Thus Rawls (1999a) and others have developed a more substantial version of equality of opportunity according to which, at least in relation to basic rights and duties, distributions should not be based on natural differences. If we follow through this line of thought then the objective of giving everyone an equal chance of obtaining benefits and avoiding burdens would seem to require extensive redistribution of resources so as to eliminate the lucky advantage of the better endowed and more fortunately situated persons.

These ideas of equality of opportunity can be extrapolated from situations of competition for scarce resources and applied to the opportunity to develop the human capacities of all individuals. A particularly attractive version of this ideal, which is presented under the label of freedom, is proffered by Amartya Sen and Martha Nussbaum to the effect that evaluative equality means equality of capabilities.[20] This position is a version of the Aristotelian model that frees equality from abstract and over-moralised conceptions of freedom and makes for something much closer to an ideal of well-being that marries the insights of pleasure-/pain-oriented utilitarianism with the sense that some human activities are more worthwhile than others. One advantage of this approach is that it can serve to articulate a range of valued properties whose significance is reached when they obtain a certain threshold or degree at which the capacities in question can be said to be exercised. This it is not so open ended as some versions of equality of well-being, although it is sufficiently selective to lay itself open to charge of cultural bias.

In contrast to these more or less egalitarian versions of equality are those that we may identify as ideals of equality in that they relate to the equal distribution of some valued property, but are compatible with very considerable social and economic inequalities. These include non-egalitarian notions of formal equality of opportunity as outlined earlier, and the associated idea of formal equality before the law which requires that everyone is subject to the same rules, in that laws do not discriminate against members of minority social groups and legal remedies are available to everyone on the same basis.

While it is not the purpose of this chapter to say how we might choose between these competing versions of the central evaluative versions of the equality ideal, we should note that the preferred situations of equality outlined in theoretically diverging models, such as equalising liberty or opportunity, and equalising happiness or well-being, can converge quite considerably when viewed in terms of their implications for the distribution of external resources. Real or full equality of opportunity requires substantial equality of resources to give the individual a fair chance in any competitive or comparative situation.[21] Conversely, ideals of equal well-being are not separable from any strong version of equal freedom since well-being is evidently crucially dependent on people being able to formulate and carry out their projects or life plans.

Given our reasons for undertaking this analysis, it is worth pointing out that conceptions of extreme egalitarianism may be hardest to ground morally in so far as they appear to veto any advances in relation to other values which are incompatible with strict descriptive equality or equivalence. Egalitarianism is more intelligible, I suggest, when the individuals being compared are taken to be members of the same community of persons. As soon as the step is made from individual to community assessment a number of dimensions enter the picture. One is the fact that benefits which accrue to individuals are generally unobtainable except through the activities of other members of the community. Another is that members of a community can more readily care for each other and be concerned about how other community members fare. Then there are emotions arising from interpersonal comparisons, such as pride and envy which flourish more readily within communities. All these dimensions of community life give rise to relevant interpersonal feelings and obligations that render the idea of complete egalitarianism within that community more understandable. It may be also that it requires shared meanings and understanding of common goods in order to make sense of such notions as equality (Walzer 1983; Miller 1993). While there are many arguments that point the other way, it is easy to see that there may be special reasons for approving substantive egalitarianism within a confined community with a shared way of life, and that such communities can most readily have the political mechanisms to agree to the adoption of egalitarian goals that in other circumstances would have unacceptably coercive consequences.

However there is a substantive overlap here of evaluative considerations that are not confined to such contexts, remembering that, on my analysis, evaluations are separated from their prescriptive implications. Thick conceptions of equal human worth that are based on identifiable foundational equalities are universal in that the positive evaluation of, for instance, all people being equally happy or equally autonomous is not dependent on any particular social context. The disagreements that arise as to what egalitarian distributive patterns are best, and what the currency for describing the desired distributions should be are equally applicable and contestable within and without community boundaries.

This means that we need not and should not be looking for radically different conceptions of equality for global as distinct from domestic use. Differences will emerge at the prescriptive level, but can be held at bay in the articulation of our equality evaluations. Thus, it is common to formulate an idea of equality for global purposes that focuses on minimum standards such as meeting basic need for nutrition and shelter, while espousing a more extensive and more egalitarian ideal for use within national communities with a shared domestic political system. However, such divergencies need not be taken to imply different normative grounds for equality ideals in the two spheres. Rather, they are better seen as largely pragmatic distinctions that bear on questions of prescriptive equality.

Moreover, as far as the choice between the competing foundational descriptions of equal worth are concerned, as these bear on our vision of equality of lives, the implications of a foundational equality based on sentience and self-consciousness do not diverge greatly from foundational equalities focused on autonomy. As a matter of fact, human happiness depends substantially on the effective opportunity to pursue satisfying projects and human autonomy is characteristically deployed in the pursuit of happiness.

It may be that there is a tendency, explicable on ideological grounds deriving from the self-interest of developed nations, to overemphasise autonomy over sentience, on the mistaken assumption that autonomy equality requires less redistribution of resources. This leads to an assumption that international justice and human rights should concentrate on the more formal and less substantial versions of equality that focus on non-discrimination, formal equality of opportunity and equality before the law, supplemented by token recognition of the need for humanitarian relief of particularly grave and unexpected disasters.

However, the limited interpretation that is given to this autonomy-based conception of equal lives runs counter to any ideal of equal human worth that is tied in to foundational descriptive equalities that include the capacity for pain and suffering as constitutive of human worth. This should not be taken to mean that there is moral justification for deploying different evaluative standards with respect to equality domestically and internationally. The core grounding of equality as an ethical ideal is essentially cosmopolitan. Indeed, if we take to heart a strong version of equality of human worth, this must serve as a basis for condemning inequalities within developed societies despite the greater aggregative wealth that may arise from a fully competitive economy. It also justifies an enlargement of the idea of the purpose of nation-states as well as civil society to incorporate a commitment to addressing issues of global inequality.

Cosmopolitan equality

In the previous section I dealt with evaluations of equality without begging questions about the extent to which such evaluations give rise to prescriptions. In general it is deceptively easy to move from the affirmation that A is more desirable than B to the conclusion that we ought to choose and promote A more than B. However, it is possible to evaluate a situation positively even though we could never act in the light of that evaluation, as when we contemplate pasts or futures that are outside our control. And even when it is feasible for us to promote that which we judge to be valuable there may be countervailing claims on our resources or a legitimate prior claim of bounded self-interest. Moreover, particularly in the case of equality, the scale of any operation to achieve equality with respect to a large number of people (and equality conceptions are in this dimension infinitely expansive), and the practicalities of action to achieve equality, particularly egalitarian versions of the same, are daunting. At the very least, therefore, there is a practical gap between valuing equality and being obliged to do or try to do something about it.

The distinction between evaluative and prescriptive equality is particularly germane in the context of globalisation. We can readily affirm the equal worth of all human beings but believe it to be justified to give priority to the welfare of our own citizens, or community, or family or friends. This has something to do with the dynamics of community membership mentioned earlier, and it also has to do with what may be regarded as our sphere of responsibility, hence the difference between our private and our public obligations. With globalisation, further questions arise, mainly about the geographical scope and changing content of our cosmopolitan public obligations.

In considering the proper responses to descriptive and evaluative (in)equality I return to the ideas of equal consideration, equal concern and equal respect. These are clearly maxims of prescriptive equality since they commend that we show respect, concern and consideration in equal measure to all human beings. Such responses seem appropriate once we have accepted the idea of equal human worth but are not clearly connected with any particular claims as to existing or potential descriptive equality, although the terms involved suggest recognition of properties relating to autonomy in connection with respect and properties relating to sentience in connection with concern.

These maxims are, however, prescriptive primarily in relation to process and attitude and need not result in any significant action to promote egalitarianism. Indeed the idea of respect often suggests a proper reserve in connection with actions that impinge on others. In this case, the idea of equal respect is readily globalisable, since we can relatively easily take such an attitude, simply because it is an attitude rather than an action, towards everyone we meet and deal with, and in principle to every person who has existed or does and will exist.

If we strengthen such maxims so that they require appropriate action when feasible then we come up against a complex of factors. Thus, to show active respect for the autonomy of another may require, in the negative dimension, non-interference with choices made, and on the positive side, active assistance in obtaining situations where choice can be made and facilitating their successful outcome. Or, to act out of concern for the well-being of others may require, on the negative side, not harming them in any way and, in the positive dimension, doing what we can to relieve their suffering and to make them happy and content. All this then has to be related to a context of other moral claims including legitimate self-interest and the practicalities of carrying out such endeavours in an equal way, that is to the equal advantage of all to whom we owe respect, concern and consideration, that is, to everybody.

It is at this point in the analysis that the major divergences between theories of social and political equality emerge, both with respect to the range of those whom we ought to have in our sights and the content of what ought to be done within this range when determining how to act out a commitment to equality. The choices depend in part on considerations of efficiency as to how wealth or well-being may be maximised, often through methods that tolerate descriptive external inequalities in the service of general welfare. It also depends on the extent to which egalitarianism is thought to be morally required by the affirmation of equal worth even at the cost of failure to maximise desired goods. Such disputes are irresolvable without agreement on a broad and deep social and political ideology. I confine myself to making a few points relating to the impact of globalisation on the idea and practice of equality.

The central point here is that for an ideal of equality to flourish outside the boundaries of nation states it is necessary to detach these ideals partially at least from arguments which base themselves in an ideal of citizenship or membership of a polity and the reciprocal obligations that arise therefrom. Thus any Dworkinian argument from political obligation to equality of concern will be inadequate to transcend state boundaries and provide a basis for global equality.

However, if we resuscitate the idea of foundational descriptive equalities then we have something on which to base transnational obligations. This takes us to the idea of human rights as a basis for universal obligations and rights, grounded in the foundational fact that the human experiences of pleasure and pain, freedom and domination, hope and fear are basically the same the world over. Indeed, this may also serve as a basis for resuscitating an egalitarian or welfare state/society within the vestiges of the nation state itself.

In this context it may seem wise to focus, not on complete equality of well-being properties, but on a conception of equal minimum well-being as a prescriptive goal that knows no national boundaries. However, this is a matter of tactics, rather than an implication of the Equal Worth Project. Pragmatically any prescriptions have to be applicable in the absence of an international organisation that can have direct responsibility for what happens within states. In a world of nation states there is currently no effective international framework for implementing a programme of minimal well-being let alone even the weakest form of general equality of well-being. Nevertheless it is an intelligible goal, and one that can lead to the formulation of a feasible objective that encompasses global perspectives.

Here the discussion passes to what globalisation has to offer by way of transnational institutions to promote the prescriptions that derive from equal worth. Unfortunately the prime answer is that the chief medium of globalisation is a regime of international trade that flourishes on a very limited and highly non-egalitarian version of equality that focuses on formal and negative equalities of choice. This includes a spasmodic commitment to the formal rule of law, legal equality of trading opportunities, good governance in relation to business needs and, perhaps, democratic procedures, with occasional reference to human rights in the area of employment.

However, this does not mean that progress cannot be made towards gaining acceptance for linking international trade agreements to the implementation of civil and political rights by all parties, tying international aid to the basics of human material well-being: nutrition, health and education. The inegalitarian trends of current globalisation are neither inevitable nor justified and there is considerable potential within the global trading community for moving towards stronger versions of equality norms through international institutions and the harnessing of global public opinion. This in turn may resurrect the salience of more egalitarian forms of equality within the politics of nation states and move us back to something like the vision of welfare state egalitarians such as Tawney. At the same time, it may stir the dominant political communities to a shared recognition of their collective global responsibilities arising from the (roughly) equal worth of all human beings.

Notes

1 Sen 2001: 'We live in a world of unprecedented prosperity – incomparably richer than ever before. The massive command of resources, knowledge and technology that we now take for granted would be hard for our ancestors to imagine. But ours is also a world of extraordinary deprivation and of staggering inequality'. Also, Sen and Nussbaum 1999: ix; Fincher and Saunders 2001: 11–27.

2 Tawney 1964: 57: 'So to criticize inequality and to demand equality is not, as is sometimes suggested, to cherish the romantic illusion that men are equal in character and intelligence'. But see 197: 'Socialism, accepts, therefore... that differences in character and capacity are of minor importance compared with the capital fact of their common humanity'.

3 I thank Keith Horton for this catchy label, and for many other helpful suggestions concerning this chapter.

4 Labelling these properties 'well-being properties' may appear to confine them to social and economic rather than political and legal equalities, the latter having to do with the distribution of rights and duties. However rights and duties are (a) types of benefit and burden, and (b) in the case of the rights and duties operative in a particular group of society, they are capable of being described and measured. For both reasons my analysis can be taken to take in positive (as distinct from moral) rights and duties as a species of benefit or burden that impact on well-being.

5 When the purpose of the description is to formulate an explanation, as when wealth is or is not correlated with intelligence or stupidity, then what may be called 'causal properties' are involved for the purpose of establishing the reasons why certain distributions of well-being properties do or do not exist.

6 Strictly speaking, assertions of identity in relation to persons (or anything else) are in order only when we are saying that a person or thing is identical with itself. We might need to do this in order to make it clear, for instance, that what we thought to be two different are in fact the same person. At this extreme descriptive equality could be taken to mean that a person is in all respects, including spatio-temporal properties, identical with himself. However, in social and political philosophy, equality is essentially a comparative concept that is used to compare and contrast persons and their circumstances rather than to explore issues of personal identity. Distinguishing the idea of descriptive equality from that of identity, the idea of a person being equal to or with herself does enable us to pinpoint one extreme in the comparative use of the concept. This occurs when one person is said to be identical with another person in all respects other than the spatio-temporal ones that are required in the case of actual identity. Thus we may speak of two different people being identical with each other, as in the purely theoretical example of identical twins in identical circumstances. In practice, being equal is rarely taken to mean being identical even in this sense although the term 'identity' can be used to make the strongest of all descriptive equality affirmations, namely equality in all conceivable respects short of actual personal identity. I call this the pole of descriptive full equality or identicality.

7 The issues that are raised as matters of relevance or appropriateness may themselves be matters of fact in that what is in dispute is an empirical question, for instance, as to which properties will bring about a desired result. However, determination of relevance ultimately involves evaluation of which properties are desirable or undesirable in themselves. In this case operative descriptive equality assertions presuppose value judgments as to what is right or good or valuable, the logic of the assertions being that two or more persons are the same with respect to the relevant properties. The category of descriptive equality is analytically distinct from but in practice inevitably embedded in an evaluative context.

8 Another way in which evaluation interfaces with questions of descriptive equality is when equality is being affirmed or denied with respect to properties that are empirically distinct but are assumed or asserted to be evaluatively equivalent. The discourse of evaluative equality includes judgments about the relative worth of different descriptive equalities. Such equivalence judgments between comparators may or may not be undertaken via a common currency, such as money or pleasure. Thus comparison of ways of life may be carried out in purely empirical terms, such as monetary value, length or happiness. However, such comparisons may involve or assume equivalences of value between distinct characteristics, so that two ways of life may be considered equally valuable even though they are descriptively different and empirically incommensurable. Evaluation comes in not only to the determination of relevance, but also to the comparison of properties. In these ways the descriptive elements of equality discourse mingle in practice with its evaluative mode.

9 It is important to note that most of these evaluations do not relate directly to the idea of equality. The initial question is: what is valuable for me and for human beings in general? Only once this is identified do we have an idea of what it is that we may be interested in seeing distributed equally. Indeed it may be that there are some valued things whose equal distribution does not concern us. In which case it is important to inquire whether equality is more important in relation to some benefit or burden rather than another. Thus attaining descriptive equality may be considered important in relation to power, perhaps less important in relation to esteem or money, and even less important in the case of love.

10 Derek Parfit distinguishes between 'teleological egalitarianism' which holds that 'It is in itself bad if some people are worse off than others' (Parfit 1996: 204) and 'deontic egalitarianism', for which such equality matters only if it is the outcome of some wrong or injustice. However, it seems incoherent to regard 'deontic egalitarianism' as a form of egalitarianism at all, unless the assumption is that being made less well off is an injury in part because it resulted in such inequality rather than for some reasons extraneous to equality.

11 The justification of inequality aspects of equality discourse merge with the discourse of justice, the difference being that equality discourse has to do more with reasons for treating people equally or in such a way as to bring about equality, whereas justice has more to do with justified descriptive inequalities, such as those that correspond to differential worthiness. Indeed, justice may be analysed as a combination of equal worth and unequal worthiness (see Campbell 2001: 27–9).

12 Interestingly, the term 'equality' often features to qualify the nature of the proper response rather than what the response is about. Thus we speak of 'equal consideration and respect' which does not in itself presuppose anything about the equality or inequality of those to whom this equal consideration and respect is given. For this reason we may prefer the alternative formulation 'consideration and respect as an equal'.

13 See Cullity, Chapter 2 of this volume.

14 Thus Ackerman 1980: 11, in propounding the ideal of neutral dialogue denies a morally privileged position to any participant in that dialogue: '*Neutrality*. No reason is a good reason if it requires the power holder to assert: (a) that his conception of the good is better than that asserted by any of this fellow citizens, *or* (b) that, regardless

of his conception of the good, he is intrinsically superior to one or more of this fellow citizens.'

15 Nielsen 1988 runs the two aspects together: equal moral standing is, for him, the thesis that everyone matters and all matter equally. This is acceptable in so far as no one will be concerned about mattering equally if no one matters at all, but it should not be taken to imply that mattering equally means that everyone matters to any particular degree. Other philosophers collapse the idea of equal worth into the very different notion of 'infinite value' or 'sacredness'. See also Vlastos 1962: 49 'something which is equally and highly valuable in all persons'.

16 This means that Kymlica is wrong to say that equal worth implies egalitarianism, if this term implies something like an equal distributive outcome (1989: 4). A better term for theories that espouse 'equal worth' might be 'equalitarian' (used in Vlastos 1962), keeping 'egalitarian' for theories which emphasise equality in distributive outcomes.

17 This is not quite correct. The capacity to be religious and the capacity to have sexual experiences and, even race, if this is interpreted as a matter of cultural identity, may be seen as ingredients of happiness or human nature, and even as sites for autonomous choice. What is excluded, however, is the view that membership of a particular race, or religion or gender is a value requirement that is relevant to human worth.

18 My own view is that elements of all of them are required to provide a convincing picture of the sense in which we think that we are, importantly, all basically the same. Such a normative amalgam has to demonstrate how it is that human beings are not just the loci of valued things, like pleasure, but are actually valued. This points to a complex composite of self-conscious and enjoyable goal directed activity, something like Vlastos's combination of 'well-being' as 'the enjoyment of value in all the forms in which it can be experienced by human beings' and 'freedom' as 'not only conscious choices and deliberate decisions but all those subtler modulations and more spontaneous expressions of individual preference which could scarcely be called "choices" or "decisions" without some forcing of language' (Vlastos 1962: 48).

19 For such a critique see McDonald 1947–48: 50: 'I affirm that no natural characteristic constitutes a reason for the assertion that all human beings are of equal worth. Or, alternatively, that *all* characteristics of *any* human being are equally reasons for this assertion'.

20 The Sen/Nussbaum conception of capabilities can, of course, feature as an Aristotelian style content in foundational descriptive equality. Indeed, one reason for the popularity of the capacities approach to the currency of equality is that it is easy to read back the idea of capacities into an egalitarian form of Aristotelianism that identifies these capacities with foundational equalities in terms of standard human capabilities.

21 Thus, Rawls required fair equality of opportunity which means that 'those who are at the same level of talent and ability, and have the same willingness to use them, should have the same prospects of success regardless of their initial place in the social system, that is, irrespective of the income class into which they were born' (Rawls 1999a: 63).

4 Moral universalism and global economic justice

Thomas W. Pogge

Introduction

Socioeconomic rights, such as that "to a standard of living adequate for the health and well-being of oneself and one's family, including food, clothing, housing, and medical care" (UDHR 1992: Article 25) are currently, and by far, the most frequently unfulfilled human rights. Their widespread underfulfillment also plays a major role in explaining global deficits in civil and political human rights demanding democracy, due process, and the rule of law: extremely poor people – often physically and mentally stunted due to malnutrition in infancy, illiterate due to lack of schooling, and much preoccupied with their family's survival – can cause little harm or benefit to the politicians and bureaucrats who rule them. Such officials therefore pay much less attention to the interests of the poor than to the interests of agents more capable of reciprocation, including foreign governments, companies, and tourists.

It is not surprising, perhaps, that those who live in protected affluence manage to reconcile themselves, morally, to such severe poverty and oppression. Still, it is interesting to examine how, and how convincingly, they do so. In this regard, earlier generations of European civilization had two noteworthy advantages over ours: first, the advanced industrial societies were then much less affluent in absolute and relative terms.[1] Fifty years ago, the eradication of severe poverty worldwide would have required a major shift in the global income distribution, imposing substantial opportunity costs upon the advanced industrialized societies. Today, the required shift would be small and the opportunity cost for the developed countries barely noticeable.[2] Second, earlier generations of European civilization were not committed to moral universalism. Their rejection of this idea was forcefully expressed, for instance, when the Anglo-Saxon powers blocked Japan's proposal to include language endorsing racial equality in the Covenant of the League of Nations.[3] Today, by contrast, the equal moral status of all human beings is widely accepted in the developed West. These two historical changes make our acquiescence in severe poverty abroad harder to justify than it would have been in the past. Still, we are quite tolerant of the persistence of extensive and severe poverty abroad even though it would not cost us much to reduce it dramatically. How well does this tolerance really fit with our commitment to moral universalism?

Moral universalism

A moral conception, such as a conception of social justice, can be said to be universalistic if and only if

(A) it subjects all persons to the same system of fundamental moral principles,
(B) these principles assign the same fundamental moral benefits (e.g. claims, liberties, powers, and immunities) and burdens (e.g. duties and liabilities) to all, and
(C) these fundamental moral benefits and burdens are formulated in general terms so as not to privilege or disadvantage certain persons or groups arbitrarily.

I cannot fully explicate these three conditions here; but some brief comments are essential.

Condition A allows a universalistic moral conception to be compatible with moral rules that hold for some people and not for others. But such differences must be generated pursuant to fundamental principles that hold for all. Generated *special* moral benefits and burdens can arise in many ways: from contracts or promises, through election or appointment to an office, from country-specific legislation, from conventions prevalent in a certain culture or region, from committing or suffering a crime, from being especially rich or needy, from producing offspring, from practicing a certain occupation, from having an ill parent, from encountering a drowning child, and so on. Only *fundamental* moral principles, including those pursuant to which special moral benefits and burdens are generated, must be the same for all persons. This condition raises the difficult question of who is to count as a person in the relevant sense: what about the severely mentally disabled, infants, higher animals, artificial, or extraterrestrial intelligences?

Condition B raises various problems about how a universalistic moral conception can respond to pragmatic pressures toward allowing the assignment of lesser fundamental moral benefits and burdens to children and to the mentally disabled and perhaps greater fundamental moral burdens to the specially gifted. It is possible that the development of a plausible universalistic moral conception requires that this condition be relaxed somewhat to allow certain departures from equality. Still, equality remains the default – the burden of proof weighs on those favoring specific departures. This suffices to disqualify traditional assignments of unequal fundamental moral benefits and burdens to persons of different sex, skin color, or ancestry.

Moral universalism is clearly incompatible with fundamental principles containing proper names or rigid descriptions of persons or groups. But fundamental principles may legitimately involve other discriminations, as when they enjoin us to respect our parents or to give support to the needy. This distinction between acceptable and unacceptable discriminations cannot be drawn on the basis of formal, grammatical criteria, because it is possible to design gimmicky general descriptions that favor particular persons or groups arbitrarily. Thus, principles meant to discriminate against the Dutch need not refer to them by name, but can refer instead to persons born at especially low elevations or something of this kind – and similarly in other cases. If moral universalism is not to be robbed of all content, we must understand Condition C as including the demand that a moral conception must justify the discriminations enshrined in its fundamental principles. An injunction to show special concern for the well-being of the needy can be given a plausible rationale – for instance by reference to the fact that they need help more than others do or that such aid yields larger marginal benefits to its recipients. An injunction to be especially concerned with the well-being of lawyers, by contrast, lacks such a rationale: why should lawyers, of all people, enjoy special care? Why not also public prosecutors, brokers, dentists?

From this reflection we can see that moral universalism cannot be defined formally. (This is why it makes sense to explicate it through an exemplary application: to the topic of economic justice.) All three conditions raise substantive questions. Who is to count as a person? Can persons differ from one another so much that somewhat different fundamental principles may hold for them? And when is a distinction made by a fundamental principle arbitrary? These are difficult questions that have more than one plausible answer. And even if we could agree on how to answer them, we still would not have achieved moral agreement: from the fact that the rule of helping the needy, for instance, cannot be disqualified as arbitrary, nothing follows about whether this rule is morally valid and, if so, what moral weight it has. Universalism is thus not a moral position with a clearly defined content, but merely an approach – a general schema that can be filled in to yield a variety of substantive moral positions. Universalism can at best provide necessary, not sufficient, conditions for the acceptability of a moral conception. These conditions amount to a call for systematic coherence in morality: the moral assessment of persons and their conduct, of social rules and states of affairs, must be based on fundamental principles that hold for all persons equally; and any discriminations built into such fundamental principles must be given a plausible rationale.

Our moral assessments of national and global economic orders

Consider two important questions about economic justice:

1   What fundamental moral claims do persons have on the global economic order and what fundamental responsibilities do these claims entail for those who impose it?
2   What fundamental moral claims do persons have on their national economic order and what fundamental responsibilities do these claims entail for those who impose it?

The prevailing opinion is that the correct answers to these questions are very different, that moral claims and burdens are far less substantial in the first case than in the second. But this discrepancy in moral assessment, much like preferential concern for the well-being of lawyers, looks arbitrary: why should our moral duties, constraining what economic order we may impose upon one another, be so different in the two cases? Let us consider whether this discrepancy stands in need of justification, as moral universalism affirms, and whether such a justification is available.

In discussions of national economic justice it is commonly mentioned that national populations, like families, may understand themselves as solidaristic or fraternal communities bound together by special ties of fellow feeling. Such ties generate special moral claims and burdens, and our responsibilities toward fellow citizens and family members may then greatly exceed, and weaken, our responsibilities toward outsiders.[4] Conceding all this does not, however, invalidate the universalist challenge, but merely gives it a different form, involving more specific versions of our two questions:

1′ What moral constraints are there on the kinds of global economic order persons may impose on others even when they have no bond of solidarity with them and a strong bond of solidarity with a smaller group such as their own nation?

2′ What moral constraints are there on the kinds of national economic order persons may impose on others even when they have no bond of solidarity with them and a strong bond of solidarity with a smaller group such as their own family?

The latter question is not concerned with the more ambitious criteria to which specific societies might choose to subject their national economic order, but with the weaker criterion of justice to which we would subject *any* national economic order, regardless of how the society in question understands itself. This weaker criterion is still much stronger than the criterion we apply to the global economic order. There is then a discrepancy between the *minimal* criteria of economic justice we apply on the global and national levels. Moral universalism demands that this discrepancy be given a plausible rationale.

Let us first examine, however, whether such a discrepancy is really widely presumed as I claim. My impression is that most people in the rich countries think of our global economic order as basically just – although this order does not meet two important minimal requirements we place on any national economic order.

The first minimal requirement is that, at least within the limits of what justice allows, social rules should be liable to peaceful change by any large majority of those on whom they are imposed. The global economic order, though it does stabilize a largely violence-free coordination of actors, nonetheless relies on latent violence in two ways. On the one hand, its stability – like that of any other realistically conceivable economic order – depends on the presence of substantial armed forces that prevent and deter rule violations. On the other hand, the design of the global economic order – in contrast to that of a democratically governed state – is determined by a tiny minority of its participants whose oligarchic control of the rules ultimately also rests on a huge preponderance of military power.

The crucial asymmetry concerns the latter point: we deem it unjust when a national economic order is coercively imposed by a powerful minority and demand that any large majority of its participants should be able to change its rules without the use of force. But few in the wealthy countries place the same moral requirement on the global economic order – most would dismiss it as ridiculous or absurd.

The second minimal requirement is that avoidable life-threatening poverty must be avoided. Insofar as is reasonably possible, an economic order must be shaped to produce an economic distribution such that its participants can meet their most basic standard needs. In regard to the global economic order, most citizens of the rich countries would reject this requirement as well. We know that billions abroad are exposed to life-threatening poverty. We think that we should perhaps help these people with sporadic donations, just as we should occasionally support the worse off in our own country. But few of us believe that this extensive and severe poverty, even if avoidable, shows our global economic order to be unjust.[5]

Some factual background about the global economic order

The moral assessment of an economic order must be responsive to information about three factors: the extent of absolute poverty, how severe and widespread it is; the extent of inequality, which is a rough measure of the avoidability of poverty and of the opportunity cost to the privileged of its avoidance; and the trend of the first two factors, that is, how poverty and inequality tend to develop over time. Let me summarize the state of our world in regard to these three factors.

The extent of world poverty

The World Bank estimates that over one-fifth of all human beings, 1,175 out of 5,820 million, were in 1998 living below the international poverty line, which it currently defines in terms of $32.74 PPP 1993 per month or $1.08 PPP 1993 per day.[6] "PPP" stands for "purchasing power parity." So the income per person per year of people at the international poverty line has as much purchasing power as $393 had in the United States in 1993. According to the US consumer price index, $393 had as much purchasing power in 1993 as $498 has in the United States in the year 2003 (www.bls.gov/cpi/). The World Bank's $1/day poverty line corresponds then roughly to an income of $498 per person per year today.[7] Those living below this poverty line fall, on average, 29.55 percent below it.[8] So they live on roughly $351 PPP 2003 per person per year on average. Now the $ PPP incomes the World Bank ascribes to people in poor countries are on average at least four times higher than their actual incomes at market exchange rates.[9] Since virtually all the global poor live in such poor countries, we can then estimate that their annual *per capita* income of $351 PPP 2003 corresponds to at most $88 at market exchange rates. On average, the global poor can buy about as much per person per year as can be bought with $351 in a typical rich country or with $88 in a typical poor one.

These are the poorest of the poor. The World Bank provides data also for a less scanty poverty line that is twice as high: $786 PPP 1993 ($996 PPP or roughly $249 in the year 2003) per person per year. Fully 2,812 million people are said to be living below this higher poverty line, falling 42.79 percent below it on average.[10] This much larger group of people – nearly half of humankind – can then, on average, buy as much per person per year as can be bought with $570 in a typical rich country or with $142 in a typical poor one.

The consequences of such extreme poverty are foreseeable and extensively documented: of about 6,154 million human beings in 2001 (www.census. gov/ipc/www/worldpop.html), 13 percent lack adequate nutrition, 18 percent lack access to safe drinking water, and 39 percent lack basic sanitation, and 854 million adults are illiterate (UNDP 2002: 21, 29, 11). More than 14 percent lack access to health services (UNDP 1999: 22). Approximately 16 percent have no adequate shelter and 32 percent no electricity (UNDP 1998: 49). "Two out of five children in the developing world are stunted, one in three is underweight and one in ten is wasted" (FAO 1999: 11). About 179 million children under 18 are involved in the "worst forms of child labour" including hazardous work in agriculture, construction, textile or carpet production as well as "slavery, trafficking, debt bondage and other forms of forced labour, forced recruitment of children for use in armed conflict, prostitution and pornography, and illicit activities" (ILO 2002: 9, 11, 18).

These percentages are depressing enough. Yet, they can plausibly be accused of making things look better than they are. By focusing on human beings *alive at any given time*, all these statistics give less weight to persons whose lives are short. Thus, if the poorest third of humankind live, on an average, half as long as the rest (which is approximately true), then they account for fully one half of all human lives. To give the same weight to each human life irrespective of its duration, all the above statistics would have to be similarly adjusted for differences in life expectancy. No such adjustment is needed for statistics about births and deaths, as they already give equal weight to every human life. One-third of all human deaths are due to poverty-related causes, such as starvation, diarrhea, pneumonia, tuberculosis, malaria, measles, and perinatal conditions, all of which could be prevented or cured cheaply through food, safe drinking water, vaccinations, rehydration packs, or medicines.[11] If the developed Western countries had their proportional shares of these deaths, severe poverty would kill some 3,500 Britons and 16,500 Americans per week. Each year, fifteen times as many US citizens would die of poverty-related causes as those perished in the entire Vietnam War.

The extent of human suffering and premature deaths due to poverty-related causes is not well known in the West. As the media presented retrospectives on the twentieth century, they gave ample space to some of its man-made horrors: 11 million murdered in the German holocaust, 30 million starved to death in Mao's Great Leap Forward, 11 million wiped out by Stalin, 2 million killed by the Khmer Rouge, 800,000 hacked to death in Rwanda. The media also give considerable attention to natural disasters. When there are earthquakes, storms, and floods, we have them on the evening news, with footage of desperate parents grieving for their dead children. Not mentioned in the retrospectives and not shown on the evening news are the ordinary deaths from starvation and preventable diseases – some 270 million people, mostly children, in the 15 years since the end of the Cold War. The names of these people, if listed in the style of the Vietnam War Memorial, would cover a wall 621 kilometers (386 miles) long.[12]

The extent of global inequality

Severe poverty is nothing new. What is new is the extent of global inequality. Real wealth is no longer limited to a small elite. Hundreds of millions enjoy a high standard of living with plenty of spare time, travel, education, cars, domestic appliances, mobile phones, computers, stereos, and so on. The high-income countries, with 15.6 percent of world population and 81 percent of aggregate global income, have annual per capita income of $26,710 (World Bank 2003: 235). For the world as a whole, annual per capita income is $5,140 (ibid.).[13] The collective income of the bottom quintile is about one-third of 1 percent of aggregate global income. This contrast gives us a sense of how cheaply severe poverty could be avoided: one-eightieth of our share is triple theirs[14] – which should give pause to those who conclude from the very large number of extremely poor people that eradicating world poverty would dramatically impoverish the developed countries.

Global inequality is even greater in regard to property and wealth. Affluent people typically have more wealth than annual income, while the poor normally own significantly less than one annual income. The enormous fortunes of the super-rich in developed societies were given special emphasis in recent *Human Development Reports*: "The world's 200 richest people more than doubled their net worth in the four years to 1998, to more than $1 trillion. The assets of the top three billionaires are more than the combined GNP of all least developed countries and their 600 million people" (UNDP 1999: 3).[15]

Trends in world poverty and inequality

The last fifty years give the impression of rapid progress, punctuated by a long series of human-rights declarations and treaties, new initiatives, summits, as well as detailed research into the quantification, causes, and effects of poverty. Such things are not unimportant. But they disguise the fact that real progress for the poor themselves is less impressive. Yes, life expectancy has risen markedly in many countries and infant mortality has fallen substantially due to better disease control. But the number of people in poverty has not declined since 1987[16] – despite the fact that this period has seen exceptional technological and economic progress as well as a dramatic decline in defense expenditures.[17] Since 1996, when 186 governments made the very modest commitment to halve the number of undernourished people within 19 years, this number has barely changed – despite a 22 percent drop in the real wholesale prices of basic foodstuffs.[18] These trends are all the more disturbing as the ranks of the poor and undernourished are continuously thinned by some 50,000 premature deaths daily from poverty-related causes.

While poverty and malnutrition are stagnant, global inequality, and hence the avoidability of poverty, is escalating dramatically: "The income gap between the fifth of the world's people living in the richest countries and the fifth in the poorest was 74 to 1 in 1997, up from 60 to 1 in 1990 and 30 to 1 in 1960. [Earlier] the income gap between the top and bottom countries increased from 3 to 1 in 1820 to 7 to 1 in 1870 to 11 to 1 in 1913" (UNDP 1999: 3).[19] There is a long-established trend toward ever greater international income inequality – a trend that has certainly not decelerated since the end of the colonial era forty years ago.[20]

So much by way of data about the world economy which is deemed tolerably just here in the developed countries.

Conceptions of national and global economic justice contrasted

Let us compare this case to that of a national society in which the various economic parameters we have considered resemble those of the world at large. No national society displays anything like the current degree of global income inequality, but because Brazil has one of the highest quintile income inequality ratios (29.7),[21] and because its PPP gross national income *per capita* is close to that of the world at large,[22] we might call our fictional country Subbrazil. The point of the contrast is to pose this challenge: if we consider Subbrazil's economic order unjust, how can we find the global economic order morally acceptable?

One may object here that the economic order of Subbrazil is not really unjust. It appears unjust to us because we imagine that most of its citizens, like most citizens of European countries, conceive of their society as being, at least in some weak sense, a solidaristic community. Subbrazil's failure to meet even weak solidaristic standards constitutes no injustice, however, because most Subbrazilians do not want their national economic order to meet such a standard. If they desired otherwise, a majority of Subbrazilians could reform their economic order through the ballot box.

This objection could be contested by asserting that we do not accept as just a national economic order that avoidably produces life-threatening poverty for a sizable minority merely because this economic order is approved by the majority. But even if we accept the objection despite this worry, the challenge is not yet dissolved. The objection assumes that the Subbrazilian economy meets at least the first minimal requirement. It assumes that, if some large majority of Subbrazilians wanted to reform their national economic order so as to reduce life-threatening poverty, they could bring about such reforms. I can thus circumvent the objection by weakening my claim. Instead of claiming that we would condemn as unjust any national economic order that does not meet *both* minimal requirements, I claim instead that we would condemn as unjust any national economic order that does not at least meet *one* of them.

Let us imagine then a fictive Sub-Subbrazil: a society whose economic order avoidably produces life-threatening poverty for a sizable minority and is also not subject to peaceful change from below, even by a large majority.[23] Such an economic order would be condemned as unjust by most people in the developed countries. (What is to count as an unjust national economic order, if not this?) And we arrive then at this reformulated challenge: if we condemn as unjust the imposition of the national economic order of Sub-Subbrazil, how can we condone the imposition, by governments acting in our name, of the existing global economic order? The latter order is, after all, like the former in the extent of poverty and inequality it produces and also in that even a large majority of those on whom it is imposed – the poorest four-fifths of humankind, for instance – cannot reform it by peaceful means. How can the flagrant discrepancy between our minimal criteria of national and global economic justice be justified?

As here explicated, moral universalism demands such a justification. In the face of this demand, we have three options. First, we can evade the demand by surrendering the discrepancy: by strengthening the minimal criterion we apply to the global economic order and/or by weakening the minimal criterion we apply to any national economic order (perhaps even reversing our opinion that Sub-Subbrazil's economic order is unjust). Second, we can try to meet the demand by defending a discrepancy of minimal criteria – by justifying the view that our global economic order may not be unjust even if it fails to meet the minimal criterion of justice we apply to any national economic order. Third, we can insist on a discrepancy of minimal criteria while rejecting the universalist demand to justify this discrepancy.

Responses of the first two kinds accept the universalist challenge and are willing to engage in the debate about minimal criteria of national and global economic justice. The third response declines to join this debate with the tripartite claim that national economic regimes are subject to some minimal criterion of justice, that the global economic order is not subject to this criterion, and that no justification can or need be given for this discrepancy. The next section focuses on this third, most antagonistic response.

Moral universalism and David Miller's contextualism

The third response can point to existing moral intuitions or convictions: our discrepant criteria of national and global economic justice are fixed points that any philosophical account of our morality must reaffirm. An account that does not vindicate our deepest convictions must be rejected for this reason alone. We are deeply convinced that we do not share responsibility for starvation abroad. This conviction, which we are more sure of than we could ever be of the merits of any complex philosophical argument, refutes any moral conception that concludes otherwise. To be sure, our discrepant standards of economic justice may seem incoherent. But the moral data (our intuitions or deepest convictions) are what they are, and coherence, in any case, is in the eye of the beholder.

In this simple version, the third response is hard to swallow. The view that moral reflection exhausts itself in compiling our favorite convictions, that what we firmly enough believe to be right is right, trivializes the ambition of leading a moral life. But perhaps the third response can be made more palatable by presenting it as including a justification for its rejection of the universalist demand for justification. David Miller may appear to develop a more sophisticated position, arguing for the anti-universalist claim that we should allow diverse moral principles to hold in different contexts without demanding any justification for such diversity.[24] I try to show that this appearance is misleading, that Miller's contextualism overlaps with moral universalism, and that moral conceptions within this overlap seem more promising than moral conceptions exemplifying more extreme variants of either universalism or contextualism. Let me add that I am here setting aside Miller's interesting and important work on national and international justice,[25] attending solely to his more general account of contextualism. Miller may appear to embrace the general statement of the anti-universalist response when he associates the contextualism he favors – "a species of intuitionism in Rawls's sense" (Miller 2002: 20) – with bald, conversation-stopping pronouncements of the form "equality is simply the appropriate principle to use in circumstances C" (ibid.: 16). He also argues against the demand for justification: attempts to construct a unified account of all of morality cannot achieve "a reasonably close fit between the theory and our pre-theoretical considered judgments" (ibid.: 6). Such attempts, he believes, lead to the proliferation of neat but implausible moral theories whose disagreements raise questions we cannot convincingly resolve and therefore foster a skeptical attitude toward morality which sets back efforts toward achieving moral progress on concrete and urgent practical problems.

I respect and share these concerns. But it is not clear that anti-universalism can do any better. Those who walk out of specific moral discussions with an emphatic declaration that C_1 and C_2 simply *are* different contexts to which different principles P_1 and P_2 are appropriate will fail to convince, and quite possibly seem offensive to, those who believe otherwise – even if they also argue in general terms that morality is too heterogeneous to yield to the universalist demand for justifications. (Think of those who, in accord with the convictions of their time, emphatically declared that moral principles appropriate to one social class simply *are* inappropriate to another.) By declining to give any specific reasons for delimiting the various contexts, and for assigning the various moral principles to them, in the way they do, such people will moreover foster a cynical attitude toward moral theorizing as the bare assertion of favorite convictions, invariably distorted by the asserter's interests, social position, and prejudices.

Miller is sensitive to these countervailing concerns when – setting his contextualism apart from conventionalism – he writes: "Contextualism . . . recognizes that we are likely to find different principles of justice being used at different times and in different places, but it argues that this variation itself has an underlying logic that we can both grasp and use as a critical tool when assessing the prevailing conceptions of justice at any particular moment" (ibid.: 12–13). This remark shows, I believe, that Miller rejects the third response by recognizing that morality is subject to an underlying transcontextual logic which may, on the one hand, provide a rationale for applying different moral principles in different contexts (e.g. under different natural, historical, cultural, technological, economic, or demographic conditions) and may also, on the other hand, serve as a basis for criticizing prevailing moral conceptions. Once we can, by appeal to such an underlying logic, formulate justifying reasons for or against the application of different moral standards to persons from different social classes, and for or against the differential assessment of national and global economic regimes, we have moved beyond *dogmatic* contextualism and the unsupported endorsements or rejections it takes to be appropriate responses to moral disagreement.

Insofar as contextualism endorses a justificatory discourse about the delimitation of contexts and the variation of principles across them – and other work by Miller (see note 25) contains plenty of argument in this vein – it overlaps with moral universalism. As explicated here, universalism does not require that, if moral principles P_1, P_2, P_3 are to apply in contexts C_1, C_2, C_3, respectively, then there must be one supreme "transcendent" principle or set of principles of which P_1, P_2, P_3 are contextual applications (as "drive no faster than 30 mph" is a contextual application of "move no faster than is both safe and legal"). To be sure, moral universalism *permits* such highly unified anti-contextualist moral conceptions, as exemplified by utilitarianism. But it *also* permits the *critical* contextualist alternative suggested in the last-quoted sentence from Miller: a moral conception holding that fundamental principles P_1, P_2, P_3 apply in contexts C_1, C_2, C_3, respectively, and offering a justification for delimiting the various contexts, and for assigning the various moral principles to them, in these ways.

I find this contextualist moral universalism far more plausible than its anti-contextualist (monistic) alternative. Regarding our general view of moral theorizing, Miller and I may converge then upon an intermediate view – critical contextualism – defined by the rejection of monistic universalism on the one hand and dogmatic contextualism on the other. We both envision different fundamental moral principles applying in different contexts, and we both seek justifications for the delimitation of contexts and the formulation of fundamental principles appropriate to them. We differ in regard to what delimitations, context-specific principles, and justifications we find acceptable.

Because the proposed intermediate view of moral theorizing is unfamiliar, I develop it somewhat further through a discussion of Rawls's work, which provides both an illustration and a violation of the contextualist moral universalism I favor.

Contextualist moral universalism and John Rawls's moral conception

Rawls wants to confine his theory of justice to a specific context: to the basic structure of a self-contained society existing under the circumstances of justice. His theory commits him to certain moral demands on the political conduct of citizens – they must support and promote a just basic structure. But Rawls wants to leave open what moral principles may apply to their personal conduct. He has been attacked for this aloofness by monistic universalists, such as Gerald Cohen and Liam Murphy.[26] According to them, any fundamental moral principle that applies to social institutions must also apply to personal conduct. Thus, if the difference principle requires that a society's economic order should erase any socioeconomic inequality that does not optimize the lowest socioeconomic position, then individuals must also be required, in their personal conduct, to erase any socioeconomic inequality that does not optimize the lowest socioeconomic position.[27]

Rawls's contextualism can be defended against this critique. Rawls has important reasons for limiting the range of his principles of justice to the basic structure. These reasons – invoking *inter alia* the fact of pluralism as well as the need to avoid overdemandingness and to achieve stability (compliance) – show that basic social institutions should be treated as a separate context to which distinct moral principles apply.[28] These reasons illustrate how limiting the range of moral principles can be justified without the invocation of any deeper, transcontextual principles from which context-specific principles are then derived. The case at hand thus shows how it is possible to justify moral principles as range-limited or context-specific even while also maintaining that they are fundamental. Insofar as the justification for the Rawlsian range limit satisfies the three conditions of moral universalism, his account of the justice of basic social institutions is an instance not merely of critical contextualism, but also, and more specifically, of contextualist moral universalism.

Whereas this Rawlsian separation of contexts instantiates contextualist moral universalism, another separation of contexts, central to his latest work, instantiates its violation. Rawls insists there on applying quite different fundamental principles to national and international institutional schemes, but fails to give an adequate justification for the separation of contexts. This failure occurs on three distinct levels.

First, Rawls strongly rejects the difference principle as a requirement of global justice on the ground that it is unacceptable for one people to bear certain costs of decisions made by another – decisions affecting industrialization or the birth rate, for example.[29] But he fails to explain why this ground should not analogously disqualify the difference principle for national societies as well. Why is it not likewise unacceptable for one province, township, or family to bear such costs of decisions made by another?[30] And if, despite such sharing of costs, the difference principle is the most reasonable one for us to advocate in regard to the domestic economic order, then why is it not also the most reasonable one for us to advocate in regard to the global economic order? Rawls provides no answer.

Rawls also fails to explain how his rejection of the difference principle for the global order accords with his argument in *A Theory of Justice*, which he continues to endorse. There Rawls discusses how a human population of indeterminate size and explicitly conceived as "self-contained" and "a closed system"[31] should institutionally organize itself. His inquiry leads to the difference principle as a requirement of economic justice. He takes this principle to be acceptable – indeed ideal – for the United States, even though this society diverges from the task description by not being a self-contained closed system. So why should the difference principle be unacceptable for the world at large, which fits the task description precisely? There is, again, no answer in Rawls.

It might be objected that this unjustified discrepancy is not important. Perhaps Rawls should concede that a global economic order designed to satisfy the difference principle is not, as such, unacceptable. But the goal of such an order is nonetheless morally inappropriate to our world, because many people oppose the difference principle and not unreasonably so.

Against this objection, one needs to point out that such opposition exists at home as well as abroad. Increasingly sensitive to this fact, Rawls continues to propose the difference principle, which he had associated with the ideal of fraternity (Rawls 1999a: 90–1), as the most reasonable one for the domestic economic order of modern liberal societies including, first and foremost, the United States. But he allows that other societies may reasonably subject their national economic regimes to other criteria. And he is even willing to concede that his difference principle is not uniquely reasonable even for the United States: his fellow citizens would not be unreasonable if they gave their political support to some other liberal criterion of economic justice.[32] At least according to Rawls's later work, then, a society that deliberately fails to satisfy the difference principle may nonetheless not be unjust. Rather, to count as just (or not-unjust), a national society need merely endorse and (approximately) satisfy *some* not-unreasonable liberal standard of economic justice.

Now if this, rather than the difference principle, is Rawls's minimal criterion of national economic justice, it defines a second level on which the challenge from moral universalism arises: Rawls should either hold that a global order, too, can count as just only if it satisfies this minimal criterion of economic justice or else justify his failure to do so.

Rawls does neither; but he suggests that one reason against applying liberal standards globally is the need to accommodate certain – "decent" – non-liberal societies. (Decent societies are ones to which, Rawls believes, liberal societies should offer reciprocal recognition as full and equal members in good standing within a well-ordered system of states.) This is a strange suggestion because, in our world, non-liberal societies and their populations tend to be poor and quite willing to cooperate in reforms that would bring the global economic order closer to meeting a liberal standard of economic justice. The much more affluent liberal societies are the ones blocking such reforms, and it is not clear how their obstruction can be justified by the concern to accommodate decent societies. Granted, these reforms are not required by decency, decent societies thus could oppose them, and liberal societies might then have reason to accommodate such opposition. But when there exists no decent society actually opposing the reforms, then the concern to accommodate decent societies cannot be a reason for liberal societies to block them contrary to the minimal criterion, and hence to every more specific criterion, of liberal economic justice.

Suppose that the foregoing argument fails or that there are some decent societies opposed to economic reform. If so, the challenge of moral universalism arises one last time on yet a lower level: Rawls should either disqualify as less-than-decent any global economic order that does not meet whatever requirements any national economic order must meet to count as decent or else justify his refusal to do so.

But again, it seems that Rawls wants to insist on an unjustified double standard. He writes that a decent society's "system of law must follow a common good idea of justice that takes into account what it sees as the fundamental interests of everyone in society" (Rawls 1999b: 67–8). Rawls is quite vague on what constraints he takes this condition to place on the national economic order of a decent society. But he does not require the global economic order to meet even these weaker constraints of decency. All he asks is that no peoples should have to live "under unfavorable conditions that prevent their having a just or decent political and social regime" (ibid.: 37). And even this demand does not constrain global economic institutions, but only the conduct of other peoples. We may impose a global economic order that generates strong centrifugal tendencies and ever increasing international inequality, provided we "assist" the societies impoverished by this order just enough to keep them above some basic threshold.[33]

Despite considerable vagueness in his treatment of economic institutions, it seems clear then that Rawls endorses double standards on three different levels: in regard to national economic regimes, the difference principle is part of Rawls's highest aspiration for justice; in regard to the global economic order, however, Rawls disavows this aspiration and even rejects the difference principle as unacceptable. Rawls suggests a weaker minimal criterion of liberal economic justice on the national level; but he holds that the global order can fully accord with liberal conceptions of justice without satisfying this criterion. And Rawls suggests an even weaker criterion of economic decency on the national level; but he holds that the global order can be not merely decent, but even just, without satisfying this criterion. Insofar as he offers no plausible rationales for these three double standards, Rawls runs afoul of moral universalism. He fails to meet the burden of showing that his applying different moral principles to national and global institutional schemes does not amount to arbitrary discrimination in favor of affluent societies and against the global poor.

Rationalizing divergent moral assessments through a double standard

Most citizens of the developed countries reconcile themselves to massive and avoidable poverty abroad by not holding such poverty against the global economic order as they would hold similar poverty within a national society against its domestic economic order. The common and obvious way of rationalizing such a divergence is through a double standard: by subjecting the global economic order to weaker moral demands than any national economic order. Such double standards are widely employed in ordinary and academic discourse. They are often dogmatically taken for granted, perhaps with a general appeal to "our moral convictions" or a general argument for dogmatic contextualism. This is the "third response" to moral universalism, discussed in section titled "Moral universalism and David Miller's contextualism."

Rawls seems willing to defend a double standard in regard to national and global economic justice and thus exemplifies the second response to the universalist challenge. But the defenses he actually provides are incomplete, because he does not face up to the comparative nature of the task. It is not enough, for instance, to provide arguments against a global application of the difference principle. One must also show that these arguments create the desired asymmetry, that they have more weight than analogous arguments against a national application of the difference principle. Rawls does not even begin to do this.

His failure is typical of academic and popular rationalizations of double standards of economic justice. There are reasons for, and reasons against, a strong criterion of economic justice. Discussions of the national economic order tend to highlight the reasons for, discussions of the global order tend to highlight the reasons against. But to justify the desired asymmetry, one must discuss the relevant reasons of both kinds in respect to both contexts. In particular, one must show that some reasons for a strong criterion have more weight in the balance of reasons concerning national than they have in the balance of reasons concerning global economic justice – and/or, conversely, that some reasons for a weak criterion have less weight in the balance of reasons concerning national than they have in the balance of reasons concerning global economic justice.

Arguments for a weak criterion of economic justice typically appeal to cultural diversity or to the autonomy of, or special ties within, smaller groups. Such arguments are often used to justify acquiescence in a global economic order that engenders great poverty and inequality. But all three factors exist within nations as well. And they can then be useful in the defense of a double standard only if one can show them to be significantly less relevant domestically. As we have seen, showing this is not so easy.[34]

In a sense this is a modest result: many different double standards could be formulated with regard to our topic, and various rationales might be offered for each such formulation. No one can anticipate and refute all conceivable such accounts. But this very impossibility of showing conclusively that no sufficiently large discrepancy of standards can be justified provides a subsidiary reason for what I have presented as an essential element of moral universalism: the assignment of the burden of proof to those who *favor* a double standard. They can bear this burden, as they need only make good on an existential quantifier by formulating *one* version of the desired double standard and then giving a plausible rationale for it. And yet, the *moral* reason remains primary: we owe the global poor an account of why we take ourselves to be entitled to impose on them a global economic order in violation of the minimal moral constraints we ourselves place on the imposition of any national economic order.

If the burden of proof indeed weighs on those favoring a double standard, then the result of my discussion is not so modest after all: we, the affluent countries and their citizens, continue to impose a global economic order under which millions avoidably die each year from poverty-related causes. We would regard it as a grave injustice, if such an economic order were imposed within a national society. We must regard our imposition of the present global order as a grave injustice unless we have a plausible rationale for a suitable double standard. We do not have such a plausible rationale.

Rationalizing divergent moral assessments without a double standard

There is another way of rationalizing the failure of the affluent to hold massive and avoidable poverty abroad against the global economic order as they would hold similar poverty within a national society against its domestic economic order. The next four paragraphs give a summary statement of this rationalization, which invokes the idea of institutional responsibility.

We tend to recoil from an institutional order described as one that is imposed upon people of whom many avoidably are very poor. But let us not be fooled by mere rhetoric. An economic order under which there is a lot of avoidable love sickness is not, for this reason, morally flawed. This example drives home that the moral quality of an institutional order under which avoidable starvation occurs depends on whether and how that order is causally related to this starvation. It depends, that is, on the extent to which starvation could be avoided through institutional modification. And it also depends on the manner in which the institutional order in question engenders more starvation than its best feasible alternative would: does it, for example, require serfs to do unremunerated work for aristocrats or does it merely fail to tax the more productive participants enough to underwrite an adequate welfare system?

This insight is relevant to our topic: we have been discussing the moral assessment of two kinds of economic order (national and global) that, in the real world, differ greatly in their causal impact. The global economic order plays a marginal role in the perpetuation of extensive and severe poverty worldwide. This poverty is substantially caused not by global, systemic factors, but in the countries where it occurs: by their flawed national economic regimes and by their corrupt and incompetent elites both of which impede national economic growth and a fairer distribution of the national product. Such domestic defects are the main reason why these countries become ever poorer in relative and often even in absolute terms and why the burdens of this impoverishment fall upon their poorest citizens most heavily.[35] Excessive poverty and inequality within countries, by contrast, are to a considerable extent traceable to systemic factors and are then, causally and morally, the responsibility of the politically and economically influential elites who uphold the relevant national economic regimes.

We do indeed judge our global economic order, under which a great deal of poverty and inequality persists, less harshly than we would a national economic order associated with similar poverty and inequality data. But these discrepant assessments do not reflect a double standard concerning the significance of extreme poverty and inequality in the moral assessment of global and national regimes. Rather, they reflect a single standard uniformly applied to both kinds of regime, yet a standard that is sensitive not merely to the incidence of avoidable poverty but also to the regime's causal role in its occurrence.

The reconciling force of this empirical rationalization depends on complex economic causalities, on the correct explanation of persisting severe poverty worldwide and of the expansion of global inequality. We must convince ourselves that the global economic order is not a significant causal contributor to these phenomena. Many citizens of the affluent countries are convinced of this, and convinced even that the global economic order could not be modified into a significant causal contributor to the eradication of extreme poverty and inequality. These people believe that, for such progress to occur, the poor countries themselves must get their house in order, must give themselves governments and political institutions that are more responsive to the needs of their populations. With respect to this task, outsiders can help only to a very limited extent. This is so because it would be morally unacceptable to impose what we think of as reasonable leaders or social institutions upon such countries and also because any resolute interference in the internal affairs of poor countries could easily turn out to be counterproductive as corrupt rulers manage further to entrench their rule by denouncing our supposed imperialism or neo-colonialism. Sad as it is, our hands are tied. We can try to alleviate world poverty through development assistance, given *ad hoc* by affluent societies and individuals or built into the global order as in the Tobin Tax proposal. But such attempts will not succeed well because we cannot prevent the corrupt elites from siphoning off much of our aid into their own pockets. Perhaps 1.18 percent of our incomes would indeed suffice to raise all the incomes of all human beings to the World Bank's higher poverty line (cf. note 2). But, as things stand, there is unfortunately no way of getting such a donation to the world's poorest people in a concentrated way.

Responding to this empirical rationalization, I do not deny the analysis sketched in the preceding paragraph. The eradication of poverty in the poor countries indeed depends strongly on their governments and social institutions: on how their economies are structured and on whether there exists genuine democratic competition for political office which gives politicians an incentive to be responsive to the interests of the poor majority. But this analysis is nevertheless ultimately unsatisfactory, because it portrays the corrupt social institutions and corrupt elites prevalent in the poor countries as an exogenous fact: as a fact that explains, but does not itself stand in need of explanation. "Some poor countries manage to give themselves reasonable political institutions, but many others fail or do not even try. This is just the way things are." An explanation that runs out at this point does not explain very much. An adequate explanation of persistent global poverty must not merely adduce the prevalence of flawed social institutions and of corrupt, oppressive, incompetent elites in the poor countries but must also provide an explanation for this prevalence.

Social scientists do indeed provide deeper explanations responsive to this need. These are, for the most part, "nationalist" explanations which trace flaws in a country's political and economic institutions and the corruption and incompetence of its ruling elite back to this country's history, culture, or natural environment.[36] Because there are substantial differences in how countries, and the incidence of poverty within them, develop over time, it is clear that such nationalist explanations must play a role in explaining national trajectories and international differentials. From this it does not follow, however, that the global economic order does not also play a substantial causal role by shaping how the culture of each poor country evolves and by influencing how a poor country's history, culture, and natural environment affect the development of its domestic institutional order, ruling elite, economic growth, and income distribution. In these ways global institutional factors might contribute substantially to the persistence of severe poverty in particular countries and in the world at large. The following section shows that this is indeed the case, contrary to the central claim of the empirical rationalization.

The causal role of global institutions in the persistence of severe poverty

My case can be made by example, and I focus on two highly significant aspects of the existing global order.[37] Any group controlling a preponderance of the means of coercion within a country is internationally recognized as the legitimate government of this country's territory and people – regardless of how this group came to power, of how it exercises power, and of the extent to which it may be supported or opposed by the population it rules.[38] That such a group exercising effective power receives international recognition means not merely that we engage it in negotiations. It means also that we accept this group's right to act for the people it rules and, in particular, confer upon it the privileges freely to borrow in the country's name (international borrowing privilege) and freely to dispose of the country's natural resources (international resource privilege).

The resource privilege we confer upon a group in power is much more than our acquiescence in its effective control over the natural resources of the country in question. This privilege includes the power[39] to effect legally valid transfers of ownership rights in such resources. Thus a corporation that has purchased resources from the Saudis or Suharto, or from Mobuto or Abacha, has thereby become entitled to be – and actually *is* – recognized anywhere in the world as the legitimate owner of these resources. This is a remarkable feature of our global institutional order. A group that overpowers the guards and takes control of a warehouse may be able to give some of the merchandise to others, accepting money in exchange. But the fence who pays them becomes merely the possessor, not the owner, of the loot. Contrast this with a group that overpowers an elected government and takes control of a country. Such a group, too, can give away some of the country's natural resources, accepting money in exchange. In this case, however, the purchaser acquires not merely possession, but all the rights and liberties of ownership, which are supposed to be – and actually *are* – protected and enforced by all other states' courts and police forces. The international resource privilege, then, is the legal power to confer globally valid ownership rights in the country's resources.

Indifferent to how governmental power is acquired, the international resource privilege provides powerful incentives toward coup attempts and civil wars in the resource-rich countries. Consider Nigeria, for instance, where oil exports of $6–10 billion annually constitute roughly a quarter of GDP. Whoever takes power there, by whatever means, can count on this revenue stream to enrich himself and to cement his rule. This is quite a temptation for military officers, and during twenty-eight of the past thirty-two years Nigeria has indeed been ruled by military strongmen who took power and ruled by force. Able to buy means of repression abroad and support from other officers at home, such rulers were not dependent on popular support and thus made few productive investments toward stimulating poverty eradication or even economic growth.[40]

After the sudden death of Sani Abacha, Nigeria is now ruled by a civilian ex-general, Olusegun Obasanjo, who – a prominent member of the Advisory Council of Transparency International (TI) – raised great expectations for reform. These expectations have been disappointed: Nigeria continues to be listed near the bottom of TI's own international corruption chart.[41] This failure has evoked surprise. But it makes sense against the background of the international resource privilege: Nigeria's military officers know well that they can capture the oil revenues by overthrowing Obasanjo. To survive in power, he must therefore keep them content enough with the status quo so that the potential gains from a coup attempt do not seem worth the risk of failure. Corruption in Nigeria is not just a local phenomenon rooted in their tribal culture and traditions, but encouraged and sustained by the international resource privilege.

Nigeria is just one instance of a broader pattern also exemplified by the Congo/ Zaire, Kenya, Angola, Mozambique, Brazil, Venezuela, the Philippines, Burma/ Myanmar, the oil states of the Middle East, and many smaller resource-rich but poverty-stricken countries.[42] In fact, there is a significant negative correlation, known as the Dutch disease, between the size of countries' resource sectors and their rates of economic growth. This correlation has a "nationalist" explanation: national resource abundance causes bad government and flawed institutions by encouraging coups and civil wars and by facilitating authoritarian entrenchment and corruption.[43] But this nationalist explanation crucially depends on a global background factor, the international resource privilege, without which a poor country's generous resource endowment would not handicap its progress toward democratic government, economic growth, and the eradication of poverty – certainly not to the same extent.[44]

Similar points can be made about the international borrowing privilege, according to which any group holding governmental power in a national territory – no matter how it acquired or exercises this power – is entitled to borrow funds in the name of the whole society, thereby imposing internationally valid legal obligations upon the country at large. Any successor government that refuses to honor debts incurred by an ever so corrupt, brutal, undemocratic, unconstitutional, repressive, unpopular predecessor will be severely punished by the banks and governments of other countries; at minimum it will lose its own borrowing privilege by being excluded from the international financial markets. Such refusals are therefore quite rare, as governments, even when newly elected after a dramatic break with the past, are compelled to pay the debts of their ever so awful predecessors.

The international borrowing privilege has three important negative effects on the corruption and poverty problems in the poor countries. First, it puts a country's full credit at the disposal of even the most loathsome rulers who took power in a coup and maintain it through violence and repression. Such rulers can then borrow more money and can do so more cheaply than they could do if they alone, rather than the entire country, were obliged to repay. In this way, the international borrowing privilege helps such rulers to maintain themselves in power even against near-universal popular opposition. Second, indifferent to how governmental power is acquired, the international borrowing privilege strengthens incentives toward coup attempts and civil war: whoever succeeds in bringing a preponderance of the means of coercion under his control gets the borrowing privilege as an additional reward. Third, when the yoke of dictatorship can be thrown off, the international borrowing privilege saddles the country with the often huge debts of the former oppressors. It thereby saps the capacity of its fledgling democratic government to implement structural reforms and other political programs, thus rendering it less successful and less stable than it would otherwise be.[45] (It is small consolation that putschists are sometimes weakened by being held liable for the debts of their elected predecessors.)

I have shown how two aspects of the global economic order, imposed by the wealthy societies and cherished also by authoritarian rulers and corrupt elites in the poorer countries, contribute substantially to the persistence of severe poverty. The two privileges crucially affect what sorts of persons jostle for political power and then shape national policy in the poor countries, what incentives these persons face, what options they have, and what impact these options would have on the lives of their compatriots. These global factors thereby strongly affect the overall incidence of oppression and poverty and also, through their greater impact on resource-rich countries, international differentials in oppression and poverty.

This result is not altered by the fact that reforms of the two privileges are not easy to devise and might well, by raising the prices of natural resources, prove quite costly for the affluent consumer societies and for other states dependent on resource imports. I am arguing that the citizens and governments of the wealthy societies, by imposing the present global economic order, significantly contribute to the persistence of severe poverty and thus share institutional moral responsibility for it. I am not here discussing what we should do about persistent global poverty in light of our moral responsibility for it.[46]

It is easier to disconnect oneself from extensive and severe poverty suffered by wholly innocent people abroad when there are others who clearly are to blame for it. My argument in this section was therefore focused specifically on how the national causal factors we most like to highlight – tyranny, corruption, coups d'etat, civil wars – are encouraged and sustained by central aspects of the present global economic order. The argument shows that, those national causal factors notwithstanding, we share causal and moral responsibility. This insight should not lessen the moral responsibility we assign to dictators, warlords, corrupt officials, and cruel employers in the poor countries any more than our initial insight into their moral responsibility should lessen the moral responsibility we assign to ourselves.

The focus of my argument should also not obscure the other ways in which the present global economic order contributes to the persistence of poverty. By greatly increasing international interdependence, this order exacerbates the vulnerability of the weaker national economies to exogenous shocks through decisions and policies made – without input from or concern for the poorer societies – in the United States or European Union (e.g. interest rates set by the US and EU central banks, speculation-induced moves on commodity and currency markets). Moreover, the components of this global economic order emerge through highly complex intergovernmental negotiations in which the governments and negotiators of the developed countries enjoy a crushing advantage in bargaining power and expertise. Agreements resulting from such negotiations therefore reflect the interests of these rich countries' governments, corporations, and populations – regardless of whether the relevant representatives of the developing countries are corrupt or are selflessly devoted to poverty eradication. And agreements that are good for the rich countries may not be good for the global poor, as is amply demonstrated in the history of the Uruguay Round.[47]

Conclusion

The previous section has shown what is obvious to people in the poor, marginal countries: that the rules structuring the world economy have a profound impact on the global economic distribution just as the economic order of a national society has a profound impact on its domestic economic distribution. The empirical rationalization is not empirically sustainable.

Spreading awareness of its unsustainability could turn out to be of great practical importance in reshaping both the explanatory and the moral debates about world poverty. As it is, the explanatory debate is largely focused on nationalist explanations: on the question what national economic institutions and policies in poor countries hamper or promote the eradication of domestic poverty. Some argue for free markets with a minimum in taxes and governmental regulations (the Asian tigers model), others for increased governmental investment in education, medical care, and infrastructure (the Kerala model). This debate is certainly important. But it would also be quite important to examine what *global* economic institutions hamper or promote the eradication of poverty worldwide. Such modest inquiries are familiar: economists and politicians debate alternative structures and missions for the IMF and the World Bank and the international impact of the 1995 Trade Related Aspects of Intellectual Property Rights (TRIPs) Agreement reached within the WTO. But with respect to larger issues, such as the international resource and borrowing privileges and the political mechanisms through which the rules of the world economy are created and revised, the status quo is largely taken for granted as a given background much like the basic natural features of our planet.

As it is, the moral debate is largely focused on the question to what extent affluent societies and persons have obligations to help others worse off than themselves. Some deny all such obligations, others claim them to be quite demanding. Both sides easily take for granted that it is as potential helpers that we are morally related to the starving abroad.[48] This is true, of course. But the debate ignores that we are also and more significantly related to them as supporters of, and beneficiaries from, a global institutional order that substantially contributes to their destitution.

If the empirical rationalization fails, if national and global economic regimes are comparable in their workings and impact, then we are after all employing a double standard when we count avoidable extremes of poverty and inequality against national economic regimes only. And we do then face moral universalism's challenge to our easy acceptance of extensive, severe poverty abroad. Without a plausible rationale, our discrepant assessments constitute covert arbitrary discrimination in favor of the wealthy societies and against the global poor.

Acknowledgments

This essay originally appeared in *Politics, Philosophy, and Economics* (2002) 1/1: 29–58, and is reproduced with permission by Sage Publications Ltd. It elaborates ideas first formulated in lectures (2000–02) presented in Eichstätt, Bremen, Beijing, Halle, Canberra, Christchurch, NYU Law School, and LUISS Roma. I am very grateful to my various audiences for their lively feed-back, to Paula Casal, Keith Horton, David Miller, Ling Tong, and Andrew Williams for extensive and very helpful written comments, and to the Program on Global Security and Sustainability of the John D. and Catherine T. MacArthur Foundation for a generous grant which has supported this work.

Notes

1 See text at note 19.
2 See notes 6–10 and accompanying text. The global poverty gap is about $43 billion annually for the World Bank's official international poverty line and $300 billion annually for their doubled poverty line. These figures correspond to 0.14 and 0.95 percent, respectively, of aggregate global income ($31,500 billion annually) and to 0.17 and 1.18 percent, respectively, of the combined gross national incomes of the high-income countries ($25,506 billion annually). See World Bank 2003: 235, reporting data for the year 2001.
3 April 11, 1919. The proposal received a majority in the relevant committee (eleven of the seventeen members present), but Woodrow Wilson, as chair, ruled that this particular amendment needed unanimous support to pass. See Shimazu 1998: 30.
4 This appeal to special ties and "priority for compatriots" is further discussed in my *World Poverty and Human Rights* (Pogge 2002), chapters 3 and 5. The appeal is usually made on behalf of societies that could easily build just and thriving national communities even in a more egalitarian global economic order. The difference would be that the remaining majority of humankind might then enjoy the same opportunity.
5 On this point we tend to depart from the *Universal Declaration of Human Rights* (UDHR 1992) which, after recognizing basic economic rights in section 25, asserts that: "Everyone is entitled to a social *and international* order in which the rights and freedoms set forth in this Declaration can be fully realized" (section 28, my emphasis).
6 See Chen and Ravallion 2001: 290 (table 2). The poverty line is further explained in World Bank 2001: 17 and 23.
7 I say "roughly", because the two equivalences cannot, strictly speaking, be combined by transitivity. The reason is that they are based on different goods: One set of goods was used to determine what amount of a foreign currency had, in 1993, the same purchasing

power as $393 then had in the United States. Another goods-basket (defining the US consumer price index) was used to determine what amount of dollars have, in 2003, the same purchasing power as $393 had in the United States in 1993.

8 Chen and Ravallion 2001: 290 and 293 (tables 2 and 3), dividing the poverty gap index by the headcount index.

9 Thus the World Bank equates India's *per capita* gross national income of $460 to $2,450 PPP, China's $890 to $4,260 PPP, Nigeria's $290 to $830 PPP, Pakistan's $420 to $1,920 PPP, Bangladesh's $370 to $1,680 PPP, Ethiopia's $100 to $710 PPP, Vietnam's $410 to $2,130 PPP, and so on (World Bank 2003: 234–5). These countries are listed here by the number of poor people they contain. For a detailed critique of the World Bank's poverty assessment methodology, see Reddy and Pogge 2002.

10 Chen and Ravallion 2001, 290 (table 2), and ibid.: 290 and 293 (tables 3 and 4), again dividing the poverty gap index by the headcount index.

11 In 2000, there were 55.694 million human deaths. The main causes highly correlated with poverty were (with death tolls in thousands): diarrhea (2,124) and malnutrition (445), perinatal (2,439) and maternal conditions (495), childhood diseases (1,385 – mainly measles), tuberculosis (1,660), malaria (1,080), menengitis (156), hepatitis (128), tropical diseases (124), respiratory infections (3,941 – mainly pneumonia), HIV/AIDS (2,943), and sexually transmitted diseases (217) (WHO 2001: annex table 2). Cf. also FAO 1999, UNICEF 2002, and USDA 1999: iii: "Worldwide 34,000 children under age five die daily from hunger and preventable diseases".

12 The Vietnam War Memorial in Washington, designed by Maya Ying Lin, is a black granite wall, 134 meters (439½ feet) long, on which the names of 58,226 fallen US soldiers are engraved.

13 This figure reflects aggregate global income (sum of all gross national incomes) of $31,500 billion annually and a world population of 6,133 million (year 2001).

14 Cf. also the figures provided in note 2. Curiously, the World Bank does not publish data about the *per capita* income or the collective income of the global poor, about their share of aggregate global income, or about the amount of extra income needed for all of them to reach the relevant poverty line.

15 "The additional cost of achieving and maintaining universal access to basic education for all, basic health care for all, reproductive health care for all women, adequate food for all and safe water and sanitation for all is…less than 4% of the combined wealth of the 225 richest people in the world" (UNDP 1998: 30).

16 The number of people below the doubled international poverty line (cf. note 10) has increased by 10.3 percent – or 21.3 percent if the special case of China is excluded (Chen and Ravallion 2001: 290 (table 2)). Global population growth during the same period (1987–98) was about 18 percent (www.census.gov/ipc/www/worldpop.html).

17 Thanks to the end of the Cold War, the high-income economies were able to reduce their military expenditures from 4.1 percent of their combined GDPs in 1985 to 2.2 percent in 1998 (UNDP 1998: 197; UNDP 2000: 217). Their annual "peace dividend" currently amounts to about $477 billion (1.9 percent of their combined GDPs of currently $25,104 billion – World Bank 2003: 239). In the same period, the same countries chose to reduce their combined net official development assistance (ODA) dramatically: from 0.33 percent in 1990 to 0.22 percent in 2001, when aggregate ODA was $52.3 billion (UNDP 2003: 290), down from $53.7 billion in 2000 (UNDP 2002: 202) and $56.4 billion in 1999 (UNDP 2001: 190). The United States has led the decline by reducing ODA from 0.21 to 0.10 percent of gross national product in a time of great prosperity culminating in enormous budget surpluses. Despite a commitment made at the 1995 World Summit for Social Development to allocate 20 percent of ODA to basic social services (www.un.org/esa/socdev/wssd/agreements/poach5.htm, Chapter 5, Article 88(c)), only 7 percent or $3.7 billion are actually so allocated (http://milleniumindicators.un.org/unsd/mi/mi_series_results.asp?rowId=592 – this is 0.014 percent of the rich countries' gross national incomes and less than one cent per

day for each person below the lower international poverty line). The remainder of ODA is spent to benefit agents more capable of reciprocation – domestic firms, for example, or strategically important governments. (As the USAID itself proclaims with disarming frankness: "The principal beneficiary of America's foreign assistance programs has always been the United States. Close to 80 percent of the U.S. Agency for International Development's (USAID's) contracts and grants go directly to American firms. Foreign assistance programs have helped create major markets for agricultural goods, created new markets for American industrial exports and meant hundreds of thousands of jobs for Americans" (www.usaid.gov/procurement_bus_opp/osdbu/book-information.htm). Cf. also Alesina and Dollar 2000. These priorities are evident when one looks where ODA goes: India, with more poor people than any other country, receives ODA of $1.50 annually for each of its citizens; the corresponding figures are $42.70 for the Czech Republic, $54.50 for Malta, $69.50 for Cyprus, $76.60 for Bahrain, and $132.40 for Israel (UNDP 2002: 203–5), which have 11 to 40 times the GDP *per capita* of India (ibid.: 162, 164, 190, 192). Cyprus, Malta, and Israel are listed as high-income countries (ibid.: 270).

18 The 1996 *Rome Declaration on World Food Security* described "more than 800 million people" as undernourished. This number has officially developed as follows: "nearly 800 million" (UNDP 1995: 16, and UNDP 1996: 20), "some 840 million" (UNDP 1997: 5), "841 million" (UNDP 1998: 49), "about 840 million" (UNDP 1999: 22), "about 790 million" (UNDP 2000: 8), "826 million" (UNDP 2001: 22). The World Bank's Food Price Index fell from 124 in 1985 to 108 in 1996 to 84.5 in 2000 (statistics from "Global Commodity Markets" published by the World Bank's Development Prospects Group at www.worldbank.org/prospects/gcmonline/index.htm).

19 These ratios are based on market exchange rates, not purchasing power parities. This is appropriate when one is focusing, as I am throughout, not on income inequality as such, but on the avoidability of poverty. The global quintile income inequality ratio is much greater, if one compares individuals (or household averages) rather than country averages. One would then, in the top quintile, replace the poorest citizens of rich countries with richer persons in poorer countries and analogously, in the bottom quintile, replace the wealthiest citizens of poor countries with poorer citizens in less-poor countries. So calculated, the global quintile income inequality ratio rose from 78 in 1988 to 113 in 1993, indicating an average annual growth gap of 7.7 percent (personal communication from Branko Milanovic, World Bank). This trend has continued. Today, the top quintile of human beings have around 90 percent of global income and the bottom quintile about one-third of one percent, which puts the global quintile income inequality ratio at about 270. Cf. also Milanovic 2002: 88.

20 The figures just cited indicate an average annual growth gap of 1.66 percent for the colonial era (1820–1960), 2.34 percent for the period from 1960–90, and 3.04 percent for the period of 1990–97.

21 UNDP 2000: 195. Outside Latin America, most national quintile income inequality ratios are between 4 and 10. For example: Slovakia 2.6; Japan 3.4; Germany 4.7; Bangladesh 4.9; Spain 5.4; France 5.6; India 5.7; Switzerland 5.8; Australia 7.0; United Kingdom 7.1; China 8.0; USA 9.0; Malaysia 12.4; Nigeria 12.8; South Africa 22.6 (ibid.: 194–7).

22 $8,810 versus $7,570 (World Bank 2003: 234–5).

23 North Korea comes to mind, China around 1960, and the Soviet Union around 1930. But none of these cases displays the extreme income inequality of Sub-Subbrazil.

24 In this general statement, anti-universalism is entirely consistent with the thesis that the two minimal requirements (conjunctively or disjunctively) apply to the present global economic order. I address such anti-universalism, then, not because it threatens this thesis, but because it threatens the way I support this thesis here.

25 See especially Miller 1999, 2000 and 2004.

26 The word "monism" is introduced in Murphy 1999. According to his usage, monism denies that there is a plurality of different contexts, or domains of value, each with its

own fundamental moral principle(s). The fundamental principles of monistic moral conceptions thus are not contextually limited in range. Such a conception could nonetheless feature a plurality of fundamental moral principles and thus need not be monistic in the more usual sense.

27 Ibid.: 280; Cohen 1997: 22–3.

28 For an elaboration of these reasons, see my "On the Site of Distributive Justice" (Pogge 2000). In accordance with his method of avoidance, Rawls would probably prefer to make the weaker claim: to have shown that the moral principles appropriate to the basic structure *may* not be appropriate to other contexts or, generally, that different moral principles *may* be appropriate to different "domains of value." See the cautious formulations he employs in his discussion of a "model case of an overlapping consensus" in Rawls 1993: 169–71.

29 Rawls 1999b: 116–18. This argument exemplifies the strategy of justifying inequality by appeal to group autonomy.

30 See my *Realizing Rawls* (Pogge 1989): 252–3, and "An Egalitarian Law of Peoples" (Pogge 1994): 211–13.

31 Rawls 1999a: 401, 7.

32 With regard to his own fellow citizens, Rawls writes: "It is inevitable and often desirable that citizens have different views as to the most appropriate political conception; for the public political culture is bound to contain different fundamental ideas that can be developed in different ways. An orderly contest between them over time is a reliable way to find which one, if any, is most reasonable." Rawls 1993: 227; see also 164 and 241.

33 This objection to Rawls's account is presented more fully in my "Rawls on International Justice" (Pogge 2001).

34 See text at note 4 for the appeal to special ties, text at note 29 for the appeal to group autonomy, and the discussion of "decent peoples" in Rawls for the appeal to cultural diversity. This last appeal comes in two variants. Cultural diversity is adduced to justify that we may suspend our moral standards in dealing with foreigners who do not share our commitment to these standards (see my *Realizing Rawls* (Pogge 1989): 269–70). But why may we then not likewise suspend these standards in dealing with compatriots who do not share this commitment? Cultural diversity is also adduced to argue that, given non-liberal cultures abroad, we may not reform the global economic order in light of liberal notions of fairness and equality of opportunity. But why may we then, despite the presence of non-liberal cultures within the United States, realize such liberal notions in the national economic order?

35 Rawls offers a version of this view, suggesting that the causes of international inequality are purely domestic: "the causes of the wealth of a people and the forms it takes lie in their political culture and in the religious, philosophical, and moral traditions that support the basic structure of their political and social institutions, as well as in the industriousness and cooperative talents of its members, all supported by their political virtues... Crucial also is the country's population policy" (Rawls 1999b: 108). If a society does not want to be poor, it can curb its population growth or industrialize (ibid.: 117–18) and, in any case, "if it is not satisfied, it can continue to increase savings, or, if this is not feasible, borrow from other members of the Society of Peoples" (ibid.: 114). With the right culture and policies, even resource-poor countries like Japan can do very well. With the wrong culture and policies, resource-rich countries like Argentina may do very poorly (ibid.: 108). Every people is master of its own fate – except only perhaps the Arctic Eskimos (ibid.: 108, note 34).

36 The spirit of many nationalist explanations reverting to history and culture in captured in Walzer's remark that "it is not the sign for some collective derangement or radical incapacity for a political community to produce an authoritarian regime. Indeed, the history, culture, and religion of the community may be such that authoritarian regimes come, as it were, naturally, reflecting a widely shared world view or way of life" (Walzer 1980: 224–5). Detailed accounts are provided in Landes 1998, and in the essays collected

in Harrison and Huntington 2001. Nationalist explanations reverting to societies' natural environments are exemplified in Diamond 1999.

37 Other aspects, though less significant, are considerably more obvious and, perhaps for this reason, currently under attack. One such obvious aspect is diplomatic immunity – recently invoked by General Augusto Pinochet – which shields crimes committed by high officials from prosecution in other countries. Another such obvious aspect is the fact that, until 1999, most developed countries have not merely considered it perfectly legal for their firms to bribe foreign officials, but have even allowed these firms to deduct such bribes from their taxable revenues. Obviously, bribes encouraged by such rules have a considerable effect on the loyalties of officials in poor countries and on what kinds of people are motivated to scramble for public office in the first place. There is hope that such bribery will now become less common. The US pioneered reform with its 1977 *Foreign Corrupt Practices Act* after the Lockheed Corporation was found to have paid – not a modest sum to some minor third-world official, but rather – a US$2,000,000 bribe to Prime Minister Kakuei Tanaka of powerful and democratic Japan. It took another 22 years for other countries, pressured by the new organization Transparency International (TI), to follow suit with a *Convention on Combating Bribery of Foreign Officials in International Business Transactions*, requiring signatory states to criminalize the bribery of foreign officials. This convention took effect in February 1999 and has been ratified by most developed countries (www.oecd.org/home). Thus far, the *Convention* has not been successful: "Plenty of laws exist to ban bribery by companies. But big multinationals continue to sidestep them with ease" – so the current situation is summarized in "The Short Arm of the Law," *Economist*, March 2, 2002: 63–5, at 63. And even if the *Convention* were to stamp out international bribery completely, the deep entrenchment of corruption in many ex-colonies would still be traceable (by way of an historical explanation) to the extensive bribery they were subjected to, with official encouragement from the affluent states, during their formative years.

38 Such a government is considered entitled to rule "its" people by means of laws, decrees, and officials, to adjudicate conflicts among them, and also to exercise ultimate control over all resources within the territory (through "eminent domain" and its taxing powers). It is also considered entitled to represent these people toward the rest of the world: to bind them *vis-à-vis* outsiders through treaties and contracts, to regulate their relations with outsiders, to declare and to wage war in their name, to represent them through diplomats and emissaries, and to control outsiders' access to the national territory. In this second role, a government is considered continuous with its predecessors and successors: bound by the undertakings of the former, and capable of binding the latter through its own undertakings.

39 As explicated in Hohfeld 1919, a power involves the legally recognized authority to alter the distribution of first-order liberties, claims, and duties. Having *a* power or powers in this sense is distinct from having power (i.e., control over physical force and/or means of coercion).

40 For some background, see "Going on down," *The Economist*, June 8, 1996: 46–8. A later update reports: "Oil revenues [are] paid directly to the government at the highest level... The head of state has supreme power and control of all the cash. He depends on nobody and nothing but oil. Patronage and corruption spread downwards from the top" (*The Economist*, December 12, 1998: 19). Despite its huge oil revenues, Nigeria's real *per capita* GDP has declined by 22 percent between 1977 and 1998 (UNDP 2000: 185).

41 In October 2003, Nigeria received a score of 1.4 out of 10 on the Corruption Perception Index, second from the bottom among 133 countries ranked (www. transparency.org/cpi/2003/cpi2003.en.html).

42 For the 1975–99 period, these countries had long-term average annual rates of change in real GDP *per capita* as follows: Nigeria −0.8 percent, Congo/Zaire −4.7* percent, Kenya 0.4 percent, Angola −2.1* percent, Mozambique 1.3* percent, Brazil 0.8 percent,

Venezuela −1.0 percent, Saudi Arabia −2.2 percent, United Arab Emirates −3.7* percent, Oman 2.8* percent, Kuwait −1.5* percent, Bahrain −0.5* percent, Brunei −2.1* percent, Indonesia 4.6 percent, the Philippines 0.1 percent (UNDP 2001: 178–81; asterisks indicate that a somewhat different period was used due to insufficient data). As a group, the resource-rich developing countries thus fell far below the 2.2 percent annual rate in real *per capita* growth of the high-income economies – even while the developing countries on the whole kept pace (with 2.3 percent) thanks to rapid growth in China and the rest of East and South East Asia (ibid.: 181).

43 See Lam and Wantchekon 1999. The empirical part of this chapter supports the hypothesis that the causal connection between resource wealth and poor economic growth is mediated by reduced chances for democracy: "all petrostates or resource-dependent countries in Africa fail to initiate meaningful political reforms... On the other hand, besides South Africa, transition to democracy has been successful only in resource-poor countries" (ibid.: 31). The authors summarize their results as follows: "In this paper, we investigate why resource abundance generates dictatorial political regimes, which in turn exacerbates the poor economic performance due to Dutch disease. We argue that the negative impact of a resource boom on democratic regimes is caused by its effect on the distributive influence of the elite. Our cross-country regression confirms our theoretical insights. We find that a one percentage increase in the size of the natural resource sector generates a decrease by half a percentage point in the probability of survival of democratic regimes... [I]n order to improve economic performance, one has to limit the power of the elite. This could be achieved by... restricting elite discretion over the process of rent distribution" (ibid.: 35–6; see also Wantchekon 1999).

44 I add this caution because coups, civil wars, and oppression may be encouraged by the prospect of mere possession of resources, even without the power to confer internationally valid ownership rights. As I have learned from Josiah Ober, this is elegantly observed already in Thucydides 1986, Book 1, chapter 2.

45 Many poor countries are weighed down by large debt service obligations that their unelected rulers incurred for unproductive purposes (including, most typically, purchases of weapons needed for internal repression). In Nigeria, for instance, the military rulers did not only steal and waste the oil revenues of several decades, but also left behind a national debt of $30 billion or 78.8 percent of GNP. Debt/GNP ratios for some other countries are as follows: Congo/Zaire 232 percent, Kenya 61.5 percent, Angola 297.1 percent, Mozambique 223.0 percent, Brazil 30.6 percent, Venezuela 39.6 percent, Indonesia 176.5 percent, the Philippines 70.1 percent (UNDP 2000: 219–21; for Congo/Zaire, the figure is from UNDP 1999: 195). When the burden of debt service becomes too oppressive, the high-income countries occasionally grant some debt relief, thereby protecting their own banks from losses and, as a side effect, encouraging further lending to corrupt authoritarian rulers.

46 See my *World Poverty and Human Rights* (Pogge 2002). Chapter 6 outlines a reform specifically of the international resource and borrowing privileges, while chapters 7 and 8 offer more general discussions of appropriate global institutional reforms.

47 "Rich countries cut their tariffs by less in the Uruguay Round than poor ones did. Since then, they have found new ways to close their markets, notably by imposing anti-dumping duties on imports they deem 'unfairly cheap.' Rich countries are particularly protectionist in many of the sectors where developing countries are best able to compete, such as agriculture, textiles, and clothing. As a result, according to a new study by Thomas Hertel, of Purdue University, and Will Martin, of the World Bank, rich countries' average tariffs on manufacturing imports from poor countries are four times higher than those on imports from other rich countries. This imposes a big burden on poor countries. The United Nations Conference on Trade and Development (UNCTAD) estimates that they could export $700 billion more a year by 2005 if rich countries did

more to open their markets. Poor countries are also hobbled by a lack of know-how. Many had little understanding of what they signed up to in the Uruguay Round. That ignorance is now costing them dear. Michael Finger of the World Bank and Philip Schuler of the University of Maryland estimate that implementing commitments to improve trade procedures and establish technical and intellectual-property standards can cost more than a year's development budget for the poorest countries. Moreover, in those areas where poor countries could benefit from world trade rules, they are often unable to do so... Of the WTO's 134 members, 29 do not even have missions at its headquarters in Geneva. Many more can barely afford to bring cases to the WTO." *The Economist*, September 25, 1999: 89. The three cited studies – Hertel and Martin, UNCTAD, Finger and Schuler – are listed in the references.

48 Singer has famously built his case for demanding obligations on an analogy to the situation of a healthy adult chancing upon a drowning infant whom he alone can rescue from a shallow pond (Singer 1972). Many others have followed his lead, discussing the question on the basis of the tacit assumption that we are not contributing to the distress we are able to alleviate.

5 Reclaiming equality in a globalised world

Duncan Kerr

Words like democracy, citizenship and equality are constantly contested. The last two centuries have seen two distinct conceptions of citizenship and equality vie for adherents within the democratic, non-communist world.

One conception is that grounded in classical liberalism, now subsumed in neo-liberal – or, in the language popularised by Michael Pusey in Australia, economic rationalism (Pusey 1991). It sees citizenship as conferring rights of equality on individuals. The state meets its obligations to equality by establishing a framework of rules within which free-market operations are to govern outcomes. In its most authentic tones it asserts in the words of Margaret Thatcher, 'there is no such thing as society'.

The alternative conception looks beyond formal rules to substantive outcomes. Advocates of this conception of citizenship and equality assert that the state should provide a foundation of common provision – a typology described by Jamrozik as a platform of legal, social and economic infrastructure and access to material goods for all its citizens, so that, being relieved of the concern for basic survival, they can pursue their individual interests but within a framework of collective provisions, interests and obligations (Jamrozik 2001).

This latter notion is the ideological foundation of the welfare state. Michael Ignatieff points out that the twentieth century has seen a struggle to transform the liberty conferred by formal legal rights into the freedom guaranteed by shared social entitlement. He notes that

> [Rights talk] can capture civil and political inequalities, but it can't capture more basic inequalities, such as the ways in which the economy rewards owners and investors at the expense of workers. The economic system may not infringe anybody's individual rights, but the whole machine ends up reproducing enduring types of social inequality. Rights talk not only fails to capture this kind of inequality, but diverts attention of the political system from it.
>
> (Ignatieff 2000: 19–20)

Thus given the inertial tendency of markets to generate inequality, the state is called upon, by its own citizens, to redress the balance with entitlements designed to keep the contradiction between real inequality and formal equality from becoming intolerable.

Globalisation, however, has caused governments throughout the world to reorientate their social policies towards the neo-liberal paradigm. This chapter looks at what has been happening, asks whether there is anything we can do about these changes and puts forwards strategies that allow for the alternative conception of citizenship and equality to be reasserted in our globalised world.

The golden straitjacket

Britain's Margaret Thatcher popularised the expression 'There is no alternative'. She was wrong and in her case the alternative was, first, John Major, then Tony Blair. But in some fundamental aspects her views live on. Ironically, the idea that there is no alternative to governments constraining their expenditure on social justice and repudiating much or all of the welfare state still underpins almost all western democratic dialogue. Much contemporary political debate seems to accept the paradigms Thatcher championed... *The Queen is dead, Long live the Queen*.

Her usurper but, in this regard, ideological successor, Prime Minister Tony Blair put it this way: 'These forces of change driving the future don't stop at national boundaries, don't respect tradition. They wait for no one and no nation. They are universal.'

This idea that citizens and nation states are powerless to alter the impact of globalisation is best captured in *New York Times*' correspondent Tom Friedman's phrase the 'Golden Straitjacket'. Friedman's phrase describes the elements of policy now required of national governments by global capital markets, to sustain the value of their currencies and to remain able to attract or even retain foreign investment.

> To fit into the Golden Straitjacket a country must either adopt, or be seen as moving toward, the following golden rules: making the private sector the primary engine of its economic growth, maintaining a low rate of inflation and price stability, shrinking the size of its state bureaucracy, maintaining as close to a balanced budget as possible, if not a surplus, eliminating and lowering tariffs on imported goods, removing restrictions on foreign investment, getting rid of quotas and domestic monopolies, increasing exports, privatizing state-owned industries and utilities, deregulating capital markets and making its currency convertible, opening its industries, stock, and bond markets to direct foreign ownership and investment, deregulating its economy to promote as much domestic competition as possible.... When you stitch all of these pieces together you have the Golden Straitjacket.
>
> (Friedman 1999: 86–7)

Yet is it all that clear-cut? If it were, I would join with those who accept the agenda of accommodating the inevitable.

But it is not. Rather, close analysis suggests we are dangerously close to throwing the baby out with the bathwater. If we run down the elements of our common citizenship and make bare the social safety net, what will be left for the dispossessed?

What will hold together societies that are increasingly being polarised between the rich and the poor?

Dani Rodrik, author of *Has Globalization Gone Too Far?* points out that until the recent past there has been an unmistakable positive correlation between a nation's openness to trade and the amount it spends on social programmes. In his view the social welfare state has been the flip side of the open economy. Its unravelling may undermine the whole edifice.

> By any standard, the postwar social bargain has served the world economy extremely well ... [The expansion of world trade] did not cause major social dislocations and did not engender much opposition in the advanced industrial countries. Today, however, the process of international economic integration is taking place against a backdrop of retreating governments and diminished social obligations. Yet the need for social insurance for the vast majority of the population that lacks international mobility has not diminished. If anything it has increased.
>
> (Rodrik 1997: 25–6)

This is rapidly becoming a much more broadly accepted view. In essays published since the influential *The Lexus and the Olive Tree* in which the Golden Straitjacket was described, Tom Friedman has given greater importance to the legacy of the social welfare state, arguing that attention to the issues of social safety nets may be a precondition to the health of the global economy.

Such opinions are not held just by academic and media commentators. They are shared by the OECD (see its landmark publication, *Global Markets Matter*), the former Secretary General of the United Nations and the head of the World Bank (Boutros-Ghali 1996: 46; OECD 1998a: 81; Wolfensohn 1999). Most importantly, they are increasingly the focus of demands by huge numbers of strongly outspoken citizens and protest groups – some violent and counterproductive, but most simply demanding an end to increasing inequality, and attention to the needs of those who have borne the costs of, not gained from, overall economic growth. They are demanding global financial architecture to protect the vulnerable from the relentlessness of the market, and they are demanding accountability and democratic participation in global institutions such as the World Trade Organisation.

It is also becoming increasingly clear that further moves towards global trade liberalisation will not be possible unless, at a minimum, issues of labour and environment standards are taken into account. Even the Business Roundtable, the association of chief executives of the United States 150 biggest companies, now accepts and advocates this.

The squeeze of the golden straitjacket: Australia as an example of international trends: Hawke to Howard (1983–)

I entered the Australian parliament in 1987. Then it was possible to imagine that Australia would resist the seductive claims of globalisation. Australia had high levels of public ownership, including a national bank. Its telecommunications system was state-owned. It had high (albeit reducing) tariffs to protect local manufacturing. The government had put sectoral industry plans in place for the car and steel industries. Australia had the best system of public healthcare in the world. State education was free and there were no fees for entry to university. There were no private universities. The government had the power to regulate the money supply. Most revenue was raised through (steeply) progressive income taxes.

Just fourteen years later Australia has been transformed utterly. Many changes were wrought by the Hawke and Keating Labor governments, in which I served – initially as a backbencher and later as Attorney General and as Minister for Justice. The conservative Howard government that came to power in 1996 – and has held office since – has contributed regressive social reform to the mix.

Australia now has low levels of public ownership. Successive governments have sold the national bank and the national airline, opened the telecommunications market to competition and partly privatised the national telecommunications carrier. Tariffs have been reduced to negligible levels. Industry plans have not been renewed. Private health insurance has been subsidised, a financial penalty imposed on those who fail to take it up and the public system allowed to run down. The federal government now provides more funds to support private education than it provides to assist state schools. Fees or charges have been introduced for universities. Private universities have been established. Governments have forgone the power to regulate the money supply. Income tax rates have been repeatedly reduced and a new regressive system of indirect taxation, the goods and services tax (GST), has been introduced.

I highlighted this social transformation in my book *Elect the Ambassador! Building Democracy in a Globalised World* (Kerr 2001). I did so because the Australian experience was so illustrative of the policy constraints that flow from an acceptance of the disciplines of the 'golden straitjacket'. My observations were neither a *mea culpa* nor a 'look back in anger'. The Hawke and Keating governments went along with the prevailing neo-liberal economic orthodoxy of their times but they preserved – to a degree unprecedented in comparable countries, with the possible exception of Canada – the key elements of the welfare safety net. The Howard Government, now a party of radical conservatism, has substantially undone that important legacy.

Whatever the merit of judgments made by governments during those turbulent years, it has become clear to me with the benefit of hindsight that Australia, in common with all its regional neighbours and most other countries, is now comprehensively enmeshed in the global economy. Australia under both Hawke and Keating, in the same manner as other nations led by social democratic governments, worldwide, accepted the need for these policies because, like Friedman, they believed they were necessary for their countries to remain internationally competitive, to attract and retain investment and to shift resources to areas of new opportunity. As a result many of the levers that were formerly central to Keynesian national economic policy-setting – the exchange rate, tariffs and control over the money supply – were abandoned and are no longer available. These key decisions are now left, unregulated, to the 'market' or made beyond the borders of the nation state by remote and unaccountable international institutions. This pattern has been repeated, with minor variants, in country after country across the globe.

I see it as destructive to identify social democracy's main task in the future as working within these constraints. Those who advocate that we rely more on strengthening the private sector and local communities and on public–private partnerships, while operating within these constraints, seem to ignore the evidence that we are running down the reservoirs of common citizenship Australians once took for granted. I will illustrate with two examples: education and health.

In education, the Australian public school system is rapidly becoming a residual structure, catering for those who do not have the means to pay for private education, those who suffer from a disability and those from low socio-economic areas. Meanwhile, in the name of choice, the private system (including the richest and best endowed private schools) has received ever more generous subsidies and assistance from government. Despite there still being a far greater number of students enrolled in the public sector, one half of all university entrants come from private schools and the proportion is greater for 'prestige' faculties such as medicine and law. Funding restrictions to public universities has seen the emergence of a private tertiary education sector and, even within the public system, the creation of places available only to full fee-paying students who would otherwise fail to meet selection criteria on merit.

In health, the erosion of the universal system continues unabated. Waiting periods for those without private health insurance may be months or years. By contrast immediate availability of service is promised to the privately insured and public funds provide massive subsidies to those taking out such insurance. Current policy is seeing members of the more affluent sections of society having little interest in the fate of a public system they rarely, if ever, use. It is leading to a two-tier system: private provision for the wealthy and a residual inadequately funded public system for the rest. In effect the reduction of the public sphere to a residual role means a loss of shared citizenship and inherently creates an excluded underclass – an echo of Disraeli's 'two nations'.

The public sector has been eroded at an escalating level because criteria of efficiency and profitability have been applied uncritically to its activities. No one would deny that the public sector must perform its functions as efficiently as possible but certain areas of its activity cannot be evaluated solely on market criteria. Access to health, education, a clean environment and a range of social and cultural provisions is a public matter, based on well-grounded rights of citizenship in a democratic society. One of these is accountability. For this reason the infiltration of the public sector by the values and attitudes of the market corrupts the (properly different) value-base of public service. The degree of infiltration into the public sector by inappropriate values is in turn manifested in people's declining interest in community activities and in political participation. The minimalist post-welfare state is in danger of also becoming a post-democratic state.

Communities can survive the occasional failure of privatised (or public) energy or water supplies, annoying and occasionally disastrous as that may be; but can real democracy survive the shrinkage of quality public education? Can we hold together as a society if the rich separate themselves physically from the rest of us and retreat to live in walled, gated enclaves patrolled by private security firms – leaving even law and order and the provision of policing as a poorly funded public residue?

Inequality between countries

Concerns about inequality are nothing new. They are as ancient as laments about the irresponsibility of youth. Yet, the dynamics of globalisation and the impact of neo-liberal economic policy-settings have given a sharper edge to recent expressions of concern about inequality.

Two major reports examining this question have been available for some time. The first is the United Nations Development Program's 1999 *Human Development Report*. The second is the OECD's 1998 report *Income Distribution and Poverty in Selected OECD Countries*. An annex to this OECD report summarises and reviews the findings of other studies covering the period from 1970 onwards on income distribution and poverty within individual OECD countries.

A key measurement tool used by the United Nations Development Program in the *Human Development Report* is a statistic devised to measure what it calls the 'Human Development Index' (HDI). This is a measurement that combines statistics on life expectancy, education and income – rather than using just raw economic purchasing power – to report on human development.

Using this measuring device, the *Human Development Report* shows that, overall, people living in the developed world have made strong gains in all areas covered by the HDI since 1975. On average, people in these countries are living longer, are better educated and have become wealthier. However, the gains that have been powered by economic growth and globalisation have not been evenly shared.

All of the ten top-ranked countries on the HDI have experienced strong annual economic growth since 1975. Norway's 3 per cent average annual rate of Gross Domestic Product growth was the highest for this group, while Sweden's 1.1 per cent was the lowest. For the developing world the picture is mixed. Some countries, such as Mauritius and Poland, have improved as places to live; others, such as the Russian Federation and Madagascar, have worsened (United Nations Development Programme 1999; Kerr 2001: 26).

The picture is far bleaker for the least-developed countries. All ten poorest nations are African countries. They are Rwanda, Central African Republic, Mali, Eritrea, Guinea-Bissau, Mozambique, Burundi, Burkina Faso, Ethiopia, Niger and Sierra Leone. Six of these ten have experienced negative annual economic growth since 1975 (Kerr 2001: 26–7). The worst outcome was for Sierra Leone, whose population was the poorest of all. It was ranked last (174) on the HDI, having suffered an annual rate of decline of minus 2.2 per cent in its GDP over the twenty-two-year period since 1975. Only four of the bottom-ranked countries achieved positive GDP growth, despite their low starting point. The best result was for Burkina Faso, which reached a growth rate of 1.2 per cent. This is only

0.1 per cent better than the rate of growth achieved by the worst performed of the ten top-ranked countries. In much of Africa the human development indicators have hardly improved at all since 1975. In many instances they have declined. AIDS has reduced life expectancy and incomes have fallen in what were already appallingly poor countries. It seems clear from this that, at least at the top and bottom ends of the HDI, the wealthiest nations are getting richer and the poorest ones are getting poorer.

A fresh insight into the rich/poor divide can be gained from analysing the impact of technological change. A major feature, and driver, of globalisation is the technological revolution that has occurred in the information and telecommunications industries. This is part of the information revolution. As with economic and financial wealth, the benefits of the information revolution have been very unequally distributed. Buying a computer would cost the average worker in Bangladesh more than eight years' wages; it would cost the average citizen of the United States just one month's income.

Surveys have shown that users of the Internet are generally the already well-educated and affluent. In the United Kingdom half of those who use the Internet have degrees. Men dominate; women constitute only 38 per cent of users in the United States (in the Arab states they constitute only 4 per cent). Users are young: their average age in the United States is 36 years old and the average user in both Britain and China is less than 30 years old. Despite only one in ten of the world's population being able to speak any English, 80 per cent of all websites are in English. The profile of the average Internet user, thus, is: young, male, from a developed nation or from the élites of developing nations, well-educated and English speaking. The Internet has had virtually no penetration beyond wealthy, developed countries (Kerr 2001: 28).

Inequality within nations

The *Human Development Report* provides strong evidence that most people in developed nations have improved their well-being since 1975. On an average, citizens of developed nations are living longer, are better educated and have become wealthier in terms of annual income.

But averages can mislead. If five boys are each given $10 per week pocket money and five other boys are given only $2 per week each, the average pocket money each of the ten children receives is $6 per week. This shows how the careless use of such averages can give a false picture. The mathematical (mean) average doesn't allow us to see the differences within the group of children. To see those differences we have to look more closely and disaggregate the data. And one consequence of globalisation has been 'the disaggregation of national economies into sometimes starkly contrasting locales or regions'. In other words, inequality has increased, not only between nation states but also within them.

Global cities such as London and New York have become resource-rich hubs in the world economy. They link economic and political elites through financial, informational and other commercial and institutional networks. In certain respects the economic importance and cultural significance of these key locations is equal to, or perhaps even greater than, the nations within which they are located. To think in terms of a globalising economy is to recognise that the processes integrating certain locales for better or worse are intensifying in transnational nodes. The global city phenomenon – so essential to the spread of the service economy and the speeding up and growth in importance of capital flows and financial exchanges – is a key indicator. But so is the phenomena of economically depressed regions within advanced industrialised nation states, which suffer from the transfer of production and extraction processes to more profitable areas of the world.

The gulf between economically advantaged citizens and those living in such regions has ironically increased rather than narrowed as a consequence of the growing ubiquity of information technology. Early hopes that the spread of technology would mean it would be just as easy to conduct business from the peripheries as the centre have evaporated. Instead, the introduction of new technologies has widened the gulf between the 'haves' and the 'have nots'. Thus, the latest data on household use of information in Australia shows that only 15 per cent of non-metropolitan Australians have Internet access, compared to 26 per cent of those in the cities. This data also reveals that only 17 per cent of households with incomes below $50,000 (AUD) have Internet access, compared to 52 per cent of households with incomes of $100,000 (AUD) or more (ABS 2000).

While Australia and the United States have relatively high internet access, this masks the hidden inequalities and the relative exclusion of the regions and the poor from the new economic opportunities opening up for those with a head-start in the information age. This is part of the reason why there is a potent latent populism railing against globalisation, even in the United States which has seen the greatest benefits from global growth. Consider the remarks of Jim Hightower, former Texas Agriculture Commissioner, at an anti-World Trade Organisation rally on 18 October 1999.

> [T]his amounts to a class war. I was two years ago outside of Atlanta Georgia, at a Lucent Technologies plant...and...we met a woman named Anna Harris, who has worked for Lucent Technologies, a $26 billion-a-year conglomerate that makes telephones and other high-tech products. She had worked there 25 years and worked her way up to $15.59 an hour. That's not bad. That's about 31,000 bucks a year. You're not going to summer in France on that but you can get a little slice of the American middle class out of that. She got that high because she was skilled, she was efficient, she was hard working, she was loyal, she was a quality employee making a quality product.... [T]he company kept messing with [Anna Harris] and said Mexico beckoned, and they needed to speed up production. And if they didn't that they were going to haul off to Mexico. And indeed they said at one point that you've got to take a pay cut. So Anna Harris and her co-workers did. She went from $15.59 per hour to $13 per hour. That took about a $5000 slice out of Anna Harris's life. Now if you're Bill Gates, $5000 doesn't matter, but if you're Anna Harris $5000 is a real piece of change. She's a single parent.

Well the company kept messing with them...and then along came NAFTA [North American Free Trade Association] in 1993 and within a couple of weeks of the passage of NAFTA, Lucent Technologies backed up U-Hauls to the Atlanta plant and hauled off the equipment and hauled off the jobs of Anna Harris and 1000 other people.... A buck an hour they're paying to Anna Harris's replacement down there. That's a poverty wage in Mexico.... Then thanks to NAFTA, as pretty as they please, they ship that telephone equipment right back into the United States, back onto our markets, right into our stores without paying a tariff, without honouring any kind of quota, without saying as much as a hidy do to us. Anna Harris, it took her several months but she did finally get another job. She got one of those 23 million jobs that Bill Clinton brags about having created since he's been in office. Hers is at Target and she gets $7 an hour not $13 or $15.59. She gets $7 an hour, but she only gets part-time work. They keep messing with her so they don't have to pay benefits.

(Hightower 1999)

Anna Harris's experience unfortunately is typical – the poor getting poorer despite living in the richest country on earth. It is confirmed by OECD studies into income distribution and poverty (OECD 1998b; Kerr 2001: 31–2).

What is most startling about the OECD's findings is that income inequality has risen sharply since the mid-1980s in almost all the OECD countries studied. Not one country recorded a decline in inequality for the period from the mid-1980s to the mid-1990s.

From the mid-1970s to the mid-1980s, and from the mid-1980s to the mid-1990s, citizens of the United States experienced a rise in income inequality. The United States was the first to show a trend to increasing inequality in the 1970s. Australia and the United Kingdom followed, the increase in inequality being particularly sharp in the United Kingdom in the 1980s. Since the mid-1980s the rise in inequality has spread to continental European countries, particularly to the Nordic nations. For the study period Canada was most successful in resisting the trend to increasing inequality. It was the only OECD country that showed no increase in inequality (OECD 1998b; Kerr 2001: 32).

Equality and the post-welfare state

Since the 1970s much debate on social policy has revolved around the constraints imposed by the free market on governments that sought to maintain 'the welfare state'. The argument initially was that these constraints had created an abnormal situation and placed the welfare state in crisis. The notion of 'crisis' was first introduced and elaborated upon by James O'Connor in his book, *The Fiscal Crisis of the State* (O'Connor 1973).

Under the relentless pressure for national governments to fit national policy into Friedman's golden straitjacket, O'Connor's abnormal 'crisis' situation has now become a *normal condition*. The welfare state, as envisaged in its ideal form by early writers, had a very short life (Marshall 1964; Titmuss 1968). While many of its features remain to varied extents in most industrialised countries, almost all of these remaining features are under increasing pressure of reduction or abolition. That is why the term 'welfare state' is no longer a strictly correct description for such societies.

The new forms of social policy that have emerged since the 1980s have one common feature, namely, an endeavour to control, and preferably reduce, social expenditure. Neo-liberal advocates have put forward two arguments in favour of this. One argument is that welfare expenditure has a negative effect on the economy, by reducing the amount of capital available for investment. The second is that it has a negative effect on the population, namely, the creation of a growing attitude and behaviour of dependency and reduced responsibility – a form of 'moral hazard' (Murray 1984).

Increasing pressure from global market forces has led governments in all Western countries, whether enthusiastically or reluctantly, to reduce their taxes and social expenditures as they seek to ensure the inflow of investment capital and to maintain their market competitiveness. Ramesh Mishra makes the link to globalisation explicit, arguing that 'globalisation weakens the ideological underpinning of social protection... by undermining national solidarity and legitimising inequality of rewards' (Mishra 1999: 99). But it is also a matter of raw survival. As observed by Ian Culpitt, governments 'are no longer ethically driven by the social needs of their citizenry but by the economic imperatives of survival'. As a result, Culpitt notes:

> Political support for traditional welfare states is no longer an obvious feature of the public rhetoric of western liberal democracies. The theoretical rationales which were used to defend the welfare state and its traditional pattern of practical social policies have been challenged....An essential aspect of this attack on the welfare state has been the complete rejection of those social ideas of citizenship rights and obligations which were encapsulated in the political and social structures of the welfare states.
>
> (Culpitt 1992: 1)

The attack on the welfare state by the neo-liberal economists has been mounted not only on economic grounds but also as a matter of ideology. The advocates of the 'free' market have represented the welfare state as a threat to individual liberty, arguing that the controls imposed by the welfare state on the 'free' market were reducing populations to a state of serfdom. True freedom, they have argued, can be achieved only through an unrestrictedly 'free' market. Those who espoused such ideas found a receptive political constituency among the increasingly affluent middle classes, who enjoyed benefits from the welfare state but resented having to pay the taxes, which the state needed in order to fund these services and benefits.

A related feature of this change was the transfer of many public services to private welfare agencies. This involved a growing acceptance of the neo-liberal argument that 'private welfare agencies can provide a more effective means to recognise distinctive individual or group claims to services'. The movement towards privatisation of welfare services paralleled the privatisation of the material infrastructure – services such as power and water supply, public transport, national airlines, the communications network and various pieces of public real-estate property. The outcome has been substantial reduction of the public sector and corresponding growth of the influence of market forces.

The role of the state has been reduced to providing the preconditions for the activities of the market and to controlling those who have been excluded from the mainstream of economic and social life – the growing 'human residue' of the market economy, people who are forced to rely for their subsistence on the state. For the majority of the population, however, the market has become the main regulating force and authority, providing a seemingly unlimited range and variety of goods and services.

In presenting this analysis, it is important to emphasise that this significant shift in policy orientation – the subjugation of social policy to the pervading ideology known as economic rationalism – is the reason the industrialised countries (or any country for that matter, perhaps with rare exceptions) can no longer be referred to as 'welfare states'. By any analysis, the period that gave the birth to the welfare state has come to an end. In this period of uncertainty it is more accurate to refer to such states as 'post-welfare states'. This is a theme that is further developed in a lucid and very readable way by Adam Jamrozik in his recent book *Social Policy in the Post-Welfare State: Australians on the Threshold of the 21ˢᵗ Century* (Jamrozik 2001).

The dominant feature of post-welfare states is that social policy is used as an instrument of support for free market economic policy – rather than to alleviate the excesses of inequality generated by the market, which was the aim of the welfare state. Government policies in post-welfare states tend to reinforce and aggravate the excesses of inequality generated in the free market. This occurs because governments have become persuaded that market activities must be given free rein, and have come to believe that the most important determining factor in the economy is the level of private profit rather than an equitable distribution of resources.

The post-welfare state is a minimalist state: it may provide a minimum income support for marginalised sections of the population but does not aspire to redistribute income or wealth. On the contrary, the post-welfare state supports and encourages inequality: its social policy is based on the virtues of competition. Post-welfare state policies, therefore, aim to reduce the bargaining power of wage earners but not to provide any restraint on the profitability of business enterprises nor on the incomes of managers and business executives. The result of these policies has been an unprecedented increase in inequity in income distribution in most industrialised nations, including Australia, and in corresponding lifestyles and life-chances.

Table 5.1 The welfare state versus the post-welfare state (Kerr 2001: 67)

Welfare state	Post-welfare state
Acceptance of responsibility for the welfare of all citizens, as a matter of deliberate policy	Acceptance of responsibility for welfare as a rather unfortunate necessity
Universal entitlements to social provisions	Selective entitlements
Aim to control the excesses of the 'free'-market economy	Promotion of market economy principles as a model to follow
Commitment to the pursuit of equality, at least in access to opportunities and resources	Acceptance of inequality as 'natural' and, indeed, desirable to achieve efficiency
Commitment to principles of collectivity	Commitment to individualism
Maintaining social expenditure at a level ensuring reasonable standards of provisions	Curtailment of social expenditure to an absolute minimum
Infrastructure of resources (such as power, water) provided by the public sector	Reduction of the public sector; privatisation of the infrastructure
Acceptance of collective bargaining in industry through trade unions	Promotion of individual work contracts between employer and employee
Distributing money, services and power through citizens' participation	Distributing money, some services but no power to citizens
Social control by the state	Social control increasingly by the market

The philosophy of the post-welfare state is that material incentives are a stimulus for higher productivity and efficiency, and high rewards are necessary for managers, who possess almost mystic powers that ordinary mortals can neither aspire to nor comprehend. Furthermore, provisions such as income support, emergency relief, or access to care services, are no longer available as a right in a post-welfare state but are stringently rationed according to need, the determination of which is the prerogative of the service provider. In the provision of these services, the criteria of 'deserving' and 'undeserving' have again become important factors.

Other significant conceptual and policy differences between the welfare state and the post-welfare state are set out in the Table 5.1. These differences produce changes in resource allocation and corresponding gains and losses for the well-being of various communities within the population.

What is at stake: conceptions of citizenship

The transformation of formerly welfare states into post welfare states is not simply an economic issue; it changes how we think about citizenship rights. Consider the contrast between the agenda offered by most recent social democratic parties and that of former (Australian Labor Party) Prime Minister Gough Whitlam. In writing about the philosophy that guided the policy of his government, Whitlam, head of government of the Commonwealth of Australia 1972–75, conceptualised citizen rights as follows:

> [My] approach is based on this concept: increasingly, a citizen's real standard of living, the health of himself and his family, his children's opportunity for education and self-improvement, his access to employment opportunities, his ability to enjoy the nation's resources for recreation and cultural activity, his legacy from the national heritage, his scope to participate in the decisions and actions of the community, are determined not so much by his income but by the availability and accessibility of the services which the community alone can provide and ensure. The quality of life depends less and less on the things which individuals obtain for themselves and can purchase for themselves from their personal incomes and depends more and more on the things which the community provides for all its members from the combined resources of the community.
>
> (Whitlam 1985: 3)

Whitlam, in turn, drew on Abraham Lincoln's assertion: 'The legitimate object of the government is to do for the people what needs to be done but which they cannot, by individual effort, do at all, or do so well, for themselves' (Whitlam 1985: 3).

The retreat to privileging the individual and treating acceptance of the responsibility for welfare as just an unfortunate necessity not only conflicts with the social democratic tradition but also threatens emptying the idea of democracy of real content. In a democratic society there are fundamental assumptions on which public services are established and expected to operate. Certain public assets constitute the core infrastructure of community services: the provision of health, education, public transport, policing, clean air and water, public libraries and other cultural and recreational facilities. The availability of this core infrastructure hitherto was seen to be essential for the adequate social functioning of a civilised, democratic society and the efficient operation of such services was seen as important because public property should not be wasted. But the main criterion for their provision, their *raison d'être*, is their effectiveness, that is, the discharge of the function for which they had been created – ensuring social rights of citizens in a democratic society. Access to the services constituting this core infrastructure is, or should be available by right to every citizen – something that in a democratic society has to be regarded as a citizen's birthright.

Uncritical acceptance by governments of free-market ideology presents a threat to democracy, one that is particularly evident in the reduction of the public sphere. If the public domain shrinks to nothing, the idea of commonality disappears with it. Without any shared public domain there is no area of life in which all citizens meet and interact as equals. It also sets in train a vicious cycle of blaming the victims.

Explanations of social problems are now being sought in the characteristics of the populations and individuals experiencing a given problem. One of the most important issues – poverty among families – increasingly has been translated into child abuse and neglect. Poverty is explained almost solely as the pathology of parents, who are then subjected to punitive methods of remedial intervention. Ironically, the methods of intervention based on this perspective have been developed as part of a worldwide movement among psychologists, psychiatrists and social workers, reinforced by regular international conferences held in attractive locations such as Rio de Janeiro, Sydney or Queensland's Gold Coast.

Cowed, frightened or willingly co-opted, social work and other 'helping' professions have come to occupy supporting roles of social control. Pursuing structural and social explanations and methodologies has become dangerous and to be avoided. Adam Jamrozik and Luisa Nocella have described the process of social issues being converted into personal problems:

> Examples... are poverty, unemployment, child welfare, and gambling addiction. The source of these problems can be identified in the pursuit of certain values and goals, and in the corresponding allocation of resources. The underlying common factor in the first three problems is inequality, and the source of the fourth is in a state-conducted and state-promoted activity. The common factor in all four problems is the methods of intervention at the operative level, which are based on perceptions of certain personal pathologies in those experiencing those problems. Methods employed entail a range of personal services of a counselling and therapeutic nature reinforced by surveillance and an implicit (and sometimes explicit) threat of withdrawal of income support, or other punitive sanctions. Even when there is some acknowledgment of structural or external causes of the problem, intervention remains in these cases at the operative level, substantiated at times by the argument that 'this is the best one can do'.
>
> (Jamrozik and Nocella 1998: 202)

The demise of the public sphere driven by the attempt to fit government into the constraints of globalisation has thus meant a reduction of the rights of citizenship. The mere possession of the right to vote for those who govern us, important as it is, is not sufficient to ensure the survival of a democratic system if the public sphere is curtailed. In applying T. H. Marshall's typology of citizenship rights, the exercise of civil and political rights might be formally maintained if the public sphere is curtailed, but social rights – that is, the rights to society's resources – are certainly lost (Marshall 1964). Furthermore, a citizen's civil and political rights are also curtailed, in practice, if they are delivered within a public sphere constrained by the same market forces.

The privatisation of such public utilities as the supply of energy or water often endows private providers with monopoly powers. State monopoly, which is subject to scrutiny by public institutions such as the parliament and the auditor-general, is replaced by a private monopoly that is outside any such scrutiny. Accountability becomes an issue as arrangements for the privatisation and contracting out of the provision of public services are usually shrouded in secrecy.

Susan Strange sees the issue of accountability as one of the dilemmas of globalisation. She says:

> The long struggle for liberty and accountability gradually made at least some states accountable to the people, but globalisation, by shifting power from states to firms, has allowed international bureaucracies to undermine that accountability. None of the new non-state authorities are accountable; few are even transparent. There is a democratic deficit, not only in Europe, but America, Japan – the entire globalised economy.
>
> (Strange 1997: 366–7)

Advancing equality and building democracy in a globalised world

There is a well-known prayer that counsels us to seek the grace to accept those things that cannot be changed, the courage to change those things that can and the wisdom to tell the difference. It is the credo of practical politicians.

In the short term the first-order challenge for any social democratic government is to retain what it can of the social safety net within the existing constraints of the global economy. But we need to distinguish between appropriate policies and programmes for a three- or five-year term of office and the wider objective of the social democratic project. To achieve that objective social democracy now needs global, not merely national, ambitions. More importantly anyone whose conception of citizenship and equality goes beyond the neo-liberal paradigm, cannot simply seek local solutions.

There has been a 'widening, deepening and speeding up of worldwide interconnectedness in all aspects of contemporary social life'. This is particularly evident in the case of economic and financial matters, but it applies equally to cultural, environmental, criminal and security matters. It also relates to the growth of transnational government. Globalisation is not going to go away, it needs to be dealt with. Nor are all aspects of globalisation abhorrent.

Globalisation and open markets have allowed resources to be used more efficiently and productively. There is strong evidence that the efficiency benefits of open trade and investment regimes have led to net economic growth. Prices have usually come down after the removal of trade barriers. Strategies that are destructive of open markets or that promote protectionism are, therefore, not only naïvely impractical but also flawed in principle. Further any developed world nation that unilaterally attempted to reintroduce tariff protection would invite retribution.

The net gain in global growth generated by globalisation, however, has come at a cost. Globalisation has been responsible for increasing inequality within nation states and between the richest and the poorest countries. The rhetoric of those who still argue that 'a rising tide raises all boats', or that gains to the wealthy will 'trickle down', has been proved wrong time and time again. The facts don't fit the theory. Trickle down hasn't trickled. Many boats have been left stranded. Millions of people have correctly concluded that their interests have been treated as marginal, their losses ignored, their job security lessened, their costs not compensated, their futures left bleaker than ever before – all because of globalisation. It is now unrealistic for citizens to expect that their national government, single-handedly, will be able to solve problems that are no longer national in character. Issues as diverse as crime, culture, labour standards, environmental responsibility, trade, taxation, financial stability and biotechnology – all once could be entirely regulated by national laws. Now their regulation requires a framework of international government.

The growing disparity of wealth between the developed and least-developed world is also a product of globalisation. The idea that there are effective national 'development' policies that can lift grossly disadvantaged nations up by their own bootstraps, and lead them out of poverty so that they can enjoy economic parity with their wealthy counterparts, has been discredited. The remedy for the problems of underdevelopment, if sought, is not just self-help. Solutions must move beyond that and be international in scope.

The regional and other disparities that globalisation has given rise to will be difficult to overcome – if not impossible – unless minimum standards on social issues can be agreed between nations. In particular, policies to sustain adequate collection of taxation are vital if the golden straitjacket of globalisation is to be refitted. This will require international cooperation and international institutions.

Social democracy can only be built on the willingness to address the twin issues of growth and fairness. That is why we must now give priority to developing international approaches that seek to tame the anarchy of financial markets, to establish multilateral agreements on minimum social and labour standards, to set global environmental benchmarks and to curb transnational tax avoidance (Table 5.2).

Only by shifting the focus of democratic debates to the international sphere can solutions for these, and similar issues be imagined. It means that the current undemocratic way in which these issues are decided must be challenged. How to

Table 5.2 The ten proposals for global social democracy (Kerr 2001: 159)

---

1 Develop a programme to deal with the negative structural consequences of globalisation.
2 Foster the evolution of transnational political groupings.
3 Establish a second, directly representative, assembly for the United Nations.
4 Democratically preselect leaders of key international bodies.
5 Introduce citizen-initiated recall provisions for key international positions.
6 Establish processes for the democratic endorsement of national nominees for international posts.
7 Require open-negotiation processes in making regional and international agreements.
8 Allow participatory involvement in key international agreements before they are made or adopted.
9 Insist that non-government organisations meet minimum standards of internal democratic accountability before they receive accreditation in international forums.
10 Elect advisory chambers for transnational regional associations.

---

achieve this, rather than seeking to squeeze the social democratic project into an ever-tighter straitjacket of what the existing order of the global economy allows is in my view the biggest question facing Labour and Social Democratic parties around the world.

These ideas, developed by me in more detail in *Elect the Ambassador!*, are intended to open a conversation that social democrats need to have, rather than to lay down a fixed plan (Kerr 2001: 112–62).

It is now commonplace to recognise that globalisation has shifted power from local and national government to transnational institutions. What then holds back social democratic parties and other citizens who place a high value on democracy from asserting the logical case for democratic control of the institutions of inter-national government? Perhaps the only answer is the natural propensity of those who hold positions of authority and influence to cling to the comfort of continu-ing business as usual. We should not be surprised when insiders gloss over chal-lenging ideas that threaten their status and power. Stephen Jay Gould, the pre-eminent populariser of science, cited Freud as the key to answering the conundrum of how it is possible for humans to know, intellectually, that an old system of thought is no longer tenable yet to continue to behave as if it were.

In a famous statement, Sigmund Freud argued that scientific revolutions reach completion not when people accept the physical reinstruction of reality thus implied, but when they also own the consequences of this radically revised universe for a demoted view of human status. Freud claimed that all-important scientific revolutions share the ironic property of deposing humans from one pedestal after another of previous self-assurance about our exalted cosmic sta-tus. Therefore, all great revolutions smash pedestals – and inspire resistance for the obvious reason that we accept such demotions only begrudgingly.

(Gould 1998: 302)

Globalisation has unleashed a 'revolution' that is smashing the underpinning of purely national politics. The way we trade, the way we communicate and the way we govern our lives – are all affected by this revolution. No national government acting alone can call a halt to these processes. But we are not just powerless pas-sengers along for the ride, whether we like it or not. Globalisation also presents us with opportunities to begin anew: building responsible and democratic institu-tions of international government.

Economic and social revolutions call on us to craft new approaches. We should heed the parallels in history. Useful analogies can be drawn between the changes now being wrought by globalisation and the information revolution and those generated by the industrial revolution two centuries ago. The industrial revolution generated vastly greater productivity and wealth than had feudalism, but it also produced the poverty and 'dark satanic mills' of Dickensian England. Like the industrial revolution, globalisation has produced greater productivity and eco-nomic growth, but at the cost of greater disparity of wealth and at the price of an increasing exclusion of the poor.

The solutions suggested by the Luddites and by Marxists to redress the cruelties of the industrial revolution were flawed. Yet, successful alternatives did emerge. Social democratic policies succeeded in creating social bargains in which the vulnerable were, at least to a degree, compensated and protected from the bleak relentlessness of the market. Globalisation has corroded and limited any single government's ability to sustain what the welfare state achieved. This is not to deny that defending and reshaping what remains of the welfare state to better accommodate new needs in education, housing, health and aged care is still a worthwhile national objective. But, increasingly, defence of social bargains will not be possible at a national level. Unless discussion of these issues is shifted into the international arena, the pressure to reduce expenditure on social programmes is likely to become irresistible. Democracy will become a hollow shell if we persist in thinking about issues of equality and rights only on a national scale. Nor is it enough to 'think globally but act locally'. Our world has changed. There is nothing unambiguously 'local' remaining. Effective democratic participation in our world is now not possible unless we both think and act globally. Some share of our energy and commitment as citizens, therefore, has to be devoted to asserting our rights as members of the global community. As former US Deputy Secretary of State Strobe Talbot correctly points out, the very word 'foreign' is becoming obsolete (Talbot 1997: 81).

The fate of democracy will be determined by how we adapt to that reality.

6   Welfare, equality and globalisation

Reconceiving social citizenship

Sheila Shaver

It is now widely argued that the welfare safety nets created in the postwar era of full employment and stable family structures are ill suited to the era of global capitalism. The impulse to welfare reform, shared across lines of political ideology and political party in much of the advanced capitalist world, flows from the belief that the welfare system has become a source of the problem, rather than part of the solution. Contemporary welfare reform is a response to this argument, and the changed economic and political conditions that give rise to it.

Welfare reform is only one facet of change in welfare state policies and programmes. Many countries are changing the way they fund and provide incomes in retirement in ways that will have profound consequences over the long term (Myles and Quadagno 1997; Ginn *et al.* 2001). Social services and the way they are organised are also changing (Esping-Andersen 1999: 103–5). Welfare reform has, however, signalled nations' most direct response to high levels of unemployment, sustained for two decades in some countries. These and other changes in economic and social circumstances have made calls on social protection much more common, and much more expensive, than was the case two decades ago. At the same time, it is now argued that social policy has a positive role to play in the adaptation of national economies to the changed conditions of post-industrial employment.

Welfare reform has the potential to change the terms of citizen–state relations in social policy, and the political values that are expressed in a nation's welfare arrangements. Among these are important ideals and meanings about the expectations that citizens may legitimately hold of one another in respect of the needs, risks and adversities inherent in capitalist social life. In the postwar period, welfare states came to represent ideals of social citizenship in which all members of society were to be assured a minimum standard of well-being that reflected and supported their status as human beings of equal worth and dignity. Politically, this minimal equality as citizens was seen as underpinning the democratic government. Taking different form in different countries, welfare arrangements have often failed to deliver on these promises, but their sustained growth into the 1980s and beyond is a sign that the promises mattered nonetheless. With the advent of welfare reform, the meaning and substance of such promises have come into question.

This chapter examines the implications of welfare reform for the meaning and substance of social citizenship. Taking Australian welfare reform as a case in point, it sees welfare being transformed from a limited social right to support provided on condition, and from the treatment of the claimant as a sovereign individual to a subject of paternalistic supervision. Together, these changes are redefining the meaning of Australian social citizenship from one affirming, however minimally, the social status of the welfare recipient as an equal of others, to one in which this equality is questionable and contingent. By no means unique, Australian welfare reform must be seen in the context of welfare state adaptation more generally. The chapter argues that Australian welfare reform is following one of a number of parallel courses of policy change. This course reflects the liberal values that underlie its liberal social policy design, and it is by these values that its meaning for social citizenship must be evaluated.

Citizenship, globalisation and the retreat from welfare

In the postwar period welfare states came to be established features of the nation states of the advanced capitalist world. These institutions provide their citizens with protection against the social and economic hazards of capitalist employment, the contingencies of the life course and the vicissitudes of personal life. The key factors explaining their growth are generally considered to be functional needs associated with the growth of industrial capitalism, political mobilisation by social democratic and/or Christian democratic parties and the interests, agendas and facilitating structures of policy-makers within the state (Wilensky 1975; Korpi 1983; Myles 1989; Skocpol 1992). By the end of the 1970s, social expenditure represented some ten (Japan) to almost thirty (Sweden) per cent of gross domestic product, and these shares have continued to grow in most countries (Figure 6.1).

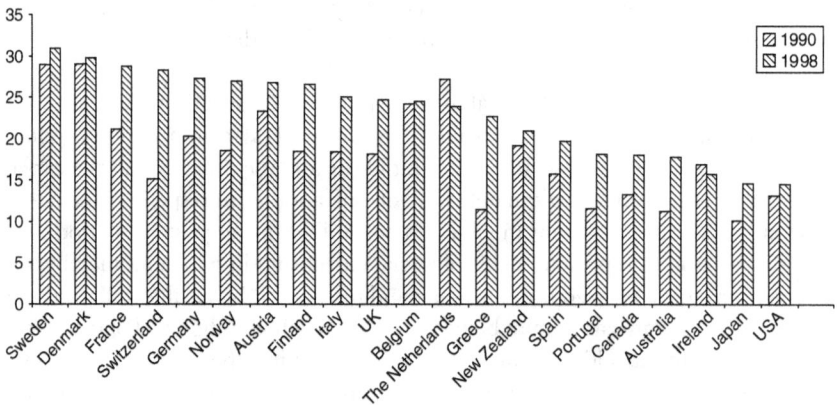

Figure 6.1 Social expenditure as per cent of GDP.

Source: OECD Social Expenditure Database 2001.

Political constituencies have formed around measures such as pensions, family support and healthcare and the levels and distribution of benefits and taxes have come to be key terms in national politics (Pierson 1994).

Equality, especially in the sense of ameliorating social and material inequalities and their effects, is a central concern of welfare states and their key institutions. This concern is multidimensional. Structurally rooted in the primary forces of class, gender and racial inequality, social policy arrangements alter the working of labour markets and employment, family and reproduction and settlement and social integration. Economically, welfare institutions effect the redistribution of command over resources in two dimensions, between income groups and over the life course. While the main direction of this redistribution is towards greater equality of income and well-being, it is important to note that social expenditure delivers significant benefits to middle-income groups (Le Grand 1982; Baldwin 1990). Much redistribution takes place from the population that is of working age to the young and the old, and in respect of family responsibilities, age, health and disability. Politically, the welfare state has been at the centre of left and social democratic strategies for more just societies, and a point of resistance by conservative and capitalist parties.

This multidimensional concern with equality is the basis of T. H. Marshall's (1963) theorisation of welfare as an historically new form of social citizenship. By social citizenship, Marshall referred to 'the whole range from the right to a modicum of economic welfare and security to the right to share to the full in the social heritage and to live the life of a civilized being according to the standards prevailing in the society' (1963: 74). He argued that the modern entitlements of the welfare state represented a new form of rights, social rights, which were equivalent to the civil and political rights that had developed before them. These rights conferred a new form of status equality by which all members, by virtue of being ensured a minimum of economic resources, could be full participants in their society. Marshall saw this limited social equality as not at all inconsistent with economic inequality, and indeed a necessary complement to it in a society dependent on competitive markets. Social security benefits particularly gave protection from risk, expressed new common experiences and perhaps most importantly treated people as individuals rather than members of social classes. As Marshall saw it, welfare state citizenship had to be universal, with all social classes sharing the same form of social protection.

Citizenship is a limited form of social and economic equality. As a concept it is fundamentally relational, positing the citizen as member in the community of the nation. This relationship has both active and passive dimensions, and entails both rights and obligations. In the economic dimension, this concept of citizenship understands equality in the limited meaning that all citizens are assured of economic well-being above a minimum standard. It endorses inequalities of income and wealth above that standard. Critically, it joins this with a social dimension in which all citizens are equal in status, dignity and capacity for democratic participation in government and the social life of the community.

Marshall's formulation of welfare as social citizenship has been criticised on a number of counts: for relying too singularly on British historical experience, for the underdevelopment of industrial dimensions, for neglect of gender, race and ethnicity in the shaping of social rights and for insufficient attention to issues concerning the obligations that accompany rights (Barbalet 1988; Turner 1992; Janoski 1998; Siim 2000: 26–30). These objections have not, however, questioned the importance of its fundamental insights, and Marshall's perspective continues to illuminate certain of the most central tensions in modern welfare states.

Marshall's approach is of particular value for the present purpose because its engagement with multiple dimensions of social equality helps to show what is at stake in contemporary welfare reform. Marshall suggests that the social provisions of the welfare state constitute the participants in an unequal economic system as equal citizens in social and political life. Welfare benefits and services ensure that all members of society are able to enjoy a minimum standard of living, secure against want for themselves and those who depend on them. The entitlement of citizens to this guarantee of minimum economic security derives from their joined interests as members of the same social community and affirms their equality with one another. Social rights thus enable citizens to participate in the social and political affairs of the society. Marshall saw social rights as the fruit of political rights and the political mobilisation of the enfranchised working class. He maintained that taken together, equality of political and social citizenship had (in the case of pre-war Britain) proven compatible with continuing inequalities of income, wealth and economic power of capitalist society. On this evidence, equality of social citizenship, including limited equalisation of income and living standards, is not necessarily inconsistent with the stability and growth of a nation's economy and moreover potentially beneficial to it. The postwar 'golden age' of the welfare state was predicated on this vision (Esping-Andersen 1996a).

Since the 1980s, however, advanced welfare states across the advanced capitalist world have been in retreat and reconstruction. The underlying causes lie in the sea change in national economies set in train by the break-up of the Bretton Woods agreement managing international currencies and the OPEC oil price increases in the 1970s. The globalisation that accelerated thereafter is part of this change, but not necessarily the most immediate factor in welfare state restructuring.

Huber and Stephens identify three dimensions of economic globalisation, these being growth in international trade, internationalisation of production and increases in international capital flows. All three inhibit the raising of state revenues to finance welfare provision, and undermine the capacity of nation states to pursue autonomous economic and social policies. Even so, some of the most generous welfare states have been built on open economies with high levels of exports, and international investment in production more often pursues access to markets than cheap labour. It is the internationalisation of capital that has been most problematic for maintaining social expenditure, because it has reduced the capacity of governments to fund deficits and stimulate employment (Esping-Andersen 1999: 95–9, 101–3; Mishra 1999; Huber and Stephens 2001: 227–30).

The effects of other economic changes not directly related to globalisation have been more immediate. According to Huber and Stephens (2001: 234–7), unemployment is the proximate cause of welfare state retrenchment or constraint. They trace this in turn to an overall decline of growth in output and productivity, the shift from industrial to post-industrial employment and maladaptive policy responses to women's increasing labour force participation. While they consider the significance of demographic change and especially population ageing to have been overstated, they note greater difficulty for governments in funding public pension systems in the changed international financial conditions. They suggest that some of the largest welfare states may have reached economic or more probably political limits to their growth.

Welfare states differ from one another. The welfare states of the advanced capitalist world appear to have developed in three broad forms. In Continental Europe, large welfare states were built under conservative political hegemony. These feature large social insurance programmes with near-universal coverage and high levels of benefits provided as of right, underpinned by tightly targeted social assistance providing a safety net of poverty relief and strong emphasis on the traditional family. The welfare states of northern Europe and Scandinavia also centre on large, generous social insurance systems, with their development under social democratic party governments reflected in a greater role in maximising employment and equalising incomes and high levels of public employment especially of women. A third, more heterogenous group of mainly English-speaking nations have smaller welfare states with lower levels of public social expenditure and more restricted access to benefits. Reflecting the common orientation to protecting the private roles of market and family and their relatively greater use of means-tested benefits, the group as a whole has often been referred to as 'liberal'. This aptly describes the United States and Canada. Some writers regard Australia and New Zealand as having followed a distinctive, Antipodean path of development relying first on state intervention in wage determination and employment standards, with welfare measures such as pensions and unemployment benefits playing a secondary role in social protection (Castles 1985, 1996; Esping-Andersen 1990, 1996c, 1999; Huber and Stephens 2001).

Welfare state retrenchment and restructuring has followed somewhat different paths in countries with welfare states of these different kinds. The large welfare states of Continental Europe have relied heavily on early retirement policies to facilitate industrial restructuring. The Nordic countries have used 'productivistic' strategies centring on re-employment through retraining and reactivation. The liberal welfare states have sought labour market flexibility through de-regulation, allowing unwanted workers to be shed onto the unemployment rolls (Esping-Andersen 1999: 120–37). One reason for such differences is that welfare institutions have been important mediators of the effects of the sea change in the international economy on national populations. A second is path dependency in welfare state adaptation, in that stakeholder groups have defended those institutions in which they have established interests. Research by Huber and Stephens (2001: 202–21) shows the rise in unemployment as decisive in triggering cutbacks to or constraints in the growth of welfare provision. Reductions in expenditures have been widespread, and some countries have also increased social insurance contributions. The trajectories of institutional change have, however, been more parallel than convergent, with variations in the scale and form of welfare provision continuing to be important (Esping-Andersen 1996a, 1999). In only two countries, Britain and New Zealand, have institutions been reshaped in significant ways (Esping-Andersen 1996c: 10; Huber and Stephens 2001: 7). Huber and Stephens (2001: 7, 240) argue that globalisation has had greater impact in Australia and New Zealand than elsewhere, because both nations opened economies that had historically been highly protected to foreign trade. The main element of convergence is a common narrowing of differences in the policy stances of political parties, mainly reflecting the movement of left parties to defend the welfare state but no longer to expand it.

Australia provides an apt case study of what the restructuring of the welfare state has meant for equality in the era of globalisation. No single country can represent the full range of national experience. The Australian case nevertheless provides an informative study of welfare state restructuring and its consequences for social citizenship and equality in a country where globalisation has been a strong force. It also provides a more specific example of these developments in countries whose welfare states have been similarly shaped in the liberal mould, and whose policy-makers have been drawing ideas from one another. Australia's period of welfare state restructuring, largely the last two decades, covers periods of government by parties of both the social democratic left (the Australian Labor Party governments of 1983–96 led by Prime Ministers R. J. L. Hawke and P. J. Keating) and the conservative right (the Liberal and National Party Coalition governments of 1996 to the present led by Prime Minister John Howard). An Australian case study thus allows exploration of the continuities and differences of strategy and emphasis between the parties, and what these have implied for social citizenship and equality.

Australia's distinctive policy tradition

Like its counterparts in the United States, Canada, New Zealand and (more contentiously) Great Britain, Australia's welfare state has an institutional design minimising the role of the state. In the result, public expenditure on welfare is low, its goals are limited primarily to poverty alleviation and its mechanisms privilege private over public solutions to economic and social problems (Esping-Andersen 1990). Australia's distinctive pattern of welfare state development has already been noted. Castles (1985) describes Australia's as a 'wage earners' welfare state', arguing that historically Australia has relied more than other countries on economic policy, and especially on central wage fixation, to ensure the social well-being of its working class. The leadership of Australia's once highly unionised working classes put their ideological faith in social democratic politics, and the use of state power to protect Australian workers through trade and labour protectionism, full employment policies and minimum wage guarantees. Social welfare provisions have been residual in part because they have been secondary.

During the postwar period Australia consolidated its welfare state development in transfer payments providing a limited but real social safety net. The centrepiece of this safety net was the social security system of cash payments to individuals and families eligible according to qualifying conditions and economic resources. These payments provided income in a range of circumstances – primarily old age, widowhood, sole parenthood, sickness or disability and unemployment – in which full-time employment was viewed as impracticable or inappropriate. There were also allowances to families with dependent children. Reflecting its genesis in the wage earners' welfare state, social security was predicated on the family model of male breadwinner and dependent spouse. The conditions of eligibility for payments assumed then-traditional ideas about the appropriate roles of men and women, and in so doing reinforced women's economic dependence on their husbands. Thus women without the support of a husband received benefits as widows and sole parents, and male breadwinners who were unable to earn received allowances for the support of their dependent family members (Bryson 1983; Shaver 1983).

What has been most distinctive about this Australian safety net as compared with others elsewhere is the predication of social security on a modernised form of social assistance rather than social insurance. Virtually all social security payments take the form of flat-rate payments with entitlement subject to a test of economic need. Although these means tests have generally been significantly more generous than the means tests used in the administration of social assistance in Europe and North America, their widespread use has given Australian welfare expenditure a distinctive profile in which the receipt of benefits is unusually concentrated among low-income groups, and the stakes of the middle classes unusually small (Shaver 1997).

Historically, Australian federalism has divided the provision of 'cash' from 'care'. Areas such as health, education and child welfare, where much assistance takes the form of personal services, are responsibilities of the state governments. Income security is a responsibility of the national government, takes the form of money payments, and is funded primarily from income taxes. Because income tax rates are at least nominally progressive and payments are means tested, the social security system has achieved a limited redistribution of income towards low-income groups. The primary dimension of this redistribution has been across the life course, from those of working age to the young and the old, with redistribution from rich to poor being much less significant (Mitchell 1991: 121–32; Saunders 1994: 44–9).

In fine, the welfare state that Australia developed in the postwar golden age achieved something like Marshall's (1963) vision of social welfare as a third dimension of social citizenship, albeit a flawed example of that vision. Because of its reliance on means-tested benefits, Australian welfare citizenship failed to achieve the universal participation that Marshall believed essential to citizenship. Its benefits were low, and application for them entailed a significant loss of privacy. Social citizenship took a more robust form in some other parts of the world. Europeans and Scandinavians were entitled to age pensions and sickness and unemployment compensation representing large proportions of their ordinary wages and which were not subject to means test (Esping-Andersen 1990). Nevertheless, Australia's commitment to a means-tested safety net has expressed a stubborn egalitarian faith in the rightness of giving priority to those who need welfare support most, and however paradoxically Australians have seen such means-tested benefits as rightful (Shaver 1991). This rather truncated version of equality in social citizenship may be compared with the more robust conceptions institutionalised in Scandinavian welfare states as universal expressions of equal citizenship and in European welfare states as reflecting their place in a stratified society by virtue of Bismarckian heritage.

The new virtues: activity and participation

In Australia as elsewhere, new themes of activity and participation began to feature in discussions of welfare and social policy in the 1980s. Versions of these ideas have gained currency across the political spectrum. Little more than a decade later, these underlie a new consensus on the directions, if not the precise programmes, for welfare reform.

The new valuation of activity lay at the centre of the 'active society' concept promulgated by the Organisation for Economic Cooperation and Development (OECD). Reflecting international policy thinking about the emergence of high and long-term unemployment in the 1970s, it sought a new complementarity between economic and social policy. This conceived of a new, direct role for social policy in facilitating labour market adjustments responding to the shift from a manufacturing to a service-led economy. The concept contrasted 'passive' measures predominantly concerned with maintaining a basic level of economic well-being, with 'active' measures intended to serve longer-term objectives. It defined the latter as measures encouraging individuals to strive towards changes in circumstance or environment to improve their prospects of social and economic integration in the future. Active measures require those in need of assistance to take an active part in measures to rectify their current disadvantage, and government to join with them in supporting such efforts (Kalisch 1991: 5–6). The active society concept thus marks a change in social citizenship, widening the focus on rights-based claims to put new emphasis on the duties associated with those rights, including the duty to invest in one's capacities for social contribution. It similarly marks a shift in the meaning of equality among social citizens, extending the equality of citizens in entitlement to benefits with more participatory notions of equality of citizens as having obligations to one another. Significantly, the active society construct does not necessarily entail a reduction in social equality as Marshall conceived of it, but has within it a communitarian element of enforced moral community.

The Australian Social Security Review, commissioned by the Labor government to advise on social security reform, took up these ideas in the late 1980s, emphasising the role of education and training in addressing barriers to labour market participation (Cass 1988). The Review recommended restructuring unemployment assistance to make the system itself an active component of a labour market strategy. Unemployment assistance was to have a dual role, supporting active job search, facilitating labour flexibility and hence the structural re-adjustment of the labour force to changed economic circumstances and redistributing income to people with reduced labour force capacities and opportunities.

The Labor government's Working Nation reforms of the mid-1990s (Commonwealth of Australia 1994) took these ideas much further. The context of these was Labor's Accord with the trade unions in which the government guaranteed to maintain minimum wages and social protection in exchange for union acceptance of wide-ranging economic deregulation and micro-economic industry reform (Castles 1996: 104–5; Huber and Stephens 2001: 288–92). Working Nation policies included youth training measures to reduce disincentives to education and training, expanded provision of labour market programmes, income test changes to reduce disincentives to part-time employment and a 'job compact' guaranteeing a period of paid employment to people who had been unemployed for eighteen months or more. For the first time, these reforms broke with the tradition of the male breadwinner family and treated the partners of a couple as separate individuals both of whom were potentially required to seek employment. Importantly, the reform package also introduced individualised case management for people who were unemployed for long periods, and with it tighter monitoring of compliance with work testing and other behavioural requirements. Among these was the first imposition of a 'reciprocal obligation' on unemployed young people to perform community service work in exchange for the receipt of an unemployment benefit.

The new valuation of activity identifies citizenship less with membership of social community than with participation in it, paradigmatically as labour force participation. There has been continuing debate about what other forms of participation should qualify. In one significant intervention, Cappo and Cass (1994, cf. Atkinson 1993) identified citizenship with social protection predicated upon and affirming the social interdependence of citizens. Central to their notion of citizenship is a view of 'work' as any form of socially useful participation that contributes substantially to public and private welfare, whether paid or unpaid. They advocated a 'participation income', eligibility criteria for which would include, alone or in combination, unemployment, underemployment, caring responsibilities, voluntary work and participation in education and training. This represented an attempt to affirm social citizenship by framing it with a discourse of active responsibility and moral community. It was an attempt to refurbish equality of social citizenship in the changed welfare environment.

Increasingly however, and especially since the election of the conservative Howard Coalition government, this valuation of activity has been voiced in the negative, as a critique of 'passive welfare' that links 'welfare dependency' with various social pathologies. While these terms had little or no presence in the first outlines of active policy strategies, they have come to be central terms in current discussion of welfare reform. Their appearance marks a discursive shift away from the neo-liberal language of economic rationalism and towards a neo-conservative analysis couched in language of character and culture. The salient themes of this discussion are the vulnerability of the welfare system to abuse through false claims, its capacity to undermine economic independence and the possibility that long-term reliance on welfare gives rise to a 'culture of dependency' (Saunders 2000).

While their meaning and validity are strongly contested, the themes themselves now dominate public discussion of welfare in Australia. Indigenous spokesman Noel Pearson (2000) has made the case against passive welfare most tellingly. Focusing on welfare dependence among indigenous Australians, he argues that 'welfare poison' has been a force for social breakdown in these communities. Pearson's argument is addressed to indigenous people, and is moreover intentionally specific to the needs and circumstances of Cape York Peninsula. It has nevertheless been persuasive among a far wider audience. There is widespread popular support for the current government's concept of 'mutual obligation' – the requirement that welfare recipients give something to society in return for welfare support – though closer examination shows a good deal of caution about applying this idea to especially vulnerable groups such as older workers and people with disabilities (Eardley *et al.* 2000). This support includes an acceptance that requirements such as literacy and numeracy education, voluntary work and 'work for the dole' may be rehabilitative for the individual concerned, and a willingness to see such rehabilitation be made compulsory. This willingness is consistent with the 'new paternalism' espoused by Lawrence Mead (1997, 2000).

At the same time, there remains substantial policy confusion about whether responsibility for the care of children is to be seen as a valid form of social participation or a source of welfare dependency. The male breadwinner family model assumed in the postwar development of social security had defined marriage and responsibility for the care of dependent children as sufficient reason for women not to be employed. Over the last two decades or so this model has been eroded incrementally, replacing assumptions of spousal dependency with recognition of responsibilities for care (Shaver 1995). The Social Security Review marked a watershed in gender expectations when it argued in favour of enabling sole parents to take up employment; previously they had been supported as full-time carers (Raymond 1987). Since then, tax and social security changes have been instituted that require some sole parents, older widows and divorcees and the partners of claimants to unemployment assistance to seek employment. Thus for women receiving welfare support, social citizenship increasingly entails obligations of the same kind as citizens who are not mothers. At the same time, however, other policies privilege mothers as full-time carers of their children. The Howard Coalition government has sought to increase support for traditional, single-earner families, and has introduced tax allowances providing higher levels of support to single-earner families than to couples in which two earners bring home the same income.[1] In the result, the tax system endorses a form of spousal dependency that the welfare system disallows. Citizens performing the same work of social care are treated differently and unequally.

Welfare reform

Activity and participation have been central themes in the present government's welfare reform initiative. The government appointed a Reference Group of welfare leaders, academics and public servants to review existing arrangements, and its reports made these themes the platform for a new direction in welfare (Reference Group on Welfare Reform 2000a,b). The Reference Group (2000a: 12) called for 'a shift in focus from simply meeting people's immediate financial needs to helping them maximise social and economic participation over the longer term'. The Reference Group argued that economic participation both increases self-esteem and yields additional income. It viewed social participation as more diffuse in its effects, but nonetheless 'essential for people to grow and flourish as human beings and to be full members of Australian society' (2000a: 13). In this conception, the entitlement to welfare support is based not on rights-based entitlement as the member of the nation community, but may be conditional on their contributing to it. The nature of their entitlement derives not from a generic status as citizens but from individual needs. There is little place in this discourse for an affirmation of citizens as equal in other than the abstract sense of having obligations to one another. While its vision is not unattractive, it marks a departure from social citizenship as Marshall conceived of it. While Marshall emphasised equality of living standards, status and dignity, the new discourse speaks of need, deficiency and capacity building among those suffering social exclusion.

The Reference Group wished to see this new orientation recognised in the renaming of 'income support' as 'participation support'. It recommended (2000b) that five features characterise a new participation support system. These are individualised service delivery, a simpler income support structure, improved incentives and financial assistance, mutual obligations and social partnerships. Of these, individualised service delivery represents the greatest departure from present arrangements. The Reference Group argued that the present system treats people in terms of the payment categories under which they qualify, rather than as individuals with varying needs and goals. It envisioned a new system in which individuals are assessed to determine their needs for income support and accompanying services, streamed according to the level of assistance required and provided with individually targeted economic and social services designed to facilitate ongoing employment or another approved participation activity. While the development of such a system is a long-term project, the government has already established integrated administration in Centrelink and a contestable market for public and private provision of job placements (the Job Network).

Simplifying Australia's complicated system of eligibility categories, payment rates, means test rules and benefit taper rates has long been desired. The Reference Group recommended evolutionary development of an integrated payment system consisting of a common base payment, needs-based supplements taking account of family circumstances, the added costs of disability, etc., and participation supplements to assist with the cost of achieving economic participation.

To maintain incentives to paid employment, the Reference Group also recommended the extension of in-work benefits, the introduction of participation supplements and measures to reduce the disincentive effects of means testing on take up of casual and part-time employment.

The Reference Group accepted the proposition that rights must be accompanied by duties, and that recipients of public support should be expected to undertake some form of economic or social participation as a condition of benefit entitlement. The Final Report recommended participation requirements for welfare-dependent parents with school-aged and older children, and more cautiously also for people with a disability. It supported the imposition of sanctions to enforce these requirements. The Reference Group was concerned to underpin the concept of mutual obligations with a wider notion of social obligations shared by government, business and employers as well as welfare recipients, but recommended these only in far more general terms. Its advocacy of social partnerships put considerable emphasis on the need for government, business and the community sector to play roles in social development initiatives, especially in poor and regional communities.

The Government's response (Vanstone and Abbott 2001) has been muted, in part because many of the recommendations advocated policy directions that were already well established. In other policy initiatives the government had already privatised public employment services and altered the industrial relations system to weaken the protection of minimum wages through central wage fixation. The 2001 Budget foreshadowed expenditure of $1.7 billion gross and $0.8 billion net on welfare reform over four years. The reform programme promises increased resources for intensive assistance services to identify and profile individual needs for assistance, and extended support services graded to levels of difficulty in the transition from welfare to work. The role of non-government organisations and contracted providers, already delivering the vast bulk of services on behalf of government, will continue to grow. A new allowance for people undergoing literacy and numeracy training is represented as a modest step towards the participation supplement recommended by the Welfare Reform Reference Group. Also foreshadowed are increased provision for training, and a 'working credit' enabling people to balance means test periods when they have earnings against periods when they do not.[2] Additional places are to be provided in Work for the Dole schemes and in childcare, and special programmes are to be created for remote and indigenous communities. The principle of mutual obligation is to be extended to workers up to the age of 49 years, and to parents of children aged six or more; the system of 'breaching' associated with these requirements, in which penalties of reduced payments for periods of up to six months apply, is also to be extended to these groups.[3]

To date, however, the legislation required to implement these proposals has been blocked in the legislative upper house, where the government lacks a majority. Many of the proposed measures, such as those for intensive assistance to individuals with particular needs, training and the working credit are supported by both major parties, but Labor and minority parties (supported by the welfare lobby) oppose the imposition of mutual obligation requirements on sole parents and people with disabilities and the extension of the breaching system to these groups. The government has refused to accept passage of less than its full bill, and the Labor opposition has been unwilling to compromise on its position (ACOSS 2002).

The new valuation of activity and participation reflects a general trend among advanced welfare states, and Australian welfare reform shares much with welfare reform elsewhere. While nations have generally responded to the continuing high levels of unemployment of the 1980s and 1990s with only marginal reductions in benefit generosity, they have moved to tighten eligibility requirements and integrate benefit rules with activity requirements. These 'activation strategies' are aimed at encouraging unemployed people to be more active in job search and to keep in touch with the labour market. Public training is the main type of active employment measure in expenditure terms, but there is increasing doubt about its effectiveness as an across-the-board approach. Countries are having greater recourse to cheaper strategies to increase job search assistance through measures such as counselling, job clubs and placement support. It is becoming usual for such assistance to be combined with increased monitoring and enforcement of job search requirements as a condition of benefit receipt. While public sector job creation has generally not proved an effective measure in its own right, its use has continued, especially in Europe, as part of a 'reciprocal obligation' on unemployed people in return for continued receipt of benefit. Temporary public employment is also used as a means of work testing claimants for benefit and as a way of enabling some unemployed people to retain their connection with the labour market (Martin 2000/1).[4] The new emphasis on the duties of social citizenship, is thus to some extent general among advanced welfare states. What this shift of emphasis means for citizenship as a social status of equality is less general, since it depends to considerable extent on how such duties are understood in terms of the status and dignity of the claimant.

Australia's active employment measures are increasingly of the 'workfare' type in which recipients may be required to work as a condition of assistance. Workfare programmes are in use in a variety of countries, with a diversity of motivations and emphases. These programmes generally reflect some mix of aspirations to reduce expenditure, to prevent individualised dependency and/or to combat social exclusion. They vary in the extent to which they confer rights on claimants to assistance through active measures, and in the relative weight of responsibility they assign to the individual and the state (Trickey 2001). In content and style, Australian welfare reform most resembles the welfare reform policies of the liberal group welfare states, although the United States and New Zealand are perhaps more extreme. It is also similar to Norwegian welfare reform in some respects. Workfare must be distinguished from Nordic employment and welfare policy, which also emphasises work as a central social obligation of citizenship. Liberal 'workfare' centres its demands on the unemployed individual, making the provision of benefits conditional on accepting work. Nordic strategies require much more of the state, to ensure that individuals have the resources and motivation they need and that work is available (Esping-Andersen 1999: 80). Because the Australian economy had long been highly protected from external competition, its deregulation has had radical consequences. These have been particularly significant for its welfare state, where much social protection previously relied on wage and employment guarantees (Huber and Stephens 2001: 296, 328–9). Their dismantling has left Australia with a residual welfare state in the liberal mould. Its limited activation agenda is designed less to increase the overall rate of economic activity and sustain generous social support than to reduce the welfare rolls and reduce their burden on a limited tax base.

Reconceiving social citizenship

I noted earlier that Marshall would have seen Australian welfare citizenship as defective, on the grounds that its central reliance on means testing divides its citizenry into groups who see themselves as primarily taxpayers or welfare claimants. For Marshall, social citizenship had to be universal, with all citizens represented on both sides of the ledger. Australia has long prided herself on the superiority of this nation's peculiar welfare tradition in delivering high levels of poverty alleviation at low levels of public expenditure and with comparatively little stigmatisation of claimants. Indeed, Australian arrangements are advanced as models that other countries might usefully emulate (World Bank 1994). It is worth noting, then, that Australia's low-level benefits and public needs testing have done very little to protect welfare from the populist resentment and political backlash driving welfare reform. The larger and more universalist European welfare states have proven significantly more secure against erosion than Australia's apparently more efficient system of income support (Esping-Andersen 1999: 147).

Contemporary welfare reform is giving institutional form to developments in ideology and policy that have been coming since late 1980s at least. However incremental, these developments nevertheless represent significant change in the nature of welfare institutions and the social citizenship they express. While the discussion here refers to Australia's version of welfare reform, the issues stem from trends extending beyond the Antipodes and are of much more general relevance.

Most fundamentally, welfare reform is changing social understanding of the meaning of welfare as a social right of citizenship. The now-excoriated 'passive' welfare was once regarded as a citizen's entitlement to support in the event of risks we all face – those of the human condition, such as old age and disability, and those of the capitalist social economy, such as unemployment. Benefit categories such as age, disability and parental responsibility have reflected social and political understandings of the circumstances under which a person can justifiably claim support from the public purse. Welfare was a safety net, although in the Australian case always a highly residual one.

Welfare reform constructs welfare as support provided not as of right but on condition. There is new emphasis on the obligations that accompany rights. As Harris (2000) observes, the obligation to participate is multiple, including self-help and the avoidance of dependence, self-improvement to become employable and 'paying your dues' to the 'community' that supports you. The concepts of reciprocal and especially now mutual obligation are explicit, literal formulations of the conditions attached to welfare support. These formulations are presented to the electorate as the public policy expression of a natural morality of fair give and take. A closer look shows the government's mutual obligation policy as a narrow, limited interpretation of the terms that might satisfy an intuitive standard of fair reciprocity. In particular, it makes the obligations of each partner strictly conditional upon the performance of the other, requires this exchange to take place at the same time and requires repayment of social obligation in the currency of labour services. In short, this version of fair reciprocity is closely modelled on the exchange of wages for work (Goodin 2001).

Esping-Andersen (1990: 35–54, 1999: 43–5) refers to this fundamental significance of a social right to welfare in the capitalist social economy as de-commodification. Because they represent a limited alternative to paid work, welfare benefits serve to put a floor under wages, and more generally to lessen the citizen's dependency on the labour market. Welfare reform attaching conditions to income support reduces the scope for welfare to endow the citizen with limited independence of employers and the labour market and to combine with others in collective negotiation of wages and conditions. The importance of this has to be seen in the context of narrowing margins between welfare and low-paid employment and the replacement of full-time, full-year jobs with temporary and part-time employment.

In and of itself, the care of school-aged dependent children, even without the assistance of a partner, no longer fulfils the conditions attached to the receipt of public support. Recipients of parenting payments, both sole parents and unemployed partners, now must show they are preparing themselves for employment in the foreseeable future when their children reach an age of relative independence. These requirements are not greatly burdensome, and it is at least arguable that they are beneficial to the individuals concerned. Their imposition nevertheless marks a new stage in the evolution of Australian income support, in which the male breadwinner family model is being replaced with one predicated on employment for all adults. As has already been noted, the opposite is happening in the social policy support offered to families who do not receive welfare. In the result, different conditions attach to the support of marital dependency and support as a full-time carer of children for different income groups.

Associated with the new conditionality of welfare support is a further shift from the provision of support as a cash payment to support coupling cash with services. The significance of this shift is reflected in the renaming and restructuring of the administering department from the Department of Social Security to the Department of Family and Community Services. Long structured in the categorical terms of social security payments, the department is now arranged in branches integrating payments and services and defined on the basis of 'customer' groups. There are branches responsible for relations with Centrelink, and for service delivery relationships with contracted and non-government service providers. The phrase 'social security' has disappeared from the lexicon. The term that has replaced it, 'income support', has fewer connotations of citizenship and social right. Australian social security had a systemic logic linking rates and conditions for entitlements attracting widespread popular support, such as the age pension, with less favoured payments. Focusing only on the 'working age' population, Australian welfare reform has weakened this systemic logic and opened the way for divergent treatment of claimant groups above and below retirement age.

Most of the welfare reform measures announced in the 2001 Budget consist of new or more generously provided, mainly employment-related services. The development of services began in the Labor period, but has grown most rapidly under the current Coalition government. The unemployed are promised individually tailored assistance from an expanded network of Centrelink 'personal advisers', employment assistance from providers contracted as part of the Job Network and community work coordinators offering places in approved community work and work for the dole schemes. For parents there is to be a new transition-to-work programme, and for people with disabilities 'disability co-ordination officers'. The government's welfare reform website (www.together.gov.au/groups/disability) claims that its commitments represent the largest increase in specialist disability employment and rehabilitation centres by any Commonwealth government.

These new forms of positive help geared to individual needs and circumstances undoubtedly represent valuable additions to Australian welfare state provision. Appropriately provided and willingly accepted, such help may enable their recipients to assess their options, address deficiencies in skills or motivations, and take up available opportunities for social and economic participation. They will not necessarily have the same value when provided as compulsory gateways for access to the income needed for subsistence. Given the individualised character of these services, it is of concern that requirements to use them may open the lives and beings of vulnerable persons to intrusion by potentially alien personal and cultural values.

Together, the shift from social rights to conditional support and from cash provision to cash linked to services changes fundamentally the relation between citizen and state. This is no less than a shift from sovereignty to supervision. Put most bluntly, the welfare claimant is no longer to be regarded as the best judge of her own needs and prospects. The basic presumption of welfare economics, shared by postwar Keynesianism and neo-liberal economic rationalism, is the value of consumer sovereignty: that utility is inherently individual and subjective, and hence best realised when individuals are able to make their own choices between alternatives in the marketplace. This presumption of consumer sovereignty has been overturned, on the presumption that welfare dependence erodes the recipient's capacity for freedom and autonomous choice of action. On the contrary, there is a new and explicit presumption that the proper role of policy is to change the way that welfare recipients behave. This impulse to behavioural engineering now finds support on both the right and the left, and is widely seen as serving the best interests of welfare recipients themselves and Australian society more generally.

Yeatman (1999) sees mutual obligation as representing a new kind of social contract, a late twentieth-century restatement of Rousseau's contention that individuals must be forced to be free. This contract is explicitly paternalist in form and intention. Made between unequal parties, it has as its goal developing the individual's capacities for self-reliance and autonomy. She sees this kind of paternalist relationship as emerging in a number of service delivery contexts, including education and disability services as well as income support.

For Marshall, it was not economics but politics that represented the active side of citizenship. As he saw it, social rights were created through the expression of democratic rights in pursuit of a basic measure of social and economic equality. What is finally most troubling about contemporary welfare reform in countries such as Australia is the separation it presumes between political and social citizenship. The new forms of income support and supplementary personal services aim at self-reliance and autonomy in the economic dimension, but lack the same concern with self-expression and social participation in political and cultural domains. Hidden in the shift from rights to conditional support, and from sovereignty to supervision, is a denial of the equality of selfhood as the price of welfare assistance.

Conclusion

Equality in social citizenship as Marshall conceived of it, and as reflected in the development of welfare states in their postwar golden age, entailed entitlement to an economic minimum and recognition as an equal in worth and dignity. He saw such equality as both essential for democratic government and compatible with the economic inequality inherent in modern capitalism. Because welfare states generally face similar shifts in the structures of risk emerging with global, post-industrial economies, they are tending to move in similar directions as they reform their structures of social citizenship.

Australian welfare reform is following a liberal path. There are marked similarities of outlook and values between the conservative Coalition government in Australia and the 'third way' models of Clinton's America and Blair's United Kingdom (Giddens 1998, 2000). These include a continuing emphasis on market and family as the preferred institutions for social support, and a newly salient appeal to moral ideas about the responsibility of citizens to be self-sustaining. The central assertions of Australian welfare reform – that all rights entail corresponding responsibilities, that passive welfare invites 'dependency' and moral hazard and that welfare should play a positive role in overcoming disadvantage by fostering willingness to take risk – are unambiguous appeals to liberal ideology.

The reform trajectories that welfare states of other types are following also emphasise activity and personal responsibility, but incorporate these in different visions of equality and social citizenship. Nordic welfare reform has kept faith with its tradition of universalistic egalitarianism. In this tradition, equality refers to social as well as economic guarantees, with the redistributive state seen as responsible for ensuring access to social resources for all. While there has been some scaling back of provision and especially of age pensions, the popular revolt against the welfare state has been avoided. The universalism of social provision, in which middle-class groups enjoy very substantial benefit, has been one source of stability. Shaped by constructs emphasising training, social investment and the morality that 'everybody works', the productivistic orientation of Scandinavian welfare discourse has been an important complement.

The impulse to retrenchment has had least effect in the large welfare states of western Europe. The least committed to goals of social equalisation, these welfare states have been most proof against welfare backlash. The institutional foundations of those lie in social insurance programmes designed to maintain status and status differentials in adversity and over the life course, and social citizenship entails only the weakest commitment to equality. Elite workers have continued to be well supported, while the brunt of welfare reform has been borne by the long-term unemployed depending on social assistance, who face an increasing risk of poverty (Esping-Andersen 1996b: 261–5).

Reflecting on the weakening of European welfare states, Offe (1996) suggests that there has been a loss of political support for class-based collective strategies for equality and redistribution of the kind reflected in Marshall's theory of citizenship. The structural disintegration of industrial society has left its members distrustful of welfare state ideals and ready to assess its institutions and programmes in the rationalist terms of winners and losers, free-riders and welfare cheats. Offe sees the changed socio-economic conditions as having fragmented and even individualised dispositions of political interest, and these acting together to generate new forms of structural and cultural plurality. He sees even the political parties of the old left as eschewing egalitarian projects in favour of libertarian, anti-statist and communitarian ideals. To date at least, welfare states have actually proven more robust than Offe's critique suggests, and are adapting their institutions to new conditions. The pattern of parallel rather than convergent change suggests that even under conditions of economic globalisation the nation states of the advanced capitalist world retain capacities to pursue distinctive types of national equality strategy. Globalisation, unemployment and the decline of social class have, however, seen a common shift of left parties toward the centre, and this may set narrower limits in the pursuit of equality through social citizenship in the long term.

Notes

1 These allowances are also available to employed sole parents, for whom they provide important assistance.
2 These last two measures go some way to restoring cuts made when the present government took office in 1996.
3 This breaching system is increasingly punitive. In the three years from June 1998, the number of penalties in reduced benefit payment applied in respect of failure to comply with activity test requirements grew by 189 per cent (ACOSS 2001; see also Moses and Sharples 2000).
4 In comparison with other OECD countries, Australia spends little on unemployment and labour market measures. Of what it does spend, a comparatively large share goes on passive measures, mainly unemployment benefits, but the difference between Australian spending proportions and those elsewhere has been narrowing. Unemployment benefit rates are comparatively generous, especially for low-wage workers, and are available as

long as unemployment lasts (providing activity test requirements are met). The narrow gap between wages and benefits weakens incentives to work, and has the potential to trap its recipients in unemployment. Within the range of active measures, Australian effort is unusually concentrated in job placement and administration through its public employment services. This concentration increased over the decade from the mid-1980s to the mid-1990s. Australian effort is comparatively sparse in the areas of labour market training and measures to assist people with disabilities (Martin 2000/1: 82–3, 94, 102).

7 Gender, equality and globalization

Gillian Youngs

Just a few statistics indicate the importance of gender to understanding of inequality in the contemporary world. Increasing numbers of women may be joining the workforce around the world but they earn only around 75 per cent of what men earn (UNDP 2002: 23). Of the world's estimated 854 million illiterate adults, 544 million are women, and of the 113 million children not in primary school, 60 per cent are girls. There are an estimated 100 million 'missing' women around the world – 50 million in India alone – who would be alive but for infanticide, neglect or sex (selective abortion). Each year more than 500,000 women die as a result of pregnancy and childbirth. Worldwide, only 14 per cent of national parliamentarians are women, with little difference between industrial and developing countries and positive exceptions including both (UNDP 2002: 10–11, 16, 23).

This chapter considers gender, equality and globalization in two main ways. First it engages in an exploration of what feminism has to offer current discussions about globalization. It assesses the distinctive role of feminist theory in addressing questions of gender and social relations of power, and introduces examination of questions of equity and difference between women and men and among women. The second part of the chapter on feminist perspectives on globalization builds on a consideration of embodied political economy to consider women's differentiated experience of globalization under conditions of global restructuring, and the dual nature of the latter as both a masculinized phenomenon of free and fast flowing capital, finance and goods and a feminized phenomenon of supporting servicing, domestic and sexualized roles, many of which are carried out by migrant workforces, who make significant contributions to home and host economies.

Feminist contributions to globalization debates

Unequal relations of power

Feminism is too often misunderstood as a theory that is solely concerned with women and their lives and possibilities, and not, as is the case, as a form of social theory that makes specific contributions to our understanding of society as a whole through an interest in the issues of gender and power. Increasingly, gender and power have been positioned as one of the intersecting facets of what might be termed the complex of identifications and power, including sexuality, race or ethnicity and socio-economic status (see e.g. Pettman 1996; Peterson and Runyan 1999; hooks 2000). Feminism is thus a set of theoretical approaches that are first and foremost relational: that is, they concern *relations of gender* and their implications for *relations of power*. Feminism's concerns with equality are set specifically within this context, that is with the problem that *relations of gender* have led to *unequal relations of power*.

The misunderstanding that feminism is just about women and not society as a whole leads to the continuing neglect of feminism's insights by mainstream (male-oriented) theory. The unequal relations of power are thus reflected as much in theoretical social process as they are in the apparently more concrete material social processes. This is especially true in the international context, where in the realm of so-called high politics and state-to-state relations, women have been historically least present in theory and practice (Enloe 1990; Peterson 1992a; Youngs 1999a).

> Feminists are arguing for moving beyond knowledge frameworks that construct international theory without attention to gender and for searching deeper to find ways in which gender hierarchies serve to reinforce socially constructed institutions and practices that perpetuate different and unequal role expectations, expectations that have contributed to fundamental inequalities between women and men in the world of international politics. Therefore, including gender as a central category of analysis *transforms knowledge* in ways that go beyond adding women; importantly, but frequently misunderstood, this means that women cannot be studied in isolation from men.
>
> (Tickner 1997: 621, my emphasis)

Feminist analysis emphasizes that unequal relations of power between men and women apply as much to the knowledge processes relating to them, as they do to the social processes in which they are involved. Thus the historical interests of feminist critique are oriented towards the discourses that maintain and reproduce gendered relations as part of the material inequality that characterizes them (for a range of discussions in this area see e.g. Harding 1998; Peterson 1992b; Youngs 2000b). In order to understand the fundamental impact of gendered inequalities, it is essential to explore the ontological and epistemological realms, for what counts as reality and the ways in which we construct knowledge about it is basic to how we think about what society is and key social processes within it.

Framing inequality: public and private

Public and private have played a central part in framing the discursive and social configurations of gendered inequalities and resistances to them. Public/private is the key dualism that has historically established a hierarchy of male identity and influence over female identity and influence. This is by no means to essentialize the nature of either men or women or to fail to recognize that they both move across public and private, playing a range of different roles in different ways and with different consequences. It is, however, to recognize the structural importance of the history of public and private to gendered realities and identities.

The public boundary defines the world of political and economic power and of decision-making and influence, to which masculine influence and identity are primarily attached. The private boundary is that which defines the world of social reproduction, of home and family, to which feminine influence and identity are primarily attached. The paid nature of work in the public sphere and the unpaid (or low paid) nature of work in the private sphere are significant definers of the unequal status of that work. Patriarchal power operates across these boundaries as the persistence of domestic violence against women demonstrates (Amnesty International 2001). When women, as they increasingly do, participate in the public sphere in political and economic activities, they do so in the context of socially and historically defined gendered relations reflecting structural inequalities between men and women. Institutionalized practices and discourses reflect such structural inequalities and are the sites through which gendered identities are forged, questioned and contested (Youngs 2000b).

Agency, equality and feminisms

Attention to agency brings macro level social processes into connection with micro level individual and collective processes. Such a focus addresses the inter-activity of individuals and social groups with historically created circumstances and structures of power. It helps ensure that all individuals, even those with less power, are considered active and determining of, as well as determined by, their social situation. It recognizes that social actors, even those with limited power, are constantly making decisions or non-decisions in relation to external circumstances, and constraints and opportunities confronting them. Such a focus opens up analysis to the ways in which individuals and groups of individuals *actively construct* their lives (thereby expressing their agency) *in the context of* formal and informal social frameworks. Questions of agency and equality lie at the heart of both different facets of feminist theory and activism, and different stages of feminist history.

The question of equality between genders remains key. Here we are talking about women being equal to men in very specific terms – for example, (equal) rights to survival, political participation and representation, education, economic wealth and status and so on. This has historically been the prime concern of Western liberal feminism, with its roots in Enlightenment thought. 'Early Western feminists such as Mary Wollstonecraft [1759–97] utilized western Enlightenment ideals of "natural" equality among men to assert women's entitlement to be recognized as human *subjects with agency and intellect*. Modern western feminism thus began with an emphasis on equality with men, a focus that has carried into contemporary western feminism and global feminism' (Hirschmann 2000: 612, my emphasis; see also Wollstonecraft 1985).

The inferior position which masculinist liberal traditions have allocated and continue to allocate to women via the public (man as subject) over private (woman as object) structure meant and still mean that women's subjectivity, and hence their agency and power associated with that, has to be struggled for and reclaimed in feminist theory and practice. Globalization has in fact extended the relevance of this struggle because the hegemonic western liberal (political and economic) ideology and principles steering so many of its key institutions, structures and processes (Hettne 1995) sit alongside and interact with other patriarchal systems that oppress women. It has been argued, for example, that 'any explanation of gender inequality in Hong Kong in terms of traditional Chinese patriarchy has to address the issue of how patriarchy complements, or has been modified by, Hong Kong's brand of industrial capitalism' (Pearson and Leung 1995a: 5–6).

Globalization is prompting us to think about patriarchy in a disaggregated yet interconnected social fashion, to consider how patriarchal structures operate across public and private spheres in political, economic and cultural senses. We need to recognize that patriarchal influences with starkly different histories and locations are merging and creating, through dynamic processes of political economy, restructured and hybrid patriarchal forms (Youngs 2000a: 51).

Agency and structure

Globalized and spatially gendered structures of oppression require us to take account of feminist critiques of public/private in ways that allow gender to be 'conceptualized in terms of an interweaving of, and recursive relationships between, personal life and conscious human action, on the one hand, and social structures or constraints, on the other' (Bondi 1994: 194). Such analysis recognizes the diverse facets of gendered spatiality under conditions of globalization, while associating structure and agency, spatiality, identity and consciousness.

The key challenge is the spatially dynamic quality of multiple linkages among public and private spheres operating frequently across state boundaries and associating patterns of oppression of different social groupings, which might superficially be regarded as *separate* on nationality, race and class bases. The global economy, traditionally interpreted as public space, can overtly be demonstrated, for example, in the case of migrant service workforces as *privatized*. Furthermore, these workers from less developed or developing economies become an explicit as well as implicit *public* force in relation to their input to both their host and home economies (Youngs 2000a: 51; see also Pettman 1996).

This dynamic understanding of gendered processes enables us to maintain a strong conceptual hold on the *constant* interaction between agency and social structure and the *active* engagement of women as subjects in managing and remaking their circumstances including aspects of their gendered identities. It recognizes that 'gender exists both as an aspect of individual, subjective identity and as an external, social construct that constrains the behaviour [and opportunities] of women and men – hence the need to combine intrinsic and extrinsic approaches', and that 'relations between women and men [and women and women] are continually being redefined and renegotiated. The tension and interplay between internalized and structural aspects of gender can be viewed as the driving force for changes in gender relations' (Bondi 1994: 194).

Agency and difference

The issue of differences between women in terms of their desires, socio-economic context, identities, goals and opportunities, has become increasingly important in both feminist theoretical preoccupations and the material conditions of globalization. The category woman remains politically potent and reflects the many shared concerns that women around the world have, but it is also problematic, particularly in its risks of essentializing and failing to prioritize sufficiently the differences among women and even across separate periods in one woman's life. These differences have become increasingly understood as central to the politics of feminism(s), and feminist theory and practice has become at the same time more challenging, contested, sensitive and subtle as a result.

At a more fundamental level in feminism there has always been strong debate about the difference issue between men and women.

> The feminist debates surrounding essentialism are political and broadly result in three positions. First, there are those who reject essentialism and argue that differences between men and women are socially constructed; challenging the social construction of gender will enable women to achieve equality with men. Second, some accept essentialism and argue that innate feminine traits are superior to masculine-determined ones and that the roles of men and women are essentially different. Finally, there are those who argue that self is fragmented and in flux, but also that difference does not preclude equality.
>
> (Abbott 2000: 615)

The debate about difference between men and women and women and women, and the extent to which difference does or does not preclude equality, will undoubtedly go on and there are many individual as well as collective perspectives on it. 'Equity feminism' and 'difference feminism' (Hirschmann 2000: 612) will continue as two key interwoven strands in the equality debate, in theory and practice. The solidarity aspect of equity feminism in representing women's collective interests, in the face of the inequities that patriarchal cultures impose on them, is clearly of profound political and strategic import. Emphasis is placed on addressing the inequalities resulting for women from patriarchal history and the public/private gendered hierarchy associated with it. It can also be argued that the recognition of differences between women and men and women and women has political and strategic import too, particularly for informing *the paths towards greater equality*. Combining equity and difference feminism perhaps leads us to 'equality based on particularity and context' (Hirschmann 2000: 613).

Women's rights as human rights

The weight of patriarchal history, and the oppression of women that has resulted from it, present a strong argument for the continuation of equity feminism as a major priority in the foreseeable future. Global political feminism is clearly informed by this, but in the strategic and grounded nature of practice-based and policy-related work, it is also informed by questions of difference, especially between men and women. The women's rights as human rights campaign has taken us beyond disembodied masculinist liberal ideology and recognized gender as an aspect of rights. The 1979 UN Convention on the Elimination of All Forms of Discrimination Against Women (CEDAW) is now a part of international law explicitly affirming women's rights and working towards their equality with men. It focuses on civil, political, economic and cultural and reproductive rights. Currently 170 countries, more than two-thirds of UN members, have ratified the Convention, which includes a country-by-country reporting process (see United Nations Development Fund for Women (UNIFEM) at www.unifem.org).

There has also been increasing attention to the elimination of all forms of violence against women and girls, including in the Platform for Action of the UN Fourth World Conference on Women in Beijing in 1995 and a series of conferences that followed it on the issue (Pietilä 2002: 27–8).

> These conferences examined violence against women as 'a male problem', as part of the male culture and its consequences to men themselves and society.... Since then, men's movements – such as the White Ribbon and others – have grown in their work against male violence in general, and violence against women in particular, in an increasing number of countries such as Canada, Namibia, New Zealand, United Kingdom, United States, and the Nordic and South-East Asian countries. Also, current research is gradually spreading and analysing the role of men and masculinity as women's research has worked on preconceived women's roles in various cultures.
>
> (Pietilä 2002: 28)

The issue of violence and the threat of violence against women and girls have so many complex structural dimensions and implications for their agency that it is graphic proof of the political potency of questions of difference between men and women in campaigning for equality between them. Amnesty International (2001), in addressing violence against women as 'torture', has extended the question of violence against women into new areas of international law, connecting private and public forms of violence that breach human rights and addressing state responsibility in both areas (for a detailed assessment of this development see Youngs 2003). The differences between women are also crucial in this area because of their varied vulnerabilities, for example, as refugees or migrants, and in custody or conflict situations. Vulnerabilities vary too due to structural aspects of social context. 'Violence against women is compounded by discrimination on grounds of race, ethnicity, sexual orientation, social status, class and age.

Such multiple discrimination further restricts women's choices, increases their vulnerability to violence and makes it even harder for them to gain redress' (Amnesty International 2001: 2).

Gender-related development

Thanks to a range of UN processes gender is increasingly being examined as integral to an understanding of patterns of inequality in globalization. Development itself, and the possibility for 'deepening democracy' (UNDP 2002) are interpreted at least partly through a gender perspective. The United Nations Development Programme *Human Development Report* has been ground-breaking in this regard. Its gender-related development index (GDI) adjusts its human development index (HDI) for inequalities in the achievements of men and women, thereby offering the kind of statistical evidence so crucial to policy-making and campaigns for improvements for women. This new methodology alone does much to concretize the problem of unequal relations of power between men and women in relation to aims for further development of societies around the world.

All statistics can only be considered estimations and they represent just part of the evidence for understanding structures of inequality, but the visibility the GDI gives to different facets of gender inequality, enables a multidimensional sense of its impact. The GDI calculations cover life expectancy at birth, adult literacy rate, combined primary, secondary and tertiary gross enrolment ratio and estimated earned income across genders (UNDP 2002: 222–5). For all countries GDI is lower than HDI indicating pervasive gender inequality and there is a significant variation in levels of inequality. For example, many countries have similar male and female literacy rates but forty-three, including India, Mozambique and Yemen – have male rates at least 15 percentage points higher than female rates (23).

The gender empowerment measure (GEM) introduced in the 1995 *Human Development Report* helps to capture the difference in opportunity and voice in society between men and women. 'Worse outcomes for women in many aspects of human development result from the fact that their voices have *less impact* than men's in the decisions that shape their lives' (23, my emphasis). The GEM takes into account seats in parliament held by women, percentages of legislators, senior officials and managers, and professional and technical workers who are women and ratio of estimated female to male earned income (226–9).

Not surprisingly, the GEM is not necessarily in any close ranking correlation to the HDI for each country. Japan, while ranked ninth highest in the HDI, is much lower in GEM terms at thirty-two. Cyprus, while ranked much lower in the HDI at twenty-six is similar to Japan in the GEM at thirty-four. New Zealand is ranked nineteen in the HDI but much higher in the GEM at nine. Of the sixty-six countries assessed for the GEM Bangladesh, which is ranked among the low human development countries, comes lowest close behind Egypt and Sri Lanka, which are ranked in the medium human development countries (UNDP 2002: 226–9). Such indicators disrupt deeply the simplistic traditional framing of successful development predominantly in terms of crude factors such as gross domestic product. They highlight the need for more complex models of measuring human development that take seriously the relative opportunities that exist for different members of society. They provide useful material for assessing how well or comparatively poorly even wealthy societies are doing in terms such as the GEM.

The GEM values range from below 0.300 to more than 0.800 with only five of the sixty-six countries – Denmark, Finland, Iceland, Norway and Sweden – achieving a GEM above 0.800 and twenty-two achieving a GEM below 0.500. The wide variation is part of the notable feature of the findings. 'Some developing countries outperform much richer industrial countries. The Bahamas and Trinidad and Tobago are ahead of Italy and Japan. Barbados's GEM is 25% higher than Greece's. The message: high income is not a prerequisite to creating opportunities for women' (UNDP 2002: 23).

The digital divide is another area affecting women across the world. While digital developments have offered new possibilities to the global women's movement(s) and individual women, they also confront major inequalities in the context of a predominantly male-dominated history of science and technology (see e.g. Youngs 1999b, 2002). Thanks to virtual links women are finding one another and working together in international contexts in ways that were never possible before, and this is as much a learning encounter about other women's lives and relationships to technology, as it is a new stage of feminist endeavour (Harcourt 1999). In other words, it is as much about changing the face of feminism as it is about taking its principles forward. Digital equity is a major new political and economic cause between North and South globally and between men and women (see Association for Progressive Communication at www.apc.org, and International Telecommunication Union, World Summit on the Information Society at www.itu.int/wsis).

Feminist perspectives on globalization

Embodied political economy

Feminist perspectives on globalization prioritize gender as an analytical category and challenge directly the disembodied traditions of mainstream masculinist analysis. These are disembodied because they omit gender as an influential element of relations of social power and thereby treat the individual in an abstract fashion. The precise meaning of abstract here relates to the failure to take account of the crucial role of gender in affecting differentiated social power among individuals. In contrast, by addressing gender directly feminist perspectives present 'embodied' political economy (Youngs 2000b). Disembodied perspectives on globalization can only offer partial approaches to agency. They are bound by their abstraction of the public over private hierarchical definition of social reality that inevitably leads to an abstract public over private framing of agency. Gender is ignored because agency in any powerful or socially significant sense is identified predominantly with the public sphere that is understood to be defined primarily by male influence, action and identity.

Clearly this disembodied notion of social reality has little purchase for women, whose lives may be shaped predominantly within the context of the private sphere, or with interactions between public and private realms, with perhaps different kinds of emphasis across them at different points in their lives. Particularly under conditions of globalization, women's embodied experience across public and private, and their strategies for coping with the complexities that result, are part of the explanation of how political economy and identities associated with it are changing.

Women's embodied agency, collectively and individually, is one of the crucial elements of the continuing struggle for equality, which as feminists have long argued, can only be achieved in full recognition of the actuality and potential of women's lives. Agency directs attention to social process and the active part of individuals and groups within it. It will inevitably link history to the future by recognizing how social context can influence the framework for potential action and encourage or inhibit consciousness leading to action. While agency can be discussed in abstract terms its material import is manifested when applied to specific times and places and embodied experience of them. The possibilities of agency are directly linked to differentiated social circumstances where gender is always an intersecting factor with other aspects of social inequality. This is as much the case for women working in the US electronic assembly plants of Mexican borderlands, as it is for men who lost their livelihoods in traditional sectors such as mining and steel in rich economies under global restructuring. One of the things that globalization has starkly highlighted is that the terms of equality do not stay the same, neither do the terms on which inequalities may be contested. Furthermore, the increasing inequality within states and across them that has been a defining characteristic of globalization (UNDP 2002), suggests that our differences are as important as our similarities in political and economic struggles.

Women, difference and globalization

It is logical that as global restructuring highlights the multiple roles of women across the globe and their highly differentiated levels of opportunity and inequality, recognition of difference of life circumstances and challenges, interests and orientations deepens. Quite simply, women are leading highly diverse lives and some are far more privileged than others, and the nature of privilege and inequality has differences and similarities across societies. In order to ask what might be possible for women in any setting or situation, we inevitably have to address that setting or situation in specific terms. This has been a common feature of feminist studies of globalization (see, in particular: Marchand and Runyan 2000; Youngs 2000c; Parpart *et al.* 2002; Kofman and Youngs 2003).

It is notable therefore that feminist studies have contrasted starkly with some of the universalistic tendencies of mainstream (malestream) discourses of globalization (Youngs 1996), and focused on the specificities of processes of globalization in place and time (see also Marchand and Runyan 2000). This can be argued as a major strength of feminist analysis of globalization that has much to offer the broader field of globalization studies. It presents detail that is frequently lost in the abstractions of masculinist perspectives and broad-brush approaches to power that thereby fail to engage with complex processes of agency. My assessment is that this is largely due to the disembodied sense of political and economic process that masculinist (public over private) hierarchies of thought produce. These lock analytical senses of reality into the public sphere and fail to take account of the public/private dynamics of feminist focus. They are disembodied to the extent that they cannot take deep analytical account of the fact that human experience is produced and reproduced across public and private spheres and that power and agency are configured in these terms (Youngs 2000b). Masculinist orientations work with a totally different sense of public and private where the former relates to the realm of public (political) goods and interests (supplied and represented by the state) and the latter to the realm of private (economic) goods and interests (supplied and represented by the market) (Cerny 2003).

Global restructuring is not confined to the masculinist interpretations of public and private as feminization of the labour force and its results indicate. The whole point about global restructuring, as only feminist analysis can demonstrate, is that the restructuring of state and market inherently incorporates the restructuring of public and private in feminist senses of these terms. Mainstream masculinist approaches ignore gender as an explanatory category of globalization, as they have traditionally of political economy more broadly. Feminist approaches signal that this makes masculinist explanations of processes of globalization limited at best and misleading at worst. If we are to take account of feminist senses of public/private, then we have to recognize gender as a socially significant factor. We also have to recognize that we experience gender as an embodied characteristic, or more specifically set of characteristics, that influences differentiated experience of public and private and their interconnections.

Feminization of labour

Feminization of labour, as a key characteristic of globalization, has been as much a story of new inequalities for women as it has been new forms of freedom, independence and status. The cleaner, lighter forms of industrial work such as in the electronics business and the many low level forms of employment in the high growth service sector may have offered many new work opportunities for women but hardly on the best of terms. Global restructuring, in which transnational corporations seek out more profitable production locations and new markets, is as gendered a process as any other (Biemann 1999; Marchand and Runyan 2000). Anne Sisson Runyan has commented on the way the business of states attracting inward corporate investment has been likened to a dating scenario that:

> symbolizes and normalizes the increasing mobility of female labour – 'girls' must 'go out' (typically to urban areas or export processing zones) and pretty themselves up or rather make themselves highly available and exploitable in order for their states to catch a 'real man' [major investor]. Alternatively, if

the states in which they reside are unable to attract foreign investor 'boyfriends', 'girls' must 'go out' of their states to catch a wage. Of course, this puerile dating is not designed for reproduction – that is, the enhancement of human and planetary life – but rather for a kind of 'love 'em and leave 'em' production, trade, and finance that enriches only a few at the expense of far too many and too much.

(Runyan 2003: 139–40)

As transnational corporate processes are reconfigured in processes of globalization, so gendered patterns of inequality are reshaped. Feminization of labour indicates the significance in processes of globalization of women's working roles outside as well as inside the home, across as well as within state boundaries.

Inequalities between women

Feminist research on globalization has shown that as more women work, inequality of opportunity and status between them, as well as between women and men, becomes of increasing importance (see e.g. Walby 1997; Chang and Ling 2000). Factors such as socio-economic and migrant status, ethnicity and educational level all come into play here in different ways. This means that even looking at women as homogenous social blocs within societies, helpful as this is in terms, for example, of the GEM discussed earlier, presents only part of the picture. We need to go further and consider how global restructuring is changing relations between women as well as between men and women both within specific local settings but also in global contexts. The interactions of political (state) and economic (corporate) processes are central to these dynamics of change that are repositioning masculine and feminine roles, identities and representations.

Kimberly Chang and Lily Ling (2000: 27) have presented a powerful picture of two faces of global restructuring. The first being the masculinized 'techno-muscular capitalism' (TMC) of the high-tech world of global finance, trade, production and telecommunications. This represents the most familiar picture of globalization in the neoliberal growth-oriented mode, where technology and increased circuits of production, trade and finance depict an ever-stronger form of capitalism. The second face of global restructuring is the less visible and 'more explicitly sexualized, racialized and class-based' sphere of 'low-wage, low-skilled menial service provided by mostly female migrant workers'.

I have argued elsewhere (Youngs 2000a) that in investigating such unequal processes it is necessary to break the 'patriarchal prism' of mainstream analysis that narrowly concentrates on the first face of global restructuring above and is unable to address sufficiently its 'intimate' (Chang and Ling 2000) interdependence with the second face of global restructuring. The first face of global restructuring is oriented towards the posited anonymous space of the global market and the free-ranging freedoms it has offered capitalist and financial operators to seek new cheaper, more flexible locations/structures for production and ever-expanding numbers of new consumers. It is an abstracted (public) conceptual framework in spatial terms and much feminist analysis has in a very real sense 'grounded' it by exposing its reliance on the second (private) face of global restructuring.

In this way feminists have demonstrated that global/local dynamics are mapped directly onto public/private dynamics and that restructuring across both is an intimately connected process. 'Labour intimacy results from and sustains TMC. Gross wage inequities increasingly casualize and informalize labor so that some workers have more means to hire others who need more economic compensation. Migrant workers toiling in the household also release cosmopolitans from time-consuming, mind-numbing, non-rewarding chores so that they may pursue their "casino capitalism".... Thus, the cycle of wage inflation and labor domestication continues' (Chang and Ling 2000: 41). Close investigation of the complex transnational role of an overseas domestic workforce such as that in Hong Kong takes us inside global restructuring in distinctive ways and demonstrates the multiple public/private connections steering it.

These workers have played a key dual role in the differentiated development of the Hong Kong and Philippine economies. They have played a vital part in supporting working households, including care of children, elderly relatives and expectant mothers in Hong Kong, while sending significant amounts of their income and goods back to their home countries. They have facilitated the growing participation of women in the Hong Kong economy (and elsewhere) during the rise of the service sector, while at the same time helping to maintain the traditional *feminized* domestic space, thereby playing a key structural part in social and economic transition (Youngs 2000a: 52; see also Pearson and Leung 1995b). The interdependence of the two faces of globalization includes multifaceted servicing functions of women within and across the public and private spheres.

Jan Jindy Pettman (1996: 185) has assessed the ways in which globalization has led to greater vulnerability for women who are 'out of place' through, for example, 'contemporary forms of international traffic in women, including women as migrant labour in internationalised domestic service, as mail-order brides, in sex tourism and militarised prostitution'. Pettman has talked in terms of an 'international political economy of sex' to signal the importance of gender and the 'implications of women's bodies being sexualised, and presumed available for men's sex and service'. But it would be a mistake to focus solely on women as objects in these processes, for as Pettman points out, their resistance, notably through NGOs, has exposed what is happening around the world and brought real change:

> campaigns... in poorer and richer states have succeeded in naming and publicising international sex tourism and child prostitution and pornography. They have directed public-education campaigns, demonstrations and boycotts aimed at the clients and at the network of interests and businesses that service them, including travel agents, airlines and advertisers. They have brought considerable pressure on states, including those that 'send' the men. As a result some states such as Australia and Germany have legislated to make their citizens liable for prosecution on return from using child prostitutes, a distinct departure from conventional understandings of sovereignty.
>
> (Pettman 1996: 204)

Resistance and empowerment

Resistance and empowerment brings us back to the theme of agency and its importance in feminist analyses of globalization. Women are involved in multiple forms of resistance in their individual daily lives, in various collective modes and through the activities of diverse NGOs from grassroots to global levels (for a range of discussions of this area see e.g. Marchand and Runyan 2000 and Naples and Desai 2002). Empowerment is a theme directly related to change because it recognizes that the roles we play in society impact on our identities and the degree to which those reflect open-ended or limited senses of the potential for leadership and participation. Role models are part of this picture because they offer imprints that can be developed or challenged by those who follow. Empowerment raises detailed issues about women's opportunities or lack of them to pursue as diverse a contribution as possible to the improvement of their societies. Empowerment links the concerns and identities of individual women to specific social processes, in which their engagement may be facilitated or inhibited by the broader social (gendered) context.

As recent commentators have argued: 'empowerment is both a process and an outcome. It is a process in that it is fluid, often unpredictable, and requires attention to the specificities of struggles over time and place. Empowerment can also be seen as an outcome that can be measured against expected accomplishments' (Parpart *et al.* 2002: 4). Critical analysis of processes of empowerment recognizes that participation can take many forms and have many meanings, not all of them necessarily related to positive change.

Jane Parpart, for example, in a recent assessment of participatory rural appraisal, gender and development, concludes that research 'cautions against a too-ready equation between participation and either individual or group empowerment. Gender inequalities, in particular, are deeply embedded in cultural as well as material patterns. Changing gender hierarchies and assumptions requires more than simply giving voice to women or including them in development activities. Indeed, many other inequalities are also highly resistant to change' (Parpart 2002: 174). Careful consideration of empowerment therefore reminds us of two key issues: the weight of history and established social structures and their impact on identity formation; and, the complimentary time and sensitivity required to work for social change in more equal circumstances while taking account of differentiated paths for different individuals and groups.

Conclusion

This chapter has demonstrated both what feminism contributes to considerations of globalization and what feminism tells us about it. I have shown that globalization should be considered in the explicit context of the history of patriarchal inequalities between men and women. I have illustrated how feminist theory facilitates our understanding of those inequalities and their bases. Feminism tells us about the persistence and refashioning of those inequalities under conditions of globalization, and the importance of inequalities among women as well as between men and women. Feminization of labour has undoubtedly brought new opportunities for women but they are often on unequal terms in relation to men, and in some circumstances, can be dependent on the supporting (racialized) 'service' roles of other women such as migrant domestic workers.

We continue to live in a world of inequalities between men and women and between women and women. The complex challenge of working for women's equality is firmly rooted in both these sets of material conditions. Equity and difference will therefore continue to be central to feminist theory and politics and to the global women's movement(s). And, as the question of violence against women so starkly demonstrates, men's identities and structural conditions are as implicated in the possibilities for change as women's. It might be useful to think of equity and difference in terms of past and future. Questions of equity relate most strongly to the legacy of patriarchal history and the unequal social structures and conditions it has created for men and women through the public over private hierarchy and differentiated masculine and feminine identity processes associated with it. Early feminist work concentrated on revealing this situation, its inequalities and impacts on women and society as a whole.

Increasingly, white Western feminism came under attack for its own hegemonic tendencies and myopia. Its sense of social context was narrowed by its own problems of privilege. As bell hooks explains:

> I can still recall how it upset everyone in the first women's studies class I attended – a class where everyone except me was white and female and mostly from privileged class backgrounds – when I interrupted a discussion about the origins of domination in which it was argued that when a child is coming out of the womb the factor deemed most important is gender. I stated that when the child of two black parents is coming out of the womb the factor that is considered first is skin color, then gender, because race and gender will determine that child's fate. Looking at the interlocking nature of gender, race and class was the perspective that changed the direction of feminist thought.
>
> (hooks 2000: xi–xii)

Feminists now work with increasingly complex senses of solidarity in theory and practice. These seek to take growing account of the range of differences that separate women as well as the similarities that unite them. Globalization has intensified this challenge because of the new opportunities and inequalities it has created. It has brought new learning curves for feminist theory and practice and new opportunities and imperatives for understanding the importance of difference. It has been a core issue in the transformation of feminism and activism linked to it, and could therefore be read as particularly influential in the present and future of feminist thought and politics.

The issue of equality does not stand still. It features continuities but also reflects the constant social changes involving political, economic, cultural and technological processes. Movements for change such as feminism are inherently themselves also confronting new challenges and undergoing change because of them. Feminism's focus on women's agency, resistance and empowerment signals the importance of women's daily and collective struggles towards change. The successes of women's movements in campaigning, for example, for women's rights as human rights, demonstrates the power of feminist politics in the era of globalization. Activism on the Internet is making such processes more transparent to wider and wider audiences and this is a notable development in the history of women and feminism. Information about their concerns and campaigns is more easily available to more people, including men, and thus there are greater opportunities to learn about how women are actually engaged in working for their communities and societies and greater equity in local and global contexts (Sreberny 1998).

Acknowledgement

I am grateful for support of this research to the Toda Institute for Global Peace and Policy Research.

8 Globalisation for a multicultural world

Bhikhu Parekh

In this chapter I explore the cultural dimension of globalisation. I begin with a brief discussion of the nature and logic of globalisation and explore some of its welcome and regrettable cultural consequences. Since culture is closely tied up with the economic and political structure of society, I end by suggesting how globalisation can be used to foster a rich and vibrant multicultural world.

The logic of globalisation

Contacts between different parts of the world are not new. Over the centuries societies have invaded, interacted and traded with each other, and borrowed each other's tools, inventions, mode of production, ideas, beliefs and practices. These interactions, however, were generally patchy, contingent and largely marginal in their internal impact. European colonisation from the sixteenth century onwards not only accelerated but gave them a new depth and pattern. European powers penetrated and shaped the lives of colonised societies at many levels, turned them into dependent economies, and divided up much of the world into more or less closely integrated economic and political units.

During the last few decades, we have entered a new phase.[1] Decolonisation loosened the earlier imperial systems and freed the countries involved to enter into new relationships. Revolutionary changes in the means of transport and communication have increased the integration of all societies, including those that were hitherto marginal, into a common system of interdependence. Developing countries desperately need the capital, technology and markets of the advanced western countries, and the latter in turn need their cheap labour and markets. This has made their integration deeper and more extensive than ever before. Such international institutions as the UN, the IMF, the World Bank, the GATT and the WTO have ensured that global interdependence is institutionalised, monitored and channelled along particular lines. As a result of all this, fates of societies separated by thousands of miles and at vastly different stages of development are increasingly intertwined. They share common interests, face common problems and need to find collectively acceptable solutions. Globalisation, understood as the increasing integration of all parts of the world into a single system of interdependence such that events in one of them directly or indirectly affect the lives of others, is a recent phenomenon.

Every country today is both the subject and the object of globalisation in the sense of both influencing and being influenced by others. Since globalisation occurs in a world of great inequalities of wealth, power, skill and productive capacities, the more powerful among them are better able to take advantage of it and make a greater impact on others. Economic, political and other forms of interaction are also more highly concentrated among the rich countries, and their political economic and cultural integration is greater than the rest of the world. Most multinationals are nationally based and only a few of them are genuinely transnational or global. None of these, however, detracts from the fact that no country, however rich or poor, is immune to the impact of global forces and is able to manage its collective life without taking full account of them.

Globalisation is not limited to the economy, though that is where it is most evident and extensive, and extends to other areas of life as well, such as the political, the cultural and the moral. And although its impact on them is uneven and varied, it is nevertheless deep, lasting and unmistakable. All states today are members of the UN, an event without a parallel in human history. Most are signatories to and bound by global protocols, conventions and agreements. They share a common political vocabulary and define their interests and resolve their differences in terms of it. Ideas, intellectual movements, the arts, literature, television programmes, the films and other cultural products travel freely across national boundaries and have a global reach. Thanks to the speedy and relatively easy modes of travel, millions are constantly on the move, acting as carriers of new ideas and experiences and helping to create, each in his or her small way, the global consciousness of interdependence.

Globalisation has penetrated our moral life as well. Travel has awakened us to the fact that, however different they might otherwise be, all societies consist of human beings like us, face common problems and share much in common. The global reach of the media brings to us vivid images of events in other parts of the world and involves us in their affairs. We feel addressed by stories of human suffering in distant lands, and translate our concern in programmes of humanitarian aid and acts of humanitarian intervention. Common environmental problems, the desire to preserve the global commons and the earth's scarce resources, the need to tackle diseases that stealthily transgress national boundaries, dangers of global warming and so on have alerted us to our shared vulnerabilities and dangers, and heightened our sense of interdependence and mutual obligations.

No society, however remote or powerful, can opt out of globalisation altogether. In some cases this is technologically impossible, for no society can totally block out access to the outside world offered by the internet, the radio and the satellite television. In other cases, stepping out of global interdependence is only possible at a price too prohibitive for any society to pay. No society can remain economically competitive without foreign technology, capital and sometimes labour. Nor can it protect itself against international crime, terrorism and infectious disease without joining appropriate global alliances and accepting the required discipline. No society can totally stop its citizens from travelling abroad or outsiders from coming in. Its citizens have also come to entertain certain expectations of life and do not easily tolerate attempts to deny them access to what the outside world has to offer. The fact that globalisation is a brute fact of contemporary life does not mean that it is self-propelling and cannot and should not be regulated. It is a human phenomenon, created, sustained and hence capable of being controlled by human beings, not obviously by any society acting on its own but certainly by all of them acting together.

Globalisation as an empirical phenomenon needs to be distinguished from globalism, an ideology which celebrates globalisation either as intrinsically valuable or as a way of solving humankind's major problems. A globalist might see it as the telos of history, the realisation of man's species-nature, or as God's plan for humankind. Whatever his philosophical or theological basis, he holds that humankind will or should come increasingly closer and eventually become a single and boundaryless community. One can accept globalisation as a fact of contemporary life and even welcome it for the good it produces without accepting the ideology of globalism. Globalism can take two forms. It can be comprehensive or partial, arguing either that humankind should become a single and closely knit community in all areas of life or only in some. In the latter case one can be, for example, an economic but not a cultural or political globalist, welcoming the economic but not the cultural or political integration of humankind.

In all areas of life globalisation has both desirable and undesirable consequences. It favours some types of society more than others, and in each it benefits some groups and harms and even ruins others. If the state fails to devise a fair sharing of benefits and burdens, such a differential impact can undermine its stability and wipe out in the long run such gains as the beneficiaries make in the short run. Since its impact on different societies cannot be easily measured and compared, and since its effects on different areas of life are inherently incommensurable, it is virtually impossible to make an overall assessment of globalisation. Our judgement on it is necessarily tentative, limited to specific areas and shaped by our values and vision of the good life.

In the economic sphere where its impact is most strongly felt, globalisation increases competition and productivity, improves the quality of products and brings them to international standards, reduces prices, increases the range of consumer choice, releases entrepreneurial energies and so on. It also, however, destroys domestic industries, increases unemployment at least in the short and medium terms, deepens economic inequalities within and between societies, creams off talent and leads to brain drain, ties national economies to the vagaries of international markets and renders them vulnerable to external manipulations.

At the political level, globalisation increases international cooperation, nurtures the spirit of human solidarity, opens up the possibility of greater collective control over the forces of the market, creates the conditions for an equitable global redistribution of resources, and provides a forum for appeal and redress against domestic tyrannies and violations of basic rights. It also, however, reduces a society's control over its affairs, weakens its democratic institutions, creates a global middle class sharing more in common with each other than with their fellow citizens and acting as a kind of multinational pressure group, weakens the sense of common belonging that lies at the heart of a political community, undermines the state's capacity to define or promote national interest and renders the poor political orphans.

Some of these consequences are inherent in globalisation; some arise from its current neo-liberal form; some others from the vast inequality of economic and political power in which it is currently embedded; yet others owe their origin to the process of industrialisation that arises independently of and is only contingently related to globalisation. Since all this is well known and is in any case not my main concern, I shall concentrate on the cultural dimension of globalisation.

The cultural impact of globalisation

As in the other areas of life, globalisation has important cultural consequences, of which four are of particular significance. First, it has resulted in what I might call sectoral convergence. As technology, institutions, ideas and practices travel across national boundaries, they tend to create broadly similar patterns of human behaviour and relationship in the relevant areas of life. All countries need and construct airports, and these are all broadly similar. They all have immigration officers, security checks, visas, luggage collection areas, location some distance away from residential areas, schemes for training pilots and a common system of communication between them and air traffic control officers. They also call for a common system of management, division of labour, hierarchy and forms of accountability, in short a common administrative and organisational culture.

Globalisation accelerates urbanisation and gives rise to cities with their familiar ethos of anonymity, traffic signals, crimes, shopping malls and so on, all carrying a broadly common meaning and requiring common patterns of behaviour. The universal acceptance of the state as a mode of constituting society brings with it territorial boundaries and disputes, the army, the police, the bureaucracy, the secret service, the flag, the national anthem and the institutionalised inequality of power. Hospitals, industries, universities, courts, armies and bureaucracies too tend to develop similar organisational structures and cultures. Despite all their differences in cleanliness, efficiency, general ethos and professional competence, to walk into a hospital, a court, a factory or a university in New York, Kuwait or Timbuktu is to encounter a broadly familiar institution and culture.

Such broad convergences in different walks of life are the result of several interrelated factors. Common technology requires common responses. Social, educational, economic, political and other institutions aim to realise common goals, and these are generally achieved in broadly similar manners. Those involved in running the institutions undergo similar training and acquire common expertise and professional culture. Most citizens are generally familiar through direct experience or hearsay with the good practices of other societies, and make appropriate demands on their own. Demands of the international community, expectations of fellow professionals in other parts of the world, cross-country comparisons and the need to compete with other countries also generate pressures for a broad global conformity.

Such sectoral convergences in different areas of life are not only inescapable but have much to be said for them, and promote further globalisation. They facilitate travel, communication, increased contacts, organised international cooperation and exchange of experiences and ideas. One would hardly wish to travel to another country, let alone establish close economic, cultural and other contacts with it, if one could not be reasonably confident that, despite all the local variations and eccentricities, its airports, hospitals, transport and bureaucracy would function in ways one could anticipate, understand and cope with. Sectoral convergences create pockets of familiarity, make the relevant areas of life in other societies intellectually and emotionally accessible, and provide the bases from which to reach out to and make sense of those that are unfamiliar, opaque. Thanks to globalisation, no society today is wholly inscrutable or closed to us.

Second, globalisation has also led to a broadly shared thin culture. People all over the world talk in the language of human rights, elections, free press, minority rights, accountability of government, democracy, national sovereignty, national interest and patriotism. At the social level, ideas of individual choice, running one's life oneself, romantic love, equality of human worth, self-respect, recognition of difference, identity and so on are a universal currency. This is not to say that these ideas are all equally cherished or even respected by all societies and all groups within them, but rather that they are intellectually accessible and intelligible to them all. In every society some groups appeal to them to legitimise their demands, and those opposed to these know what they mean and involve and why they are considered important.

The thin global culture also extends to several other areas of life. Coca Cola, McDonald's and such consumer goods as Nike, Adidas, Rolex, Chanel and Levi-Strauss jeans are almost universal. Michael Jackson and Madonna are global icons. Yoga, techniques of meditation, acupuncture, karate, judo, alternative medicine, etc. are familiar to all societies. Dress, the unmistaken traditional marker of a group's identity, especially in relation to women, now crosses national frontiers in a manner unimaginable earlier.[2] More and more men the world over dress alike, traditional clothes being confined largely to rural areas, indigenous peoples and self-consciously nationalist regimes. Even women are beginning to dress alike and try out new fashions. Uganda legislated against miniskirts, but in vain. The Iranian Mullahs put women back into the chador, but that too is not working and jeans and trousers are fairly common. Such commonality is also to be found in architectural style, interior décor, hobbies and forms of sexual self-expression. In many of these cases western influence is obviously most dominant, but not entirely. Indian, Chinese, African and other cultures have also influenced the West, including matters of dress, hairstyle and the ideas of male and female beauty.

Third, as a result of cultural interaction brought about by globalisation, cultural boundaries have become porous, leading both to the multiculturalisation of each cultural tradition and the emergence of new cultural forms that neatly fit into none of them. Although cultural interaction is uneven and heavily dominated by the West, it is not an entirely one-way process. Other cultures too take advantage of globalisation and impact on each other as well as on the West. Indian films are a powerful presence in the Middle East, Central Asia and parts of Africa and now increasingly in the West. Indian cuisine, forms of spirituality, yoga and music, are popular in the West and to a lesser extent in other parts of the world. This is equally true of Chinese cuisine, martial arts, dance forms, systems of medicine and herbal remedies, and of African and Latin American music, arts and literature. Islam is a fast growing religion in the world, and Buddhism too has made a considerable impact. Brazil's Rade Globo exports its telenovelas to more than eighty countries around the world, and one of the biggest TV hits in Russia is a Mexican soap opera called *Los Ricos También Lloran* (The Rich Also Cry). Australian television programmes such as *Neighbours* are watched in scores of countries. Just as there is globalisation of India, China or Africa, there is also, albeit to a much lesser extent, Indianisation, Sinisation or Africanisation of the globe.

Thanks to the greater exposure to other cultures and the willingness to interact with and borrow ideas from them, there is a considerable crossover and fusion of styles, images, cultural idioms and sensibilities. African percussion rhythms and Indian music are combined with western pop music. Western designers plunder Indian, Chinese and African styles in search of a 'seasonal look'. Writers and artists experiment with the genres and images of different literary and artistic traditions, Indian, Chinese, Middle Eastern and other culinary traditions have incorporated western ingredients, vegetables and styles of cooking even as the latter have incorporated theirs. Jokes and styles of humour of one culture find their way into another, and are either retained as a welcome alien presence or bought into a creative interplay with their local counterparts. Children grow up reading stories of distant lands, learning something about their peoples, myths and legends and imaginatively confronting and combining them with their own. Religions too borrow each other's ideas of God, spirituality, sacredness, after life and the meaning of life and death and suitably redefine their own.

This process of cultural fusion, which is not limited to the creative minds and goes on consciously or unconsciously in the lives of millions of ordinary men and women, has no doubt gone on for centuries, but it has received a new depth and momentum under globalisation. As a result, each culture carries elements of some others, develops curiosity about and respect for them and does not feel unduly obsessed about its purity and authenticity. This is not to say that cultural communities do not worry deeply about their identity and boundary, but rather that it is shadowed by the widespread recognition that cultural fusion is inescapable and necessary for their culture's ability to survive and flourish in a globalised world. Nor is it to say that we are moving towards a single musical, artistic or literary or culinary tradition, but rather that each tradition is becoming porous, that they all share different elements in common and display family resemblances, and that they are now part of a global cultural *mélange* (Pieterse 1995).

Thanks to this, few educated persons in any part of he world today are or would admit to being ignorant of at least some of the great literary, artistic and musical achievements of other societies. There is in this sense a minimum level of global cultural literacy. It is true that intercultural interaction is still heavily one-sided, relatively fragile and resisted in many parts of the world. However it is well under way, has its own momentum, and is just as common as economic and technological globalisation. It is also true that the interaction is largely limited to the middle classes. However it is spreading to other sections of society, who sometimes embrace it even more enthusiastically and use it to overcome their social inferiority, assert their modernity and to liberate themselves from oppressive social norms. The multicultural literacy is likely to increase as it becomes part of the educational curriculum all over the world and gets transmitted to succeeding generations.

As a result of intercultural borrowing, no culture is wholly strange to us. At least some areas of it, be it music, cuisine, literature, myths or beliefs, are familiar to us not only because we have learned about them in schools, films or television programmes or read them about in books, but also because we find their influence in our own traditions. Such familiarity provides a platform from which we prise open the obscure or unfamiliar areas of other traditions and make these accessible to us. This gives us the confidence to relax in their presence, delight in their otherness, and to enjoy the adventure of exploring their complexity yet further. For the first time in history, it is possible to say that today we not only inhabit a common earth but are beginning to share a common world. As we do so, we build bonds with other cultural communities and come to recognise and appreciate our shared humanity.

Finally, globalisation is leading to the pluralisation of all societies. Thanks to the movements of ideas, technology and cultural products, all societies are exposed to different cultures. And thanks to the movement of people, many are also exposed to different cultural communities that are settled in their midst. While human beings have always known that different people live and think differently, their knowledge was largely vague, abstract, hostage to traditional prejudices and elite manipulation. Today they see these people on television, observe their customs and practices and form their own views. When outsiders are settled in their midst, as they generally are, they interact with them to varying degrees, have a direct knowledge of their food, music, dress, habits, customs, values, norms of behaviour and grasp their humanity in all its pleasing and bewildering complexity. Unlike earlier societies in which cultural homogeneity was the norm and differences lay beyond their boundaries, human plurality and diversity is today a persuasive and tenacious fact of life. Difference is so much in the air we breathe that it is widely accepted as an almost quasi-ontological feature of human existence. While there is growing homogeneity or uniformity *between* different societies in some areas of life, there is *within* each of them a considerable degree of pluralisation. Both are part of the same general process. Almost all contemporary societies are plural or multicultural and are likely to remain so for the foreseeable future.

The depth and impact of multiculturality vary greatly, and different societies respond differently to what I might call their multicultural predicament. Western societies are culturally self-confident and convinced of the superiority of their culture. They do not therefore see non-western cultures as rival sources of moral authority. They expect non-western cultures to accept the basic western system of meaning and values, and take all conceivable measures to ensure that they do. In other areas of life they not only leave them free but encourage them to flourish. Non-western cuisines, music, films, theatres, arts and literature are widely enjoyed in the West, and even influence the dominant taste.

Such a neat division of spheres does not often work in practice, partly because they cannot be easily separated and more importantly because non-western cultural communities have different ideas on their place in western societies. They make cultural demands, seek recognition of their cultural beliefs and practices, press for multicultural education and so on. This is sometimes perceived by sections of society as a threat to western culture, provoking resistance and even opposition. Not surprisingly, an influential body of opinion in the West has mounted a strong attack on multiculturalism and the alleged dilution or destruction of national culture. Since the threat posed by non-western cultures is relatively feeble, western societies by and large have had little difficulty coping with such tensions as they generate.

The situation in non-western societies is quite different.[3] The dual strategy of western societies is not available to them. They have no problem copying what one might call the relatively superficial aspects of western culture. They enjoy western films, television programme, popular music, literature, food and so on, and many even adopt western dress. When it comes to the western moral, political and economic culture, they do not have the luxury of keeping it at bay. Thanks to their colonial history, they lack cultural self-confidence and often view the powerful and prosperous western culture as superior. As we shall see later, international institutions on which they depend for economic assistance require them to adopt it as its necessary precondition. The western moral, political and economic culture is not and cannot therefore be confined to the margins of non-western societies. It penetrates their vital institutions and shapes their moral lives. It is a serious cultural interlocutor, challenging the basic assumptions and categories of their ways of life and thought, and introducing a powerful destabilising element.

Non-western societies thus are multicultural or plural in quite a different way to their western counterparts. The western culture competes for moral authority with the indigenous culture in the public space as well as in the minds and hearts of their citizens. Each is a powerful presence in their lives and has its appeal. They must therefore find ways of accommodating both until such time as their tensions are successfully resolved either by a synthesis or by the defeat of one of them. In their social lives non-western societies define themselves in communal terms; in their political and economic lives in individualist terms; and their moral lives display sympathies towards both. They have one sense of time when they go to office or place of work or take children to school, and a very different one when visiting temples, attending social functions or meeting friends. Firms, government buildings and offices represent one way of structuring space; private homes, community centres and temples a very different one. Caste or tribal membership matters much in social life but is positively frowned upon in political and economic relations. In short, space, time, social relations, moral values, ways of relating to oneself and others are all informed by competing systems of meaning and involve constant conceptual leaps. It is hardly surprising that almost all non-western societies display varying degrees of cultural disorientation and nostalgically yearn for a non-existent homogeneous national culture. Like their western counterparts, they too find multiculturalism troubling, though for different reasons and with far greater justification.

American hegemony and national culture

As we saw earlier, although cultural globalisation is a truly global and not a narrowly western phenomenon, it is heavily dominated by the West, especially the United States.[4] Two factors are largely responsible for the US domination. American cultural industries have the advantages of vast resources, scale of production, a large domestic market, control of global media, an extensive network of distribution facilities, aggressive marketing, early start in mass production and, of course, the political prestige and support of a hyperpower. While these advantages are considerable and should not be underestimated, they are not by themselves enough. They would not, for example, succeed in turning Indian films into global blockbusters or give the Chinese popular music global popularity. Conversely, they have not succeeded in pushing American arts, theatre and literature high up on the scale of global popularity. American domination of global culture is largely limited to some areas, such as the films, the soaps, television programmes and popular music.

Another important factor responsible for American domination has to do with the character and content of American cultural products. Being a multicultural and multi-ethnic society whose citizens are drawn from almost every country, the United States is a microcosm of the world. Its cultural producers come from many different countries, either because they are sons and daughters of immigrants or because they have been attracted to American centres of cultural production. They are receptive to other cultures and willing to experiment with them. They also think, work and live in a multicultural society, and bring to their work a well-developed multicultural sensibility. Since immigrants from different parts of the world continue to come into the country, American cultural producers are constantly in touch with changing global tastes and cultural forms. Given their domestic multicultural audience, they have the added advantage of trying out their products on it. If these win their approval, they can be reasonably confident that their products have a good chance of satisfying much of the rest of the world.

Thanks to all this, American products tend to cut across traditional cultural boundaries and appeal to a wide variety of tastes. They do so in one of two ways, representing two different forms of universality. They deal with what all cultures share in common, are culturally as neutral and bland as is humanly possible and require no more cultural sophistication than is universally available. Or they are culturally eclectic in their appeal, multicultural in their orientation and have enough in them to engage different cultural tastes in different degrees. Most American films fall in the first category, much of popular American music in the second. In either case American cultural products, especially those meant for a mass market, have a built in globalisability. And when they cannot be globalised in their original form, they have enough cultural elasticity to be suitably adopted to local circumstances. It is this inherent or adjustable globalisability that is exploited by the massive and well-researched American centres of cultural production. The globalisability of their content is not enough to ensure their globalisation. Some other countries too produce globalisable cultural objects and activities, but their potential remains unactualised for lack of the kind of power wielded by the American cultural industries. The nature of the product and the power of the producer are both important. The United States profits as much from its capitalist economy as its multicultural society.

Globalisation, particularly the American cultural dominance, is widely perceived as a threat to national culture, and is sometimes referred to in such lurid terms as cultural invasion, onslaught and imperialism. The truth is more complex. National culture is never a homogeneous and tightly knit whole. It is composed of different strands, and impacts differently on different groups. What appears threatening to one group might seem emancipatory to another. Western ideas of social, gender and racial equality threaten the beneficiaries of the dominant hierarchical, patriarchal and racist culture in non-western societies, but are most welcome to women, indigenous peoples and other oppressed groups. The depiction of nudity, scanty clothes or sexuality in western films and television programmes that deeply offends middle-class sensibility is acceptable to the urban and rural poor, who have long been accustomed to it by their poverty, social customs or traditional lifestyle and who even welcome it as a way of challenging middle-class snobbery and superiority. Even so far as the middle classes are concerned, the situation is quite complex. Although most loud in their complaints, they are also often the keenest viewers of such films and programmes. Their prudishness is generally a recent phenomenon, being the product of a particular way of defining the national identity in the course of colonial struggle, and often has no deep roots in their culture. Indian middle-class puritanism, for example, goes back no further than the nineteenth century, and sits ill at ease with its long tradition of celebrating sexuality evident in its erotic temple architecture, popular religious stories, sexual exploits of gods and goddesses and an extensive erotic literature of which the famous *Kamasutra* is only one example. This is also the case with many Muslim societies whose puritanism is relatively recent and at odds with the exuberant sensuality evident in their literature, music and social practices.

The talk of cultural invasion wrongly assumes that the indigenous culture is passive and powerless before outside influences. It generally has the resources to engage in a critical dialogue with them and to decide what to reject, what to accept, how to indigenise or neutralise the impact of what it is powerless to resist. A society might accept western dress, food or manners but deny them dignity and status by limiting them to culturally marginal areas or socially insignificant occasions. India, China and Middle Eastern countries are full of McDonald outlets and prestigious western restaurants, but would not generally serve their food on occasions associated with major lifestyle events such as birth, marriage and death. Similar restraints are applied to western dress and music. These strategies of cultural survival and self-reproduction do sometimes break down or are voluntarily abandoned, not so much because of the pressure of global forces as because they make less sense in an increasingly industrialised and urbanised society or because of the decline in the authority or the rigidity of the cultures involved.

The impact of western especially American films and television programmes should not be exaggerated. When the Soviet Union was dissolved, Russians, who were long denied access to them, embraced them with great enthusiasm. As their country settled down and faced problems of national reconstruction, domestic films and television programmes, which sensitively explored these problems, began to enjoy far greater popularity than the western imports. Similar things have begun to happen in India. The national television, long used to the mono-poly of the domestic market, produced boring, unimaginative and technically poor programmes. It improved considerably under foreign competition and began to produce films and serials that not only won over the alienated domestic market but also enjoyed overseas popularity.

In India, Russia, China and elsewhere, Hollywood films and western television programmes are popular, but largely among the middle classes and the urban youth. Even among them surveys of primetime scheduling around the world show that domestically produced programmes always top the ratings during peak view-ing hours, with American imports filling in less popular slots during the day (Dziadul 1993). What is more, unlike the domestic programmes western imports rarely become subjects of serious formal and informal public or private discus-sions among their viewers, and are seen as forms of entertainment rather than sources of cultural norms. This is so because western imports do not relate to their society, deal with its problems, represent them, articulate their cultural, eco-nomic and other anxieties, use culturally evocative images or guide them on how to survive and flourish in their kind of environment. Viewers do not feel person-ally addressed by them, and naturally do not critically engage with them. It is not enough for western imports to indigenise themselves. They need to take up domestic issues, use native talents and handle their themes in a culturally intelligi-ble manner. This requires localised production, and then they cease to be western except in their sources of funding.

Even when foreign films and television programmes are widely viewed, that does not mean that they are necessarily popular in the sense of viewers approv-ing of or even liking them; they might watch them simply because they have noth-ing else or better to view or do. And even when they are popular, they are not always influential in the sense of shaping viewers' attitudes. American films are hugely popular in France, grossing nearly 60 per cent of the total cinema revenue, but there is no evidence that they have shaped the French attitude to the United States. Indeed, people may watch and even enjoy American imports and yet think low of the country for producing them. They might feel or be made to feel ashamed or guilty, at enjoying programmes they really ought not to enjoy, and might blame the United States for corrupting them. This seems to be the case in some Muslim countries such as Saudi Arabia, where the television and cinemas show little but American imports without inducing much respect or love for their country of origin.[5]

The culture of a society is embodied in and transmitted through its religion, literature, language, songs, food, dress, music, newspapers, films, radio and television programmes, the arts, body language, manners, children's comics, morals and so on. It is striking that those worried about the integrity of the national culture do not generally mind foreign imports in such areas as music, dress (except in relation to women), newspapers, food, literature, the arts and radio programmes, largely because they think that these areas are either marginal to culture (e.g. food and dress) or involve only the educated and presumably therefore culturally reliable elite (e.g. literature, the arts and radio programmes). They see religion as central to their culture, but know that it is least open to foreign influences. They feel the same way about the country's language, except when a foreign tongue threatens to overwhelm and replace it as in Quebec and to some extent in India. For various reasons what seem to worry them most are the films and the television programmes.

Sometimes the pressures of commercial interests are responsible. In France opposition to American films was led by, among others, the French *Gaumont* company whose head insisted, without any sense of embarrassment, that the French film industry should be protected 'if France wants to be the home to new Prousts in the future'.[6] Other reasons, especially in non-western societies, have to do with the fear that since films and television programme reach out to the illiterate masses, who are believed to be particularly vulnerable to the influence of the visual media, they must be carefully monitored. The first assumption is correct, as the films and especially the television are the main sources of entertainment and information for the masses in developing countries. The second assumption is dubious. It underestimates the shrewdness and maturity of the masses who are not as easily taken in by what they see on the screen. As we saw, they are also generally less engaged by foreign imports and often use them as a pleasant but inconsequential pastime. Furthermore, the attempt to protect the masses in the name of preserving the national culture often springs from a self-interested desire to ensure that they are kept away from ideas that are likely challenge the established social order.

In the light of our discussion the attempts to protect a society's culture are *prima facie* suspect. They do not generally arise from a democratic debate and enjoy a broad consensus. Protectionist measures are likely to be unduly restrictive, biased towards vested interests and to prevent critical ideas and social change. They are also generally too crude to cope with the subtle ways in which cultures deal with new challenges and undergo change, and too paternalistic to trust the good sense of those they seek to protect. In spite of these and other dangers there are, however, two situations in which a society's culture might need some defence against global forces, namely when they are unfairly advantaged and when they impact with such force that they undermine a society's ability to cope with change.

Guiding globalisation

When foreign cultural imports enjoy and exploit their unfair advantages, they tend to wipe out large areas of domestic cultural production. The US film and television industries recover most of their costs from the domestic market, and export their products at extremely low prices with which their domestic rivals cannot compete. It is often cheaper to buy and distribute third-rate American films than to produce native ones. Domestic producers, who are generally keen to make quick money, have no incentive to make films of their own, leading to the closing down of national studios. Rich and powerful American companies also take over domestic cinemas and use them to show their films, denying outlets to domestic films. On its opening weekend, *Jurassic Park* took over nearly a quarter of France's screens in large towns and cities and provoked a legitimate outcry. Indonesia had long protected its film industry, and produced some excellent films. The situation changed when the United States demanded easier access for its film exports in return for guaranteed Indonesian textile imports. In 1992, sixty-six out of eighty-one cinema houses showed only the foreign, mainly American films. Domestic gems such as *My Sky, My Home*, which won awards in France, Germany and even in the United States, could not secure a domestic outlet.[7] Although films require a large financial outlay and are therefore particularly vulnerable to foreign domination, similar things also tend to happen in other areas such as popular music, television programmes and political and lifestyle magazines.

Societies can cope with foreign cultures when they are able to do so at their own pace, have some sense of control over their affairs, and are fairly stable and self-confident. When they are subjected to a rapid and relentless flow of foreign cultural products which they are powerless to control, they feel paralysed, confused, helpless and lose their normal capacity to take change in their stride. The norms, values and social practices, which have long held them together and guided them through difficult situations, are weakened, creating a pervasive sense of disorientation, anomie and moral panic. Unless they are able to regulate foreign cultural imports, they either passively watch the disintegration of their society or fall for the seductive appeals by the all too familiar pedlars of a fundamentalist return to a non-existent idyllic past. This is, for example, what happened in Iran when the Shah opened up the country to massive western influences and created a panic. His ruthless attempts to suppress the inevitable protests only intensified the opposition, leading to a vicious cycle of violence which the Mullahs exploited. Every culture can and should be criticised, and benefits from interaction with others. However it needs to change slowly, at its own pace, from within, through an internal dialogue and reform and with the willing consent of its members. This requires an environment in which the process of change can occur without being harried, hurried or manipulated from outside.

One might ask why it should matter if a society's cultural industries disappear and its members view only the foreign films and television programmes, listen only to the foreign music and read only the foreign magazines.[8] Legitimate national pride and self-respect as well as the economic interests of the cultural industries and the country as a whole are important but not decisive. There are at least two crucial cultural reasons why the disappearance of domestic cultural production is to be deeply regretted and avoided.

First, out of disinterested intellectual curiosity as well as for reasons of stability and self-reproduction, every society seeks to and indeed needs to develop some conception of itself, of the kind of society it is, how it has come to be what it is and what it wishes to be. This is particularly so when it is undergoing profound changes, which is the case with all societies in our globalising age. It is subject to a complex process of transformation and undergoes a bewildering variety of experiences, which it needs to understand and incorporate into a coherent and periodically redefined account of itself. Otherwise it feels confused, has no sense of direction, does not know what changes to embrace and how to integrate them into its way of life and lacks the capacity to reflect upon, criticise and reform itself.

Although ordinary men and women in their own tentative and informal ways seek to make some sense of their society, creative minds play an indispensable role. Being part of the society, they share its experiences, participate in its moods and tensions, and understand its needs and aspirations. They comprehend their society from within, critically engage with it, inspire it, give voice to neglected experiences, uncover the inner structures of prevailing forms of consciousness, interpret different groups to each other and build common bonds between them. In these and other ways they render the society transparent to itself and bring it the great gifts of self-consciousness, self-understanding and self-criticism. Foreign cultural producers by definition cannot do this. A society deprived of thriving cultural activities has no voice and mind of its own, and suffers a grievous and irreparable moral loss. Lacking self-understanding, it is also unable to engage in and benefit from a critical dialogue with its foreign cultural imports.

Another reason why domestic cultural production matters has to do with the dangers of cultural homogenisation and the virtues of cultural diversity. Every culture embodies a particular vision of the good life, cultivating one set of capacities, emotions, attitudes to life, values and ideals and marginalising, rejecting or repressing others. It needs other cultures to correct its biases and limitations, and to deepen its understanding of the possibilities of human existence. Every culture, further, has a tendency to see itself as the only normal, rational or truly human way to live and hence to absolutise and universalise itself. It therefore needs a dialogue with others to appreciate its specificity, contingency, strengths and limitations and to learn to respect the legitimacy and integrity of others. The diversity of cultures also alerts each to that within it. Being sensitised to the fact that the good life can be defined and lived differently, it begins to appreciate that it too can contain differences, that its shared vision can be interpreted and lived differently and even that it is itself a historical precipitate of diverse influences. This prevents it from taking a homogeneous and singular view of itself and creates a space for tolerance and internal dialogue. Cultural diversity thus is one of the most important conditions of human freedom, rationality, creativity and well-being. It cannot therefore be left to the precarious mercy of the market. It is in the interest of the humankind as a whole that like equality, freedom and justice, cultural diversity should be recognised as a collective good and, consistently with other values, nurtured.[9]

Both the interests of every society and of the humankind as a whole require that while globalisation should be welcome, it should not be allowed to undermine a society's capacity to manage the process of cultural change. This is not censorship, because its purpose is not to ban the flow of external influences, nor is it a policy of cultural protection because its aim is not to prevent cultural change and freeze the existing forms of cultural diversity. Rather its purpose is to enable each society to interact with others on equal terms, change at its own pace, develop its own cultural forms and to bring its own unique gifts to a global intercultural dialogue.

A country should be free to regulate its cultural imports when they are in danger of overwhelming it or wiping out its essential cultural industries. It should also be free to encourage and subsidise the latter when they are too young, weak or diffident to compete on equal terms or too vital to its way of life to be allowed to die. In order to ensure that domestic cultural industries do not exploit the protected market or become dependent on state help, such a policy should be time-bound. Since cultural diversity is a common human good and the cultural stability of a society is in the interest of all, we may legitimately require the culturally dominant countries to exercise self-restraint. They could voluntarily limit their cultural exports, or stop giving them direct or indirect subsidies in the form of export credit and tax breaks. They could also encourage cultural imports by requiring their cinemas and television companies to show a certain percentage of them. If this should prove unacceptable, they could at least encourage and assist cultural industries in less developed countries with appropriate technical advice and financial grants. There is no reason why foreign aid, whether channelled through national governments or international institutions, should not encompass culture. Part of it could be earmarked for building up local cultural infrastructures, encouraging local creative outputs and nurturing local talents. Since foreign aid is limited in amount and involves balancing competing priorities of which economic development is naturally the most urgent, it might be a good idea to set up a global cultural fund.

Since the culture of a society cannot be dissociated from its economic and political life, no society can manage cultural change without the freedom to choose its appropriate path of economic and political development. Developing countries are unable to do so because the capital and the technology of the advanced western countries that they desperately need is given on condition that they follow a prescribed set of policies embodied in the Washington consensus. The latter is based on the ideology of market fundamentalism and involves such policies as deregulation, liberalisation, privatisation and unregulated foreign currency transactions. It assumes that there is only one proper way to organise the economic and political life, and only one correct path to it, and insists on a universally common and economic and political culture.[10]

The policies required by the Washington consensus take no account of the society's traditions and historical experiences, abstract the economy from its wider cultural context and concentrate on it to the neglect of other areas of life.[11] They were never followed by western societies during their decades of development, and not surprisingly they have rarely worked in the developing societies. They subject the latter to a rapid and massive process of social and economic change while simultaneously weakening their ability to regulate it. The result often is political instability and social dislocation. Since the economic and political institutions structure, shape and set the tone of other areas of life, these policies lead to global cultural homogenisation. If we value cultural diversity and stability, we need to challenge the Structural Adjustment Programme and the Washington consensus. While requiring the developing societies to respect the minimum necessary financial and fiscal discipline, we should leave them free to follow their own paths of development, make their own trade-offs between economic growth and other values, and encourage them to utilise the local knowledge and grass roots experience rather than rely exclusively on imported professional expertise.

Although the IMF is beginning to appreciate all this, it is too heavily dominated by the G7 to break with the past. If the development assistance were to be more generous than the current mean figure of 0.27 per cent of the GNP of the OECD countries, developing countries would be less dependent on the IMF and less timid in challenging its prescriptions. Another desirable measure is to give a greater role to the World Bank after ensuring that its governing structure is more representative in its composition and more democratic and transparent in its decision-making. It could then act as a truly independent body, helping and listening to those who need its advice and funds, respecting cultural differences, encouraging new experiments and accountable for its decisions to such international institutions as the UN.

Unless development assistance is embedded in a programme of global justice, it remains patchy, precarious, subject to manipulation and perceived by donors and recipients alike as a form of charity. Global justice involves sharing resources with those who need them with a view to creating a world in which all human beings can lead decent and fulfilling lives. A strong case for it can be made on several grounds. Poverty, despair and degradation address us all, and no moral being can remain deaf to their appeal. In our globalised and interdependent world, interests of different societies are closely tied up, and the problems of one inevitably affect others. Moral and cultural panic caused by the massive changes brought about by global forces destabilises societies and turns them into nurseries of hatred and terrorism that threaten us all. Cultural diversity is a vital human good whose loss diminishes all. And it can be nurtured only if every society is confident, stable and prosperous enough to evolve its own unique cultural forms. Fundamental interests of human beings the world over require a just and culturally varied world, and make its pursuit the supreme moral imperative of our globalising age.

Notes

1 For a good historical account of globalisation, see Held *et al.* 1999.
2 For a further discussion, see Roberts 1999.
3 See Cvekovich and Kellner 1997. The article by Axtmann is particularly relevant.

4 For an excellent account of globalisation, see Giddens 1990.
5 For a sensitive account of the way US films and television programmes dominate the world, see Barber 1995.
6 Goddard 1993: 14. See also Tournabouni 1995. Baerollueci even talks of the world hegemony of American films leading to 'a dreadful monoculture, a kind of cultural totalitarianism' (ibid.). See also Negus 1996 and Ritzer 1996.
7 Barber, op. cit.: 88 ff.
8 For a balanced evaluation of the cultural impact of globalisation, see Tomlinson 1997.
9 For a fuller discussion, see my *Rethinking Multiculturalism* (Parekh 2000): 163 f.
10 For a brilliant insider's critique, see Stiglitz 2002.
11 Ibid.: 12, 224 f and 250 f.

9   Environment, equality and globalisation

Giorel Curran

Globalisation has posed the problem of environmental justice. This is because the global economy's expanded requirement for resources and raw materials, along with the pressures of global population growth, intensify environmental risks. These risks fall on the shoulders of some individuals, communities and countries more than others. There is thus an inequitable distribution of environmental risk, despite the risk faced by all in the face of critical environmental problems such as climate change. Environmental justice requires a more even distribution of environmental benefits and burdens across and between generations – while at the same time valuing other species and nature itself.

This chapter argues that achieving the objective of environmental equality requires more adequate conceptualisation of the problems of globalisation and environmental inequality and more fulsome responses to them. In defending the objectives of environmental justice, the following discussion draws from some eco-philosophical and eco-democratic discourses it considers particularly useful in confronting the conceptual and institutional requirements of environmental equality.

The chapter is in two parts. In the first section the chapter explores the connection between globalisation and environmental risk through identifying the increased environmental stresses generated by a global economy. It then examines some of the elements of environmental inequality by exploring its domestic and international dimensions, as well as highlighting the communities this inequality most affects. The second section examines some of the global justice principles shaped by environmental equality considerations before exploring the new theoretical attempts to generate equality. Since it is argued that process as well as outcome is important, the chapter identifies and synthesises useful democratic and institutional responses to environmental risk.

Dimensions of the new equality

Environment and globalisation

Globalisation exacerbates environmental stresses. Location has a significant impact on all kinds of inequalities, from the quality of the air one breathes, to the capacity of the environment to provide sufficient and clean water. Few environmental

risks are not induced or exacerbated by the pressures of rapid economic development. Even the ferocity and frequency of floods and storms can be influenced by
events such as climate change. Environmental hazards linked to human activities
are usefully divided into two categories – the 'traditional hazards' of undevelop-
ment and the 'modern hazards' of unsustainable development (Mason 2000: 80).
The first refers to the well documented link between poverty, rapid population
growth and environmental risks such as poor sanitation and unclean water. These
factors are often exacerbated by the unintended consequences of the survival strategies of these populous poor nations – for example, the air pollution and respiratory
complaints arising from widespread fuel combustion for cooking and heating.

Modern hazards refer to the 'development and unsustainable development of
resources and are exacerbated by absences of safeguards and policies of proper
environmental control', including intensified industrial, agricultural and urban air
pollution and climate change (Mason 2000: 80). Modern hazards such as unsustainable development are linked to the production and competitive pressures of
industrialisation. These pressures induce the vigorous and environmentally risky
pursuit of economic development in both the developing and the developed
countries, as well as in the economic interrelationship between them. The rapid
deforestation and burning of large tracts of land for cash crop exports in countries such as Indonesia has contributed to the smoke and particle haze that engulfs
large areas of east Asia, with serious health and environmental consequences
(Montgomery 2002). These hazards account for the intensification of air, waste
and chemical pollution and bio-diversity loss that ensues from rapid and environmentally risky development. Developing countries usually cannot afford more
efficient, environmentally clean technologies, and are not infrequently pursued
for their 'pollution haven' potential. In their struggle to compete and survive in
the face of these competitive demands, some of these countries end up as the
dustbin of the global economy. In addition a 'risk transition' from 'traditional' to
'modern' hazards generally occurs as part of the economic development cycle
(Mason 2000: 80).

Environmental problems are linked to the production and consumption patterns
of industrialisation and of the market economy. The resource intensive demands
of the market economy – especially its reliance on exhaustible and degradable
resources – create significant environmental stresses, generating tension between
the demands of economy and ecology. Environmental stresses arise from this
imbalance between production and consumption on the one hand, and the provisions of natural systems on the other. The capacity to deal effectively and equi-
tably with such issues is complicated by the nature of environmental problems
themselves. The most important and complicating features of environmental
problems includes their common goods character; externality and displacement
features; transboundary nature; irreversibility concerns; and equality considerations –
features that will be referred to in the discussion that follows.

Globalisation has complicated this already difficult scenario. The global economy has driven a significant global increase in production and consumption,
accelerating demands for already depleted resources such as timber, minerals

and water. This in turn has exacerbated environmental risks by significantly increasing levels of pollution and toxic waste, as well as accelerating the reduction of biological (and cultural) diversity. Current global population growth and intensified urbanisation also contribute significantly to depletion of natural resources and increased levels of pollution. The new technologies that have enhanced life for many have been accompanied by risks unprecedented in their temporal and spatial reach. These developments have combined to form a 'risk society' where the successes of industrial and technological developments transform into the very qualities that will – if left unchecked – destroy it: by 'their nature [environmental risks] endanger *all* forms of life on this planet' (Beck 1992: 22). For Beck, this has generated new notions of equality and inequality. Indeed, the risks and inequality of a risk society has replaced those of a class society. Whereas wealth and other resources could overcome the inequality of class, in a risk society wealth is no longer a sufficient buffer against contemporary environmental hazards. Thus, while the poor suffer more directly from these intensified risks, Beck's claim is that wealth and privilege no longer affords its traditional protection from risk. Despite the poorer nations' disproportionate exposure to environmental risks, Beck points out that these risks are also generalisable: that is, if left unchecked, such risks could eventually affect all planetary inhabitants *equally*. A 'boomerang effect' ensures that the hazards the developed countries transfer to the poorer nations rebound in the form of imported toxic foods and products (Beck 1992: 44). While pollution might not be as 'democratic' as Beck at first claimed, the fact remains that 'the present tension between those who *produce* risks and those who *consume* them' could, in the long term, be replaced by an 'equal' risk to all in the face of events such as nuclear contamination (Beck 1992: 46). In this case, wealth or privilege would afford limited protection.

A starker connection between environmental risk, globalisation and inequality has also been made by Shiva (1999) who describes globalisation as a form of 'environmental apartheid' primarily operationalised through 'restructuring the control over resources in such a way that the natural resources of the poor are systematically taken over by the rich, and the pollution of the rich is systematically dumped on the poor' (1999: 53). The competitiveness demanded by globalisation's capital accumulation processes has generated more active worldwide sourcing of raw materials, enabling the location or relocation of production units to regions or countries that provide the comparative advantages of less rigorous environmental and labour regulations (Beck 1992; Shiva 1999). To this degree, economic globalisation is a 'normative process that replaces all value by commercial value' (Shiva 1999: 47). This 'apartheid' is complicated by the globalised power relations that sees some powerful multinational corporations significantly influencing the development decisions that were ordinarily the province of sovereign governments. The debate about diminishing national sovereignty in the face of globalisation is both a familiar and contentious one. One of the primary concerns is the implications for democratic practice of the increasing influence of multinational corporations over economic decisions that carry significant social and environmental impacts. A major criticism of the recent 2002 Earth Summit in Johannesburg was the perceived corporate domination of its agenda (Leake and Hodge 2002).

The issue of climate change highlights many of the environmental equality concerns raised earlier. Climate change arises from, or is intensified by, the accelerated development pressures of a global economy. It raises very direct equality issues and highlights the often inequitable global power relations that underpin both the development of climate change as well as preferred remedial measures. It also raises questions of where responsibility for climate change damage lies: who (including both present and future human and non-human individuals and generations) are likely to suffer the most? Who should bear the costs of remedial action and what global institutional measures would best deal with the risks? Hamilton (1999: 91) sets out the factors well:

1   The problem of climate change is one of global commons... [P]rogress is possible only with international cooperation.
2   The increased concentrations of greenhouse gasses in the atmosphere are due overwhelmingly to the activities of developed countries... an essential component... of [their] wealth.
3   Poor countries... will suffer the most significant impacts of climate change.
4   Developing countries will become the dominant emitters of greenhouse gasses in twenty-to-thirty years' time.
5   [T]he major impacts of climate change will not be felt until the middle of [the 21st century] and beyond.
6   There remain major uncertainties about the type, extent and locations of changes in climate and the impacts on humans.

Some of these equality issues were taken into account in the original 1992 Framework Convention on Climate Change (FCCC). This translated to the West taking most of the initial responsibility and bearing most of the costs in the initial stages of greenhouse gas reductions. This approach acknowledged the West's disproportionate emissions of greenhouse gasses (80 per cent) as well as the wealth they built on the back of this environmental degradation. This wealth also afforded the West the financial capacity to undertake remedial action. The next stage (post 2010) would involve the institution of remedial measures by the developing countries as well, since they are increasingly big greenhouse gas emitters. Since western countries largely created the problem it would be unfair and inequitable to expect the developing countries to contribute equally to its resolution, at this point of time at least. It could also be considered unfair for the poorer countries to deal with the consequences of the inequitable distribution of the problem without some form of compensatory redress. Environmental risks such as climate change thus contain a number of interrelated domestic and international dimensions.

Domestic equality considerations

The impacts of globalisation discussed earlier generate many domestic and international implications. We turn to the domestic first. In most developed western countries, residential property located on main arterial roads, abutting railway lines and adjacent to heavy industrial areas is usually less expensive. Such property is also likely to be environmentally hazardous, with more direct exposure to air, noise and chemical pollution. There is thus in developed countries a link between economic opportunity and the exposure to environmental risk. The less well-off are more likely to risk environmental harm than the more wealthy. This scenario is repeated – albeit more bleakly – in the divisions between the richer and the poorer countries worldwide as well in the stark divisions between a small wealthy elite and an impoverished mass in some otherwise poorer nations.

By way of illustration, let us begin by considering the fictitious story of the Delawares. Escalating city property prices forced the Delaware family to locate to the city fringes. The most affordable homes were in suburbs that surrounded the heavy industrial estates located there. The home they purchased was in a low lying suburb that trapped both the heat and fumes that stemmed from the neighbouring industries. The only consolation was the proximity to work for Mr Delaware – the sole wage earner in the family – who was employed by one of the local factories. In the middle of an unprecedented heat wave – attributed by many to climate change – their home was particularly hot and oppressive. They could not afford air conditioning and had to restrict the use of electric fans in order to curb their escalating electricity bills. Their general discomfort was compounded by the health conditions of one of their children who suffered from asthma, as did both their parents. Mrs Delaware's worsening asthmatic condition exacerbated her already troubled pregnancy. A better and healthier diet would also have helped but this was beyond the family's financial reach. She often despaired of the weakened constitution she was bequeathing her children. The heat, unbalanced diet and proximity to industrial fumes exacerbated all these conditions. Financial strain was further compounded by the Mr Delaware's growing illness, with his increasing sick leave putting his job in jeopardy.

The Delawares' relative poverty ensures them a significantly unequal exposure to environmental risk. The US Environmental Justice movement focuses on the inequitable distribution of both environmental risks and benefits, pointing to the clear link between environmental risk and race, class and gender (Bullard 1990, 1993, 1997). In the United States the Delaware family is more likely to be black, since race is a disproportionately overrepresented factor in the poverty statistics. Bullard's claim that '[m]any economically impoverished communities [in the US] . . . are exposed to greater health hazards in their homes, on the jobs, and in their neighbourhoods when compared to their more affluent counterparts', reinforces the link between poverty and environmental degradation (1997: 1). One of the features of Beck's risk society is the 'social risk position' it generates (Beck 1992: 23). While this risk position mirrors the 'old' inequalities of class and stratification they introduce a 'fundamentally different distributional logic' and thus the notion of a new inequality. The 'new' logic replaces the 'old' distributional logic based primarily on class, wealth and associated resources since, sooner or later, the risks of modernisation also 'strike those who produce or profit from them' (Beck 1992: 23). Nonetheless, while wealth might not, on its own, shield one from environmental risk altogether, it continues to provide a significant buffer. The fact remains that in the advent of an environmental illness epidemic that strikes rich and poor equally, it is better to be rich and sick than poor and sick. While it is indeed the case that the poor and rich can both die from food stress – the former usually through lack of food and the latter often from too much food – the rich nonetheless retain choices denied the poor.

It is clear that in the developed countries environmental risk and – to continue our example of climate change – the consequences of climate risk are also likely to disproportionately affect the less affluent members of an otherwise affluent society. This can include escalating insurance premiums, unaffordable flood and storm damage, more illness in an increasingly privatised or privatising health system and loss of jobs in areas affected by climate change such as agricultural work. The Delawares fell victim to most of these consequences. These consequences affect future generations as well as other species. On a direct, domestic level, the consequence of their poverty means that the Delawares risk passing on intergenerational health risks to their children.

On a broader level, while intergenerational equity considerations are now well integrated in the discourses of major international environmental institutions – with many global environmental treaties and protocols negotiated within this longer term framework – short-term economic considerations continue to dominate national decision-making. This is demonstrated in the decisions of Australia and the United States to not ratify the Kyoto protocol on the grounds that, on balance, the costs would significantly exceed the benefits (costs and benefits largely conceived in the shorter term). Some economists even promote the acceleration of global warming on the grounds that there are significant benefits and positive tradeoffs in a warmer planet: the losses in snow skiing, for example, could be replaced by an increased investment in water skiing, and so on (Hamilton 1999: 100).

International equality considerations

While often paralleling the domestic, globalisation also intensifies international equality considerations. Let us next consider the fictitious story of the Nanuians. The Nanuians live on the (fictitious) Pacific island of Nanu where they are quite isolated and remain relatively untouched by modern development. Their small island provides their tiny population with the resources for a sustainable, if meagre, existence. Their post-colonial experiments with democracy are still embryonic and, despite the inflow of aid monies, their economic and political institutions threadbare. A focus on the practicalities of survival, along with their limited communication resources, has ensured that the global climate change debate has effectively bypassed them. Yet the Nanuians stand to lose the most: as a very low-lying island, Nanu is threatened with inundation by 2050. The

Nanuians have contributed nothing to – nor have they indirectly gained from – the development processes that have generated global warming. Regardless of culpability, they do not in any case have the resources necessary to alleviate such potential calamity. There are also other potential losers from inundation. Their island houses a number of unique and rare species of fauna and flora. Sensitive to even relatively minor changes in temperature, some species of fauna and flora already face extinction. The unique properties and inhabitants of an ecologically and aesthetically wondrous piece of the global commons are threatened with impending ruination.

The Nanuians and their island's inhabitants clearly bear an unequal share of international environmental risk. In confronting the environmental justice issues of climate change directly, Shue (1992) would be clear in his defence of the Nanuians. He considers it manifestly unfair that the vital, 'survival' interests of the poorest nations be sacrificed to protect the West's 'trivial' interests (1992: 394). It is also unfair that the poorest nations be asked to direct the limited resources available to them away from their own development in order to help fund the seeming excesses of others. In resolving the threat posed by climate change, Shue argues that it can never be just to slow the development of countries already facing starvation 'just so that the affluent can retain more of their affluence than they could if they contributed more and the poor contributed less' (1992: 397). Indeed, since 'in an emergency one pawns the jewellery before selling the blankets', it can never be just to require that the poorest nations 'be told to sell *their* blankets in order that rich nations may keep *their* jewellery' (1992: 397). Environmental justice would thus 'prevent negotiations from being the kind of rational bargaining that maximizes self-interest no matter what the consequences are for others' (Shue 1992: 385).

The example of environmental refugees underscores these points. One of the consequences of global environmental problems is the creation of increasing numbers of environmental refugees. There is currently considerable worldwide antipathy to refugees and 'asylum seekers' with many countries working actively on policies to exclude them. Such policies are justified on the grounds of protection of sovereign borders against the perceived illegitimate asylum sought by the non-citizens who would traverse them. Little national attention is paid to whether domestic policies contribute to the plight of such refugees and the responsibility claims such complicity would thus generate. However, '[q]estions about the nature and extent of our responsibilities towards migrating human populations take on a new meaning when many of these migrations are "forced"; induced by the adverse environmental effects of development policies' (Semmens 2001: 72). One effect can be the de-territorialisation of increasing numbers of environmental refugees, forced to flee their homes as a result of 'development-induced environmental degradations' (Semmens 2001: 74). Economic globalisation policies often intensify such development-induced environmental risks and the accelerating environmental destruction that takes place contributes to the displacement of millions of people from both their homes, their communities and their sustenance bases (Shiva 1999: 55).

While sovereignty legitimates national and international policies on both climate change and refugee movements, these policies alone cannot contain such movements – despite the efforts of an array of global institutions designed to address such issues. This raises complicated notions of obligation. Let us return to a now inundated Nanu. Prior to its inundation, Australia and the United States refused to ratify the Kyoto Protocol on global warming. They resisted a more vigorous reduction of their (proportionally high) levels of greenhouse gas emissions on the basis that this would disadvantage their citizens economically. Such legitimate sovereign policies, however, contributed in no small way to the warming that saw the eventual inundation of Nanu. These same sovereign policies prevent Nanuians from landing on the lawful territories of these nations and pressing for some form of redress. This raises difficult dilemmas. Shue (1992), as we saw, would argue that the richer countries have an obligation to compensate the Nanuians in some way since justice in climate change policies requires the mitigation of international distributional inequalities. The Alliance of Small Island States urged, unsuccessfully, the establishment of such a fund at the original FCCC negotiations (Paterson 2001: 123). Despite the best application of international distributive policies to climate change, compliance still depends on whether international agreements complement the national policy preferences of participating sovereign states. The result is not always an environmentally just one. Expanded notions of rights and obligations in the context of a more cosmopolitan and deliberative institutional setting could thus provide a more reasonable assessment of the distributional inequalities raised by climate change and other environmental risks. Before we turn to the theoretical attempts to deal with this new inequality, we need to identify more directly the communities most affected by environmental inequality as well as confronting the added complexity they raise for meeting the new equality claims.

New environmental communities

As we noted in the Delaware and Nanu stories, the effects of environmental inequality go beyond their immediate families or communities. Environmental inequality raises novel and complex considerations. In the not too distant past, equality and justice considerations were always negotiated between humans and for (usually present) humans. Environmental concerns now introduce new actors to the negotiation table – future humans, non-human species and the biosphere as a whole. This is aside from duties to many (present) human 'others', usually located in the planet's poverty belts. There are thus three main categories or communities affected by the inequitable distribution of environmental benefits and burdens: disadvantaged present humans, future humans and non-human entities.

The first category seeks to address *intra*generational equality between members of the present generation, particularly in seeking to minimise the poverty and misery of the world's poorest countries. Divisions between the wealthy and the poorer countries – often conceptualised as the rich 'north' and the poor 'south' – reveal the most glaring inequalities, as we noted with the Nanuians. These inequalities are revealed both in terms of socio-economic resources as well as environmental degradation, especially in response to the rapid globalisation of the world economy. Aside from 'North/South' considerations, intragenerational justice also refers to equity considerations between classes of people within affluent societies, as demonstrated by the plight of the Delawares.

The second, and related, category is *inter*generational equality – the extension of distributive equality and justice to future generations. The issue of addressing distributional equality and justice across generations is a long-standing one, with many economic tools such as 'just savings rate' designed specifically to address it. When applied to environmental considerations, observing intergenerational equality in the presence of unprecedented environmental risks such as climate change and enduring toxicity, becomes particularly problematic. As resources are consumed more rapidly in populous globalised economy, and as environmental risks intensify, present generations could be bequeathing future generations an inadequate asset base on which to build equitable future livelihoods. At the very least, future generations ought be left sufficient resources with which to conduct adequate livelihoods; a planet in good ecological health; and the necessary ingredients of individual and community well-being. This could take the form of conferring rights – or equivalent guarantees – directly to members of future generations.

The third, arguably most contentious, category is that of *interspecies* equality – a category that also emerges from these rights claims. More benignly this is understood as human respect for non-human species, including respect for the integrity of the biosphere as a whole (see Callicott 1982, 1985). A more contentious application is a moral extensionism that allocates moral standing and 'rights' to other sentient creatures such as animals. Ecocentrism remains the most contentious ethic. This ethic extends moral consideration and intrinsic worth to nature as a whole, as well as its individual non-human entities such as rivers, mountains and trees. The ecocentric attribution and distribution of value has generated considerable controversy in the areas of environmental ethics and political ecology (Luke 1988; Elkins 1989–90; Tokar 1990; Goodin 1992).

Despite degrees of controversy, these communities' equality claims have generated considerable theoretical attention, facilitated by the strengthening of democracy and rights claims that have paralleled globalisation. In this way, intergenerational equality is viewed as an extension of individual rights – where individual well-being includes not only the right to a clean and healthy environment in the present, but also the capacity to pass such assets on to one's children. This view recognises that individual well-being is in part determined by the knowledge that the future of one's children, or one's community or one's heritage is assured. Some of these theoretical attempts to defend environmental equality have generated some of the pertinent discourses to which we turn next.

Democratic responses to environmental equality

Conceptualising environmental justice

The globalisation and environmental risk nexus has stimulated some important new discourses that defend the claims of environmental justice. The political ecology discourses that have emerged over the past three decades have attempted to accommodate the extended equality and justice claims of the communities identified earlier, by conceptualising environmental equality and justice in a number of innovative ways. Each of these discourses conceptualise differently the concepts of rights, just desert and needs-based distribution that underpin the environmental justice narrative (Low and Gleeson 1998: 49). Most of these discourses have been a reaction against what was conceived as a narrow, instrumental utilitarianism underpinned by human and cultural chauvinism. These instrumental approaches were considered indifferent to justice considerations and to the trashing of both ecology and society. In compensating for the limitations of more 'traditional' applications of justice, some ecological discourses offer useful insights into, and broaden out the terrain of, environmental justice considerations.

The most radical – and arguably the most novel – is the introduction into justice discourses of notions of intrinsic value, biotic egalitarianism and animal rights. These notions seek to extend the rights of previously disenfranchised communities into the domain of rights and respect. Some animal rights advocates, for example, use the tools of utilitarianism to defend the moral considerability they extend to sentient animals (Singer 1972a). Singer builds on Bentham's quite controversial utilitarian principles as applied to the moral standing of animals: 'The question is not, Can they *reason*, nor, Can they *talk*, but, Can they *suffer?*' (Bentham 1960, ch. 17, sec. 1). For some, Singer relies on an 'enlightened' utilitarianism that overcomes some of its traditional limitations. Nonetheless, Almond (1995: 5–6) considers that Singer adopts a broader, less short-term view of the 'overall balance of good effects over bad' than the 'unreflective approach' of a shallow utilitariansism, even if the 'question of *who* or *what* should be included [in the moral universe] is in the end a line-drawing exercise'.

Deep Ecology expands the scope of relevant communities to which environmental consideration applies, as was noted earlier. Its notion of biotic equality has been revised and tempered since it first emerged several decades ago – in response to the difficulty, complexity and unanticipated consequences of its application. Its ecocentrism nonetheless continues to defend a radical moral extensionism, attributing intrinsic worth to non-human nature – that is, valuing nature in and of itself, separate to its instrumental value for humans. The general claim of ecocentrism is that the expanded identification with the cosmos it facilitates enables the development of commonalities that in turn enhance a harmonious relationship with the natural world. Once personal identification with all other living entities has taken place, an 'assault' upon the integrity of non-living human organisms and the cosmos as a whole 'is an assault upon our integrity' (Fox 1990: 250). In contrast to personal identification which moves outwards from the individual to take in the remainder of the natural world, cosmological identification begins with the cosmos and 'works *inward* to each particular individual's sense of commonality with other entities' (Fox 1990: 258). In this way, an ecocentric ethic based on extended identification with the natural world paves the way for a philosophical and practical shift from an environmentally ruinous human-centred instrumentalism. To this extent, the arresting of environmental depletion requires a new way of 'being' in the world.

This, however, need not be applied in the extreme. Deep Ecology quite correctly identifies instrumentalism and anthropocentrism as key values that can undermine ecological integrity. Attributing equal value to all entities is nonetheless problematic. An anthropocentrism conceived in a narrow biocentric fashion can collapse humanity into a reductionist and homogenous whole that is at odds with Deep Ecology's support of diversity. It also fails to distinguish the differential consumption patterns of diverse human communities. Such a perspective overlooks – albeit not intentionally – the very different experiences of environmental (and social) injustice by various human groups, communities, classes and nations. Nonetheless, Deep Ecology has opened up the environmental ethics and environmental justice debates considerably by expanding moral considerability beyond the traditional claims of instrumentalism and human chauvinism. Others strenghten ecocentrism's core by making it more theoretically coherent and consistent. Callicott, for example, avoids some of the untenable 'logical conclusions' of an 'untempered holistic environmental ethic' that pits the survival of human beings against the survival of endangered non-human entities. Callicot's ecocentric ethic substitutes the language of biotic rights with that of 'respect', thus avoiding untenable 'either/or' scenarios:

> Respect adds a moral dimension to relations with the natural world...The conventional wisdom of Western society tends to offer a false dichotomy of use versus respectful non-use...of using animals, for example, in the ways characteristic of large-scale mass-production. What is left out of this choice is the alternative...of limited and respectful use.
>
> (Sylvan and Plumwood, as cited in Callicott, 1982)

Other eco-philosophical theorists also conceptualise the relationship between ecology and society more coherently and consistently. For Mathews (1991, 1995) this relationship is best encapsulated in notions of 'ecological selves' and 'relational selves'. Here the relational self of ecocentrism is opposed to the 'separate' and autonomous self of liberalism. A relational self is noted for qualities of empathy and altruism while the separate self encourages a more limited, self-directed individualism. The claim is that relationality enhances the ecological identity necessary to the functioning of an ecocentric community. By encouraging 'a form of identity defined not in terms of its independence from others but rather in terms of its relationships with them', this community 'would provide a more appropriate ontological foundation for an ecocentric polity' (Mathews 1995: 74). Understood this way, relationality is consistent with the conception of ecology as an interrelated web of diverse and interdependent relationships. Individual identity is thus determined by relationship *with* rather than separate *from* others. 'Others' include the human others of present and future generations as well as other species and nature as a whole. In this way, it is 'the "relational self", rather than the "separate self" of liberalism, that regards the interests of others as inextricable from its own', ensuring that the identities of ecocentric individuals 'are logically intermeshed with others' (Mathews 1995: 74).

Despite their limitations, these discourses contribute significantly to the expanded conceptualisation of the relationship between ecology and society that adequate environmental equality and justice frameworks require. These discourses would thus seek to respond more sympathetically to the plight of the Delawares and the Nanuians, together with the Nanuians non-human co-inhabitants. These eco-philosophical reconceptualisations of nature and justice also go to the heart of citizenship and democratic process since they each redefine – either implicitly or explicity – the nature of citizenship and the rights and obligations that attach to it. Significantly, they highlight the importance of process as well as outcome. They raise the question of whether current political institutions, and the notions of democracy that underpin them, are up to the task of incorporating the expanded principles and practice of citizenship considered necessary to environmental justice.

Equality, citizenship and democracy

In a rapidly integrating global economy, transboundary environmental risks raise implications for democratic practice and challenge traditional notions of citizenship as currently practised in sovereign nations. Sovereign state systems complicate the capacity to respond to the externality features of many contemporary environmental risks. Such externalities occur when the negative impacts of the actions of one party – in exercising their legitimate rights over the use of ecological common property – are transferred to another. The intensified development activities and integration of the global economy exacerbate externalities. Yet for the legitimation of policies that may well have negative impacts on other communities, other nations and future generations, the democratic sovereign state generally only requires the consent of those members of the present generation it deems citizens of its sovereign borders. Externalities and their consequences thus challenge the fundamental principle of consent on which the legitimacy of liberal democracy rests. Pateman articulates the dilemma well:

> The straightforward assertion that liberal democracies are based on consent avoids the 'standard embarrassment' that occurs when theorists attempt to show how and when citizens perform this act. This assertion also avoids the question of who consents, and therefore glosses over the ambiguity, inherent in consent theory from its beginnings, about which individuals or groups are capable of consenting and so count as full members of the political order.
>
> (1980: 150)

While Pateman is referring specifically to the exclusion of women from early democratic practices, her critique applies equally to excluded 'ecological others'. These 'ecological others' include the non-citizens, citizens of other nations, future generations, environmental refugees, and non-human entities who reap the negative environmental consequences of the (legitimate) behaviour of other actors. Political obligation and citizenship rights were usually conferred to specific members of a bounded geographical terrain, thus restricting legitimacy claims to bounded territoriality (Curran 1997). 'Others' outside this terrain – no matter how affected – had limited claims or rights, despite the potential redress of international law. Hence the plight of the Nanuians. While this scenario is far from historically unprecedented, the extensive geographical and biospheric impacts of many global environmental problems complicates the issue of not only *who* consents, but also *who should* consent. Environmental issues thus broaden the applicability of notions of consent by extending the boundaries of relevant communities.

In liberal democracies consent as legitimation is premised on a bounded community. The rapid economic integration of the global economy, however, blurs boundaries and borders. Economic, cultural, political and now ecological borders are particularly affected. Thus 'the idea of a community which governs itself and determines its own future... is, accordingly, deeply problematic', since it is increasingly difficult to determine if the relevant community has provided the relevant consent (Held 1995a: 99). Held elaborates:

> Whose consent is necessary and whose participation is justified in decisions concerning, for example, AIDs or acid rain, or the use of non-renewable resources, or the management of economic flows? What is the relevant constituency: national, regional or international? To whom do decision-makers have to justify their decisions? To whom should they be accountable?
>
> (1995: 102)

These are important questions. Most environmental and industry policies stem from properly elected governments with legitimated policy programmes. The legitimate citizens of a sovereign state confer policy power to their elected political body. But what legitimate form of redress remains for those who are harmed by the legitimate policies of another sovereign state? The implications of such scenarios are extensive, 'not only for the categories of consent and legitimacy, but for all the key ideas of democracy: the nature of a constituency, the meaning of representation... political participation, and the relevance of the democratic nation-state as the guarantor of the rights, duties and welfare of subjects' (Held 1995a: 102–3). Indeed, since consent is a 'notion applicable only within the limits of a *particular* community or political system', its limitations induce people to look 'beyond the boundaries of their own societies to extend such notions to a more internationalist conception of justice' (Almond 1995: 8).

We have established that environmental problems raise many equality considerations. Environmental justice thus demands the resolution of, and compensation for, environmental risks that transcend the territorial borders to which sovereignty pertains, and from which traditional citizenship is derived. Such resolution would respect both the integrity of affected present and future humans and the integrity of the planet and its non-human inhabitants. Considerable attention has been paid to resolving these dilemmas. We will draw from three models of democracy that are useful in processing some measures of environmental justice: cosmopolitan democracy, planetary citizenship and ecological democracy.

Cosmopolitan democracy

As a model of international governance, cosmopolitan democracy is premised on universal principles of justice that would ideally be universally applied. Despite the limitations of the principle of universality, it is an important notion in realising the inclusive goal of environmental justice. It builds upon the notion of rights underpinned by the overriding value of autonomy. Cosmopolitan democracy theorists such as Held (1995a, 1996) and Archibugi and Held (1995a) extend this notion to one of global or 'transnational' democracy. The aim is to strengthen the current international political system by extending cosmopolitan democracy across the globe. For Held cosmopolitan democracy is a model of global democracy that seeks to consolidate 'democratic autonomy on a cosmopolitan basis' (1996: 353). Building on the key principles of autonomy and equal rights, Held argues that 'people should enjoy equal rights and, accordingly, equal obligations in the specification of the political framework which generates and limits the opportunities available to them' (1995a: 147). There is, however, a tension between the principles of sovereignty and autonomy: 'The operation of states in an ever more complex international system both limits their autonomy (in some cases radically) and impinges increasingly upon their sovereignty' (Held 1995a: 135). What is needed therefore is a new and varied mix of cosmopolitan democracy that protects personal autonomy. This cosmopolitan democracy would incorporate several key institutions: a global parliament; a new charter of rights and duties linked to political, social and economic power; deliberative economic and political assemblies, a global legal system and the transfer of coercive and military power to regional and global institutions in preparation for the 'transcendence of the war system' (Held 1995b).

Held applies fundamental liberal democratic principles to the global political order. He does not seek to override liberal conceptions of sovereignty and rights but simply to limit them where necessary so that the autonomy and rights of a plethora of international others are also considered. Thus Held would institute a new 'Charter of Rights and Obligations locked into different domains of political, social and economic power' (Held 1995b: 279). This new Charter would be achieved by deepening and strengthening current international institutions so that they are more responsive to the rights and equality claims of others. Held does not refer specifically to any of the three categories of environmental justice identified: intergenerational, intragenerational and interspecies justice, even if one of his universal rights is that of a clean and sustainable environment. Nonetheless, Achterberg (2001: 194) claims that 'we can infer what more he would or could say if he had given thought to the matter'. It would not be difficult to locate some environmental justice requirements in the seven clusters of rights Held identifies: the body, welfare, culture, civic associations, the economy, coercive relations and organized violence and legal and regulatory institutions (Achterberg 2001: 194).

Held's cluster of rights are important in that they encapsulate and address the complexity of contemporary socio-economic life. Nonetheless, the notion of cosmopolitan democracy is also problematic, and we can censure it on several grounds. The institutional centralization of a cosmopolitan political order can weaken community integrity and decentralised decision-making. This centralization could have the effect of disempowering rather than empowering communities. These centralized institutions – including many global institutions established precisely for dealing with the transboundary and transnational pressures of a globalised world – are considered by some environmentalists to be complicit in both human and environmental abuses and therefore cannot be the same institutions for resolving such abuse. An over-zealous universalism can thus weaken particularity and runs the risk of being another grand narrative that privileges dominant discourses and exercises of power. In this way, the 'ideals' of cosmopolitanism can mask unequal power relations and political and cultural hegemony. Furthermore, universal values can become decontextualised and mask 'the real moral motivations of individuals' which centre around 'the communities they identify with – their nation, state, religious group, clan, tribe or family', communities they are likely to consider 'they are ethically justified in giving priority to' – regardless of the pull of universal values (Thompson 2001: 137).

The notion of individual human rights that underpins cosmopolitan democracy is also problematic. One is often left with the impression that environmental rights can simply be tacked on to the end of the human rights list. If so, this limits it to humans and to present generation humans. This dilemma can be resolved by separating individual environmental rights from ecological rights and environmental justice from ecological justice. Low and Gleeson (1998), for example, define environmental justice as the fair distribution among humans of environmental amenity, while ecological justice extends this distribution to all planetary inhabitants. Bosselmann (2001) adds environmental rights to the traditional human rights model and continues to circumscribe or restrict rights only insofar as they impinge on the rights of other humans. Ecological rights, on the other hand, takes a more relational approach whereby rights are modified and restricted according to their impact on other entities and on the integrity of nature as a whole (Bosselmann 2001: 119).

The approaches of both Bosselmann (2001) and Low and Gleeson (1998) help temper the limitations imposed on the rights discourse by liberalism, especially by its emphasis on rationality (albeit defined in particular and exclusive ways) and capacity to choose. Indeed, 'if reason and capacity to choose are essential conditions for rights and hence for access to justice . . . it exclude[s] other species from the liberal's moral universe and also . . . confine[s] the application of the theory to the human beings currently alive' (Almond 1995: 8). If the capacity to include duties to future generations, other species and to the integrity of nature is thus compromised, this represents a significant constraint on the development of a robust, ecological notion of justice. Other discourses have sought to address this shortcoming by expanding the notion of citizenship on which cosmopolitan justice rests.

Planetary citizenship

Thompson's (2001) conception of planetary citizenship seeks to overcome some of the limitations of the cosmopolitan democracy model, even as she argues for a form of cosmopolitanism. Thompson believes that the transboundary nature, as well as spatial and temporal interconnectedness of environmental matters, requires some form of cosmopolitanism. Given this interconnectedness, cosmopolitanism can be understood as the extension of citizenship beyond regional and national borders to incorporate a form of global or 'planetary citizenship' (Thompson 2001). Since citizenship implies both rights and obligations to specific communities, extending citizenship principles to the planet may indeed encourage notions of environmental obligation to one's global co-citizens and to the planet as a whole. According to Thompson (2001: 139) world citizenship could provide 'a promising moral basis for environmental global governance' by extending global notions of solidarity and reciprocity. Even so, there remain serious obstacles:

> The present world political order is not conducive to the solution of global environmental problems. Political boundaries, and identifications and attitudes associated with them, encourage moral parochialism. Citizens of states are not generally willing to take responsibility for what happens outside their borders, and governments are reluctant to pursue policies that require sacrifice of the 'national interest'.
>
> (Thompson 2001: 136)

Unlike Held's model, a planetary citizenship model of cosmopolitanism would directly address the specifics of environmental problems and bridge the autonomy/ solidarity divide. Thus, a cosmopolitanism motivated by environmental as well as social obligation would entail rights to both liberty and resources, in a manner that views the two sets of rights as inextricably linked through a 'generational continuum' (Thompson 2001: 141). Individual well-being is thus linked to the capacity to pass on both cultural and ecological heritage to future generations. Importantly, individuals are thus more than 'merely autonomous actors pursuing their own self interest'; rather they are members of several communities – families, cultures, traditions – whose self-interest is intermeshed and dependent on the well being of others (2001: 142). Thompson also identifies institutional benefits since '[i]ndividuals who conceive of themselves as participants in a generational continuum will be more inclined to demand or accept political means for achieving common goods' (2001: 143). While acknowledging the utopianism of planetary citizenship, she nonetheless views it as the inevitable 'evolutionary development' demanded by our new intergenerational and interspecies environmental obligations. A planetary citizen would thus become more willing to take responsibility for the environmental quality his own and subsequent generations experience. This conception of citizenship extends beyond individual human rights to require that individuals act responsibly both in their own interest and with regard to the responsibilities they share with their fellow citizens (2001: 145). It is in its conflation of self-interest with responsible behaviour that this conception of planetary citizenship draws it particular strength. Indeed, 'since the basic concern of everyone is the achievement of a good', the conflicts generated between different conceptions of rights and justice 'are more likely to be resolved than are conflicts premised on the primacy of autonomous individuals or communities' (2001: 145).

Thompson, however, does not focus on process. Since this chapter argues that process is integral to the achievement of environmental equality, planetary citizenship can thus be enhanced by the procedural considerations of an eco-democratic model.

Ecological democracy

We could merge the planetary citizenship cosmopolitan model with Dryzek's deliberative ecological democracy – a model that focuses directly on process (1987, 1997, 1999). We should keep in mind that Held recommended deliberative economic and political assemblies as one of cosmopolitan democracy's key processes and institutions. This assumes that inclusive, deliberative processes are more likely to generate sustainable and equitable environmental outcomes. Dryzek (1999: 266) defends this link by claiming that 'democratic equality that extends across the perpetrators and victims of environmental risks makes displacement less likely and so promotes ecological rationality'. Deliberative and participative decision-making processes, institutional designs and normative bases are thus considered more socially and environmentally 'friendly'. This is because deliberation's inclusive practices are more likely to acknowledge the many 'others' that a territorially and temporally bounded democracy can exclude – such as the three categories of 'others' we have already identified. In this way, rights, principles and interests are reviewed in light of their impact on both the integrity of the social and physical environment as well on the integrity of democratic practice. The administrative and political tendency to disaggregate, externalise and displace environmental risks is thus overcome. Dryzek would also like to strengthen Held's cosmopolitan democracy – a workable but 'benign proposal' – by injecting a stronger role for 'transnational civil society in this global democratic project' (1999: 268). The claim is that a 'globalisation from below' can counter the market liberal 'globalisation from above' (1999: 268).

There are of course constraints in instituting deliberative practices into indifferent institutional cultures. Despite well designed deliberative forums, imbalances in resources, skills and experience still sees some exerting unequal influence over proceedings. Nor are community based deliberative forums always the best for dealing with complex, transboundary environmental problems that require more sophisticated coordination capacities. Nonetheless, as Plumwood (1993: 457) argues, '[a]n elite dominated polity which silences messages those in power do not wish to hear and pushes on regardless with elite-benefitting projects... [is] as unconcerned about damage to its surrounding natural world as it is to its social world'. Dryzek (1987, 1997) reinforces this sentiment by claiming that the successful resolution of environmental degradation requires that decision-making systems be sensitive to feedback signals in order to ensure quick and effective remedial action. When exploration of policy solutions takes place in a collaborative setting it is likely that at the very least 'any particular interests that are raised must survive the test of discursive scrutiny' (Dryzek 1994: 194). The strength of an ecological democracy so conceived is its cognisance of the limitations of all kinds of boundaries and its firm underpinning in deliberative process. This could make it harder to ignore the displacement across boundaries of both social and environmental risk. As Low and Gleeson (1998: 119) aptly point out, NIMBY – not in my backyard – could be replaced by NIAEE – not in anyone else's either – as well as NOPE – not on planet earth.

Conclusion

Globalisation makes environmental justice more pressing. Environmental justice seeks a more equal distribution of the benefits and burdens of environmental goods across a broader range of relevant communities – present, future and non-human. It would seek a better future for both the Delawares and the Nanuians, including their non-human co-inhabitants. The achievement of environmental equality depends on process as well as outcome. Cosmopolitan institutions under-pinned by deliberative process and broader notions of citizenship, including plan-etary citizenship, go some way towards accommodating a notion and practice of justice that respects our three categories of interested communities and thus responds more adequately to the relevant equality claims. While still considerably utopian and ideal, these models raise a useful range of concepts and stimulate an important discourse.

Notions of equality nonetheless remain easier to apply to present and future humans than to non-human nature and nature as a whole. Notions of equality and fairness, after all, are largely anthropomorphic when applied to nature. Concepts of relational selves and planetary citizenship, which attempt to extend obligations, however imperfectly, beyond humanity to ecology are thus useful. Paradoxically, the achievement of environmental equality can also come at a high ecological cost. This is because the more equitable distribution of environmental burdens and benefits among humans might place additional pressure on fragile ecological systems and the flourishing of other life forms (Low and Gleeson 1998: 183). In the end, however, a commitment to reducing the current inequality of environmental risk might be a commitment to the protection of everyone's (and 'everything's') future equally. In ensuring the Delawares' and the Nanuians' futures we may well be preserving our own.

10 Legacy of danger

The *Kyoto Protocol* and future generations

Henry Shue

Introduction

Rapid climate change is capable, if not controlled soon, of causing massive harm not only to humans but to many other species of animals and plants (see J. T. Houghton *et al.* 2001; Mahlman 2001). Even slowing the now-accelerating rate of climate change will be expensive (McCarthy *et al.* 2001). This urgent effort must be paid for by a world already containing extreme inequalities in wealth and power (Shue 1999). But no inequality in power is greater than the inequality between those of us alive today and those who will come after us. This chapter explores the dangerous implications for inequalities among generations of an institutional innovation, the Clean Development Mechanism (CDM) under the *Kyoto Protocol*, that is supposed to deal with climate change in a manner that takes account of present inequalities among nations.

Least-cost-first and later generations

The negotiations about whether to take effective action concerning climate change are conducted by national governments; and measurement and reporting of sources, sinks, and net emissions are all categorized in national terms. Consequently it is difficult to overlook the fact that distributive justice has dimensions that are spatial: the international distributions of costs and of emissions. Many debates about the international division of the benefits and burdens have reflected pure conflicts of national interest, even when sometimes clothed in the rhetoric of fairness. International justice will be attained only if powerful national states aim explicitly at it; nothing supports any hope that the pure clash of national interest will somehow lead to international justice. There is no Invisible Normative Hand at the international level transmuting national interest into international justice. Nevertheless, even the nations that are too weak to defend themselves successfully against unfair treatment at least have official representatives at the negotiations, however little their voices are in fact heard.

The temporal dimension of justice is more easily forgotten, but nothing will affect more human beings than the intergenerational distributions of costs and of emissions. Indeed, future generations are usually the unrepresented, and therefore most vulnerable, parties of all, in spite of the fact that the often unnoticed other side of the coin in most of the decisions made about how much burden the current generation will handle is how much is consequently left for succeeding generations to bear. They are liable to the most unequal treatment of all: being completely ignored. For example, every decision about the relative emphasis to be placed on present mitigation efforts as opposed to future adaptation efforts is also a decision about the intergenerational allocation of effort and resources. Two connected tendencies deeply engrained in the current approaches to climate change by the national governments who do the negotiating especially strongly shift burdens forward toward our grandchildren, and their grandchildren.

The first tendency is the largely unquestioned assumption that it is only rational for governments always to pursue least-cost-first solutions to mitigation. While this may often be rational if no interests are given full weight except the interests of the current generation, it is far from evident that such solutions are rational in light of the interests of future generations or fair to them. This first danger to the future has two aspects. First, if the level of expenditures were somehow fixed independently, then the choice of a least-cost-first approach would mean that, for the level of expenditure set, the most would be accomplished. In reality, however, nothing keeps expenditures fixed, and consequently many parties will choose to accomplish the same mitigation for a lower expenditure rather than accomplishing more mitigation for the same expenditure. The result of this employment of the tactic of least-cost-first is not that more is accomplished to slow climate change but only that less is spent now. The appeal of this to electorates, and thereby to governments, is obvious, but it effectively transfers costs forward in time to those who succeed us. This forward transfer would fail to occur only if some costs that we chose not to pay now would 'evaporate' if they were deferred long enough.

Now deferred costs can disappear in one sense, namely one discovers later that some task that one earlier believed needed to be performed turns out, on the basis of better knowledge, not to have been necessary after all. If one had acted sooner, one would have done something that did not need to be done, as would later have been realized. Thus, one's own generation would have borne some costs itself, but would not have saved future generations any costs because the future generation would have known better than to have done what one did and so would not have borne these costs in any case.

This, however, is not a reason generally to follow the principle of least-cost-first. It is, most simply, a reason to try to get things right and not implement mistaken measures. Of course, if one is going to follow a mistaken policy, it is better to make a cheap mistake than to make an expensive mistake: if your only options are two dumb policies, choose the cheaper one. But obviously the main thing is not to make mistakes, any more often than necessary. The point is not to be cheap, it is to be smart. If the science is actually inadequate to the point that we do not know which measures are likely effectively to mitigate climate change, then we should invest in more research, not in dubious mitigation measures. The principle of choice is smart first – if possible, smart always – and it is not least-cost first.

The second aspect of this first dangerous tendency is that least-cost-first can mean higher-cost-later, unless technological advances that reduce the costs of the currently more expensive tasks at least keep pace with the passage of time. That is, it is not merely that future generations will have to pay to perform the tasks that this generation does not pay to perform, but that the tasks that they are left to pay for are likely to be the more expensive, in real terms, among the total set of tasks that need to be done. A policy of least-cost-first is likely to be a policy of 'cherry-picking', that is, grabbing the big juicy options – the ones, to switch metaphors, with the biggest bang for a buck – and leaving the scrawnier options, in which a larger investment brings a smaller pay-off, for later generations. This is not necessarily the case, however, and we should remember that mitigation tasks are, after all, not as static as cherries.

If one defers options that are more expensive now but will become less expensive later because of improvements in the technology required for the task, both the present generation and the future generation may be better off. The future generation is, then, better off because we will have meanwhile invested our resources on other tasks for which our technology was already good, and so accomplished more than we could have with an inferior, soon-to-be-supplanted technology, and they can then employ their superior replacement technology that has, by hypothesis, emerged in the interim and accomplish the deferred tasks more cheaply, in real terms, than we could have. We avoided wasting money by using inferior technology that would shortly be replaced.

As on the previous point, however, the sensible principle of choice does not actually turn out to be least-cost-first. This time it is something more like most mature – most productive – technology first. And while spontaneous technological advances might occur in time to contain costs for future generations, simply to assume net technological progress would be a largely groundless gamble for which future generations will be the ones to pay if it turns out badly. Therefore, if one judges that no mitigation technologies are mature, one ought not simply to do nothing and leave all problems to future generations, but instead to invest whatever is one's fair share of contribution (which I have here said nothing to specify) to solving the overall problem in the creation of the better technologies needed. When our generation cannot effectively mitigate because our technology is inferior, it can invest in better mitigating technology for future generations. Principles of justice among generations do not tell us whether to mitigate using the technology we have or to invest in research on better technology – that is a technological and scientific judgment, not an ethical judgment. Good research may well be preferable to ineffective action. Principles of justice only tell us not merely to do whatever costs us ourselves least irrespective of the consequences of such a policy for others who are affected, including future generations who may be affected profoundly.

So far I have merely sketched one obvious point, with two aspects. The approach to the mitigation of climate change favoured by governments tends to assume uncritically that the principle of choice should always be the least-cost option first. The least-cost-first approach does not necessitate, but encourages, two readings that are dangerous for future generations: first, spending less now rather than doing more (and better) now for the same cost, and, second, 'cherry-picking'. Each of these dangers is a distortion of a single sensible caution: don't just 'do something' if that means merely thrashing around in expensive and ineffectual ways – be smart and try to determine whether it is better for everyone affected, including future people, if you invest in creating a better technology that they can employ rather than using the technology at hand.

Intergenerational fairness and innovative technology

A deeper point about the politics of technology lurks beneath the surface here. The basic decisions concerning climate change are choices about energy technology. We face climate change because, like the cavemen, we still generate a great deal of our energy by setting fire to lumps of coal and – slightly more sophisticated but less of an improvement than one might think – igniting gasoline in the combustion engines of our SUVs. Like the cavemen, we burn fossil fuel, spewing carbon sequestered beneath the earth for millennia into the atmosphere as carbon dioxide. Choices about which nations are to bear the current costs of technological transitions obviously implicate international fairness; but choices about the rate of technological innovation deeply affect intergenerational fairness in a less obvious way, which we can now explore.

A second tendency ingrained in current approaches to climate change, then, is not to abandon fossil-fuel technologies until their continued retention becomes too expensive for the then-current generation and meanwhile to avoid investing very much in research or development of alternative energy technologies, investments that would hasten the day when alternative technologies become competitive with fossil fuel. Most obviously, this favours, within the current generation, those who own, transport, process, and distribute fossil fuels, and those whose existing capital stock burns these fuels, such as the electricity generators that burn coal. Yet this reliance on the existing atmosphere-distorting technology also strongly favors the current generation more generally, compared to policies on which we would bear the costs of developing alternative energy. The issue of fairness is whether this favoritism toward ourselves is unreasonably strong. This political commitment to consume fossil fuels until they become so scarce that their prices rise significantly – a day that is at least decades, if not at least a century away – and the first tendency to select lowest-cost-first solutions are related; the first supports the second – it is correctly believed to be cheaper to continue to spread into the less-developed states the current form of industrialization that runs on fossil-fuel than to create and develop alternative energy sources. But many other factors, including immensely powerful, entrenched political and economic interests and lack of imagination, also underwrite retention of the familiar fossil-fuel technology that is overwhelmingly the most important contributor to climate change. The primary issue of intergenerational fairness here is not, however, merely the first one already sketched of deferring costs so that they fall upon generations later than one's own, although that remains an issue too. I want now to try to uncover a deeper issue.

The date of technological transition

Sooner or later human societies will make a transition from a reliance dominantly upon fossil-fuel-driven technologies to reliance on one or more alternative energy technologies. The fundamental questions are: at what point in history should this transition be made (substantive intergenerational fairness)? and how should this date be determined (procedural intergenerational fairness)?

From this point on I shall refer to 'the date of the technological transition'. By 'the date of the technological transition' I mean the year in which the burning of fossil fuels ceases to add greenhouse gas to the earth's total atmospheric concentration of greenhouse gases. In theory, this could be the year in which effective technology for carbon sequestration became so widely used that, although vast quantities of fossil fuel continued to be burned just as it is now, the carbon dioxide produced did not escape into the atmosphere. One cannot rule out the possibility of effective technology for carbon sequestration, although to my knowledge there are no particularly promising developments in this direction. Vegetative sinks are certainly not the answer. So, leaving aside the bare possibility of sequestration technology, which would enable continued fossil-fuel burning to avoid its current damaging expansion of the atmospheric concentration of gases, the date of technological transition refers to the year in which the quantity of fossil fuel burned drops below the level at which the planet can re-cycle the resulting carbon dioxide without any further increase in the concentration of carbon dioxide in the atmosphere. The date of technological transition is the year in which we stop enhancing the greenhouse effect by adding greenhouse gas to the atmospheric total from the burning of fossil fuel.[1]

Next we need to remind ourselves about two scientific phenomena involved in climate change that have, believe it or not, features that are directly relevant to the issue of intergenerational justice. First, once molecules of carbon dioxide reach the upper atmosphere they remain for an average of approximately a century – carbon dioxide is a very long-lived gas. This means that the date at which humans stop adding to the atmospheric concentration is by no means the date at which the atmospheric concentration significantly declines, if indeed it declines at all. If we simply reduce our annual production of carbon dioxide to a quantity that does not add to the atmospheric concentration, but no less than that – what we might call an equilibrium production – the atmospheric concentration might of course stay the same indefinitely. If annual total human emissions dropped significantly below an equilibrium level, then the atmospheric concentration would eventually decline. But the point is that no matter how low the annual human production of carbon dioxide, the atmospheric concentration can at best decline only very slowly, because the carbon dioxide already in the upper atmosphere degenerates only very slowly. In this sense the atmospheric concentration has great inertia against downward movement – it can decline only over decades because individual molecules disappear, on average, only over a century. Upward, of course, is a different story: the accumulation can rise as fast as we spew more molecules into it. We are adding carbon dioxide far, far faster than it degenerates. The atmospheric concentration is now rising rapidly – and more rapidly every year than the year before: the increase is accelerating.

Second, obviously the atmospheric concentration can stabilize at any of quite a few different absolute amounts. At the beginning of the Industrial Revolution the absolute amount of greenhouse gas was roughly the same as it had been for centuries. With the currently accelerating annual increases in emissions we are now only a couple of decades away from a doubling of the pre-Industrial-Revolution atmospheric concentration. And until political action is taken to see to it that annual emissions are held to an equilibrium amount, that is, an annual amount such that the total accumulated in the atmosphere ceases to grow, as it now grows every year, the atmospheric concentration will increase indefinitely – with nothing to stop it from re-doubling. The pre-industrial concentration of carbon in the atmosphere, which had been the same for millennia, was 280 ppm; if we burn all currently known reserves of fossil fuel – all the coal, oil, and gas – thereby injecting into our atmosphere all the carbon now harmlessly buried in our earth, the atmospheric concentration is expected to be between 1,100 and 1,200 ppm – slightly more than two doublings of the pre-industrial level. It matters much less how rapidly we burn it than how much of it we burn all together (Kasting 1998). This is because, once the carbon dioxide is sent into the atmosphere, it stays such a long time.

The arithmetic here is exactly like the arithmetic of national population size. If a nation's population has been expanding, it will of course not become a stable size until the fertility rate drops to the replacement rate. The longer the fertility rate remains higher than the replacement rate, the larger the total population size at which the population will stabilize. In exactly the same way, the longer the annual total emissions exceed the equilibrium amount, the larger the total accumulation at which the atmospheric concentration will stabilize, if it ever does. To return to the notion of the date of the technological transition, then, the later the date of the technological transition, the larger the atmospheric total of greenhouse gas at which stabilization will occur. This is, not advanced atmospheric chemistry, but simple arithmetic: for every year that the total continues to grow, the larger the total will be when it stops growing. This is exactly like world population: the longer it continues to increase, the larger it is when it stops growing and stabilizes. This much is simple.

What is far from simple, of course, is the relation between the total atmospheric concentration of greenhouse gases and the extent, and types, of climate change. Climate involves many poorly understood feedbacks, positive and negative; and we know very little about the range within which changes tend to be incremental and where abrupt switches and reversals occur, although we do know from studies of Greenland ice cores reflecting the Younger Dryas, 10,000 years ago, that extremely abrupt switches have in fact occurred (Alley 2000). Further, climate is determined in part by factors totally independent of atmospheric chemistry, including the basic geometry of the solar system, with its cycles within cycles within cycles. Nevertheless, while there are many factors to be equal, we do have fairly good grounds for believing that, other things being equal, the higher the atmospheric concentration of greenhouse gases, the more severe climate change is likely to be. At the very least, the higher the atmospheric concentration of greenhouse gases, the farther we will have rushed, without a map, into planetary *terra incognita*. Consequently, fully acknowledging how little we really know, it still appears that the safest generalization, until we know much more, is this: the later the date of technological transition, the more dangerous the world we will have made and bequeathed to future generations. The later the date, the greater the danger.

I believe that a description of our actions regarding future generations only this rich in scientific detail, even though it is still quite superficial, transforms our understanding of the nature of the normative choices we face. It is still true, as we noticed in the beginning, that we face an issue recognizable as a fairly standard question of intergenerational distributive justice, namely does the amount of effort and money that we are investing in either the direct mitigation of climate change, or in research on better technology for future more effective mitigation, represent our generation's fair share? I have of course said nothing here to answer that question, but it is at least a relatively familiar type of question. I will not devote space to that question, because I think the deeper issues about the date of technological transition are more basic and more significant.

A legacy of risk of harm

If we adopt policies that delay the date of technological transition, then, as far as we know, we create a more dangerous world for our grandchildren and subsequent generations. We subject them to risks of unknowable probability but of enormous possible magnitude, including radical change in the very conditions of life, human and non-human, on this planet. It is vital not to make the mistaken assumption that if the size of a risk is unknown, the risk must be small – as if it could be unknown only if it were too small to see. If someone told you that there was an animal behind a closed door but that the species of the animal was not known, would you be wise to assume it was a small animal?

The imposition of such risks – of unknown (not necessarily small) probability and large magnitude – seems to me to be an inexcusable wrong. I assume that it is wrong to harm other persons without adequate reason, such as the harm's being unavoidable in self-defense and, even at that, not radically disproportional.[2] This 'no-harm' principle is of course not undeniable without contradiction or certain in any other sense. I simply take it to be an extremely compelling principle and one found in anything clearly recognizable as an ethical code. And I take it to be less uncontroversial, although equally correct, to say that it is wrong to impose a risk of harm on other persons without adequate reason. It is not as wrong to impose a risk of a harm, as it is to inflict the same harm, but it is still wrong. And if the harm would be serious, the imposition of the risk is seriously wrong, even if not as seriously wrong as the infliction of the harm itself would be.

To choose policies under which climate change will probably be more severe than it will be under other feasible policies is to choose to risk additional human deaths and other disasters, not to mention additional extinctions of species, damage to coral reefs, and many other kinds of destruction of the natural world. Perhaps this would turn out in the end to be, so to speak, all risk and no harm – that is, perhaps not a single one of the harms risked will actually occur. Nevertheless, if the best information we have suggests that simply continuing to burn more and more fossil fuel will increase the maximum accumulation of greenhouse gas in the atmosphere and that increasing the accumulation of greenhouse gas is likely to produce more severe climate change that will endanger human beings, then choosing to burn more fossil fuel than we must, by relying upon it longer than we must, is, as far as we know now, choosing to endanger future persons – choosing to impose risks upon them that could be avoided by other policies. It could, for all we know, somehow turn out well, but we would still have acted wrongly, just as I would have acted wrongly by playing Russian Roulette with your head even if luckily the revolver did not fire. And, of course, we would be responsible for the occurrence of any actual harms the risk of which we avoidably chose to impose.

Future generations are completely vulnerable to whatever risks of harm we impose by our choices. This is an extreme inequality in power. We are the only representatives or trustees they have – or can have. One perspective from which to see the stringency of our responsibility not to impose risks of serious harm is to notice how dramatically different the content of decisions about intergenerational responsibility has become in the case of climate change from its content as traditionally understood. For centuries the focus of intergenerational responsibility has been intergenerational justice in the literal sense of distributive justice, and specifically the issue of the just rate of savings. At what rate ought we to save on behalf of future generations, in light, especially, of the fact that they would probably be generally better-off than we are? Economic progress was built into the assumptions underlying the problem in a way that now strikes those aware of environmental limits as quite naive. One of the motivations for discounting the present value of future commodities was, in effect, to protect ourselves from saving too much for the people of the future who would enjoy all these commodities and thereby to avoid unfairly depriving ourselves of consumption that we are entitled to enjoy. So 30 years ago in *The Theory of Justice* John Rawls took the problem of intergenerational justice simply to be the problem of the correct savings rate (Rawls 1999a: 251–8). Twenty years ago, with the 'oil crisis' of the 1970s between him and Rawls, Brian Barry could plausibly suggest that the appropriate norm for conduct affecting future generations was an intergenerational analogue of the Lockean proviso: leave the next generation no worse off than you were – in particular, substitute for non-renewable resources that you unavoidably consume improved technology and greater knowledge that will enable future generations to live at least as well on a different, and smaller, resource base (Barry 1991). What the science of climate change now suggests is that it may actually be naive to think even that we can leave the next generation as well off as we are. My generation may have had it as good as it gets. The appropriate question appears to have become, not how can we leave them *no* worse-off, but how can we avoid leaving them *much* worse-off? How can we avoid undermining the stability of the very climate to which they, and all the other living things that they value and on many of which they depend, are adapted? How can we – to return to the earlier language – avoid imposing upon them risks of serious harm?

Thus part of the basis of the stringency of the responsibility to control the extent of the harms imposed is, in effect, how low the bar has now fallen. Not long ago it was taken for granted that we ought to leave future generations better-off – and of course this is still the dream most parents have for their own children. The only question then seemed to be: *how much* better-off ought we to leave future generations: what is the just rate of savings, the rate at which we ought to forgo consumption of our own, for their sake? Some then lowered their sights to: how can we avoid leaving the future worse-off? If one accepts that past emissions of greenhouse gases have already created an atmospheric commitment to some climate change, then, at least with regard to the climate, the question has now become: how can we avoid leaving the future *too very much* worse-off? Or, in other words, how can we avoid imposing on them the risk of serious harms? We have thus lowered our goal so much that it is difficult to believe that we should not go to considerable lengths to attain it.

The Kyoto Protocol

Much more could be – and probably needs to be – said entirely at the abstract normative level, but I want now to connect these abstract normative issues to fundamental political and institutional issues concerning one central element of the *Kyoto Protocol*. For better or for worse, the attempts to slow climate change have copied the largely successful effort to protect the ozone layer against CFCs, copying the form of the solution even where the problems are different. In the earlier case of ozone destruction, an initial vague, largely hortatory, and now mostly forgotten 1985 *Vienna Convention for the Protection of the Ozone Layer* was put into business by the specific requirements spelled out two years later in the 1987 *Montreal Protocol on Substances that Deplete the Ozone Layer*, and the protocol's amendments in 1990 and 1992. Like the *Vienna Convention*, the 1992 *Framework Convention on Climate Change (FCCC)* simply identifies the problem of anthropogenic climate change and enunciates some important principles to guide action concerning the problem. But the *FCCC* does not require any nation to do anything any more than the *Vienna Convention* did. The 1997 *Kyoto Protocol* is intended to do for the *FCCC* what the *Montreal Protocol* had done for the *Vienna Convention*, namely, spell out who should do what. The Third Conference of the Parties to the FCCC, meeting in Kyoto in 1997, had spent a long Friday night with the diplomatic clock stopped, teetering on the brink of collapse, but had tilted away from the cliff in a compromise constructed partly on the spot by sleep-deprived negotiators around a proposal that accordingly came to be known as 'the Kyoto Surprise' – more formally, the CDM (Grubb *et al.* 1999: 101–3).

Here are the first three sections of Article 12 of the *Kyoto Protocol*:

1   A clean development mechanism is hereby defined.
2   The purpose of the clean development mechanism shall be [A] to assist Parties not included in Annex I [poor states] in achieving sustainable development

and in contributing to the ultimate objective of the Convention [FCCC], and [B] to assist Parties included in Annex I [rich states] in achieving compliance with their quantified emission limitation and reduction commitments [emission caps] under Article 3.

3   Under the clean development mechanism:

   (a) Parties not included in Annex I will benefit from project activities resulting in certified emission reductions [CERs]; and

   (b) Parties included in Annex I may use the Certified emission reductions [CERs] accruing from such project activities to contribute to compliance with part of ['supplementarity'] their quantified emission limitation and reduction commitments [emission caps] under Article 3, as determined by the Conference of the Parties serving as the meeting of the Parties to this Protocol [COP/MOP].

(bracketed material added)

We need to take a couple of steps back in order to appreciate what is going on in *Kyoto*'s Article 12. While the treaty terminology is impenetrable, the situation is fairly simple. The achievement of the *Kyoto Protocol* was to have been the first imposition upon the wealthy industrial states of required reductions in greenhouse gases (GHGs): the quantified emission limitation and reduction commitments mentioned in sections 2 and 3 of Article 12, are actually imposed by Article 3. The *FCCC* of 1992 had an Annex I, which is essentially a list of the wealthiest states. Wealthy states (Annex I) have obligatory emissions reductions (or, in exceptional cases like Australia, which negotiated a cushy deal for itself, limits on increases); and poor states do not yet have any reductions or limits.[3] Poor states are for the time being allowed to increase GHG emissions without restriction. Emission caps were defined as annual emissions averaged over the five-year period 2008–12, which is known as the first commitment period.

The CDM is intended to be the first functioning bridge between poor states and rich states. The CDM was an imaginative solution to a problem that will never go away, namely, on what terms can rich and poor cooperate on slowing climate change? While I have some other profound disagreements with David Victor, I agree with him that the CDM is a crucial issue (Victor 2001). Victor asserts that 'the CDM is essential to the Kyoto treaty – and to any successor to Kyoto...'. (103). I would put the point more skeptically: that the CDM is one possible answer to a question that must have an answer. Either there will be some mechanism to differentiate between but coordinate rich and poor states, or there will be no effective international initiative to slow climate change.

In general, far more was flexible than fixed in the *Kyoto Protocol*, thanks to the insistence of the OECD states, led by the United States, on introducing market, and quasi-market, mechanisms wherever possible in accord with the general post-Cold-War *Zeitgeist* of globalization. The most important elements of the *Kyoto Protocol* are its multiple 'flexibility mechanisms' – the 'flex mechs' – the best known of which may be the proposed future international trading in assigned amounts of emissions (AAs) (popularly referred to as 'emissions permits'), but the most important of which may be CDM, the 'Kyoto Surprise', which David Victor, who is relentlessly critical of international emissions trading, rightly believes must survive in some form (Grubb *et al.* 1999). Flexibility is often a great virtue in complex institutions of the kind that any global GHG regime will certainly be, especially if it proceeds along the trajectory of complexity launched by *Kyoto*. Even if it be the case that, other things equal, flexibility is a good thing, other things are, of course, rarely in practice equal – and certainly not in the case of the CDM, as we shall now see.

The CDM may be the nearest possible analogue in a bilateral form to a market in tradable emission permits (strictly, AAs). But, of course, nothing bilateral can be a very close approximation to a market, because one of the greatest virtues of a true market is that the availability of multiple sellers and multiple buyers avoids one of the worst potential failings of a bilaterally negotiated transaction, namely that a great inequality of power between (single) buyer and (single) seller will allow the superior power to dictate the price to the inferior power. Thus, all-too-common references to CDM as 'bilateral trading' are seriously misleading, if not literally incoherent, since any bilateral exchange is a negotiation, not a market; and genuine trading, by contrast, needs to be reasonably multilateral on both sides. However, CDM is the only one of the 'flexibility mechanisms' for which the *Protocol* text of December 1997 provides an Executive Board (Article 12.4) that could in principle formulate and try to enforce rules of fairness, and minimum standards for the acceptability of CDM projects, that might prevent the exploitation of inequality in negotiations over the terms of projects, so the concern about CDM's being bilateral rather than multilateral need not be pressed until the procedures of the Executive Board have been set. It is possible that the CDM will follow a more multilateral, 'portfolio approach', if the Executive Board can become more than the mere clearinghouse for negotiated exchanges that the rich states mostly favor (Yamin 1998: 54–6). What Farhana Yamin called the 'gaps and ambiguities contained in the Protocol text, much of which is compromise language crafted to paper over what appeared in Kyoto to be unresolvable differences of views' still partly remain to be crystallized (54).

Now, let us tie together these concrete strands about CDM and the earlier abstract strands. Recall our conclusion about the date of the technological transition: the later the date, the greater the danger. The further into the future the date of technological transition, the more dangerous the world we will have made and bequeathed to future generations, because the larger the total sum of carbon we will have moved from beneath the surface of the planet, where it does no harm, into its atmosphere, where it does the great harm of fueling climate change. Many other things equal, the more carbon injected into the upper atmosphere, the worse climate change will be. Rather than maxi–min, this is mini–min: making the worst as bad as possible. What does this have to do with CDM?

CDM is a flexibility mechanism; what this really means is that it is a way for rich states to save money. They save money by avoiding any need to reduce their own emissions beyond the money-saving no-regrets reductions that are economically rational in any case. They avoid needing to reduce their own emissions by instead paying for CDM projects in the poorer states, which will be much cheaper per marginal unit of emission reduction, and subtracting the credits they receive for their CDM projects from any reductions they would otherwise be required to make at home. Why are emissions in the poorer states generally cheaper? Naturally, there are multiple factors, including generally lower standards of living, lower wages, lower health and safety standards, and so on. One of the biggest factors, however, is that the current technology in the richer states that would need to be replaced in order to reduce emissions – at high costs in replacement of capital stock before the end of its useful life – may well constitute a technological advance over current technology in the poor states, certainly in the poorest parts of the poor states. In purely economic terms, it is much more efficient to replicate current rich-state technology in the poor states than it is to replace current rich-state technology in the rich states with technology that would be superior measured in terms of its emissions. CDM has great short-term efficiency – it is, precisely, a least-cost solution.

Is this as clever as it may appear? We (this generation) are saving money. When one turns from efficiency narrowly construed to technology, the kicker appears. What is this familiar, easily transferable technology? It is the very fossil-fuel technology that is bringing us climate change: technology fueled by coal, oil, and gas. CDM may also be a way to guarantee that fossil-fuel technology will continue to be used until all the fossil fuel is gone – gone from beneath the earth, that is, with the carbon injected into the atmosphere, providing one pre-condition for the worst possible degree of climate change.

Yet, CDM is far from all bad. Actually, it is difficult to assess on balance even only in terms of international distribution. For it is not only achieving something good but bringing it about in a superior way. CDM will contribute to desperately needed economic development in poor states, although probably not the very poorest. It will achieve that development with relatively fewer emissions than would be required, if it could be achieved at all, without the technology transfers motivated by the CERs to be awarded to the rich states – strictly, firms located in the rich states – who finance the projects. In other words, at least some of the technology transfers demanded in the 1960s and 1970s as a matter of justice as part of the NIEO (New International Economic Order) but never granted out of any sense of justice on the part of rich states might now take place out of national, and individual firm, self-interest.

Some of this economic development in poor states might well be a good thing. And assuming only that each CDM project would enable something to be done with fewer emissions than it would otherwise have generated, if it could have been done at all, relative reductions in emissions would be generated. Indeed, it is precisely these relative reductions – reductions relative to a hypothetical development path minus the technology transfers brought about by CDM – for which the CERs are to be issued. This is the good news: (1) economic development – at least, more energy, which does not of course necessarily mean development, which, in turn, as we all know, does not necessarily mean a better life for poor people – and (2) fewer emissions per unit of development, compared to any development that hypothetically might have occurred without CDM. A worthwhile goal achieved by a better means.

But the bad news is also double. First, CDM will actually increase greenhouse gas emissions. Every development project it makes possible will produce emissions that would not have occurred if there had been no project. Now of course a CDM project may produce relatively fewer emissions than the hypothetical alternative project without CDM, which would hypothetically use inferior technology with higher emissions. But in fact in most cases the hypothetical project is simply a fantasy project, because without CDM there would be no project at all. If the poor state had been going to carry out the project on its own, in many cases it would by now already have carried it out. Development with CDM will be cleaner than it might have been, in some counterfactual world, but in this world the only real alternatives are the CDM project and no project. Many CDM projects will therefore lead to an absolute increase in emissions.

Few seriously pretend otherwise, although I think that calling the payments that rich states receive Certified 'Emission Reductions' is a slippery bit of public-relations terminology – it would have been far more straightforward to have named them 'Certified Smaller Emission Increases', which unfortunately does not have quite the same ring. But the relative reductions, compared to what might otherwise have happened in future, are absolute increases, compared to what is in fact happening now. One political justification is that this is the development half of the environment/development bargain. Stockholm 1972 was the UN Conference on the Environment; Rio 1992 was the UN Conference on the Environment and Development. There was no way that the poor states were going to be a part of any climate change initiative that did not provide for their further development. From a political bargaining stand-point, CDM is at least theoretically part of the pay-off for the poor states, although in fact the satisfaction of the rich states' determination to pursue least-cost-first strategies was, I think, even more important in the wee hours of the critical Friday night at Kyoto. CDM had – perhaps still has – some of the makings of a grand bargain of the kind that can keep diverse coalitions functioning. In any case, insofar as CDM projects actually contribute to a genuinely human development that improves the quality of the lives of the planet's poor, no sensible person is going to be against them. One might say that the absolute increase in emissions is in nearly the best possible cause, improving the lives of at least some of the poorest.

What is troubling is not the CDM projects themselves, at least not what could be the best of them. The worries arise at the other end, in the rich states whose firms would be financing the CDM projects. The reward for carrying out projects in the poor states – for doing more abroad – is doing less at home. This obviously is why the projects would lead to absolute increases in emissions. One could avoid the absolute global increases by requiring domestic reductions – reductions in the firm's home country (or elsewhere) – to balance out the additions in the poor state. But that, of course, would destroy the narrow economic rationale for CDM projects. If a firm would still have to achieve reductions at home equal to the increases produced abroad by the CDM project, it could just skip the CDM project entirely and simply bring about the required domestic reductions. Adding in the option of CDM (a) saves money, and satisfies least-cost-first (providing one is willing to play the game of counting relative reductions as if they were absolute reductions) and (b) promotes development assuming the CDM projects are well-chosen, perhaps under the watchful eye of a multilateral Executive Board with significant poor-state participation – all of which remains to be seen.

Nevertheless, the second element of bad news, and the central point of this chapter, is this: the CDM seems likely to contribute to significant delay in the date of technological transition. The ultimate motive behind the CDM is least-cost-first: spending as little as possible ourselves for any given reduction in emissions. Which will be cheaper for the current generation: spreading fossil-fuel-driven technologies to the ends of the earth or replacing them with a superior alternative technology not based on fossil fuel? There is every reason to think that the *status quo* is cheaper for us, at least until existing capital stock has operated for its normal expected life. The complete dynamics of the technological transition need fuller exploration, but, as far as I can see, the best that one could hope for with CDM would be the very gradual replacement of fossil-fuel-driven technology at the end of the expected life of the capital stock using it, but only after the installation of much more fossil-fuel-based capital stock across the poor states. If this is not the surest way to prolong the consumption of fossil fuel for the longest possible time, it comes close.

Whether CDM would contribute to international justice is, I think, not easy to judge. Much clearly depends on who exactly benefits in which respects from the projects. But insofar as they might constitute the diversion of investments from projects that would enhance the lives of the affluent, to projects that would improve the lives of the poor, there is something to be said for them from the standpoint of international justice. At present, however, there are no explicit requirements that CDM project benefit the poor people in the poor states. By contrast, insofar as CDM delays the date of technological transition – delays the date when human activity stops making climate change worse – it imposes an unknown but quite possibly rather great risk of harm of significant and potentially even unmanageable kinds upon future generations. By my lights the risk of harm to future generations seems considerably more clear and serious than do the possible benefits to our impoverished contemporaries, whom we are in any case quite free to assist in ways that do not entail worsening climate change. We certainly need not reduce international inequality by increasing intergenerational inequality. If we faced an unavoidable choice between the 'present poor' and the 'future poor', that might be a difficult or even tragic choice. But only the CDM is forcing that choice upon us, and the CDM is fundamentally about letting the rich states adopt policies toward climate change that are, for them now, least-cost. The real choice is between the present rich and the future poor, the most unequal pair of all.

Alternatives

Two intellectually simple but politically difficult – furiously rejected by the US government – stratagems are available to reduce the risks imposed on future generations: the 'positive list' and 'supplementarity'. The positive list would specify acceptable types of technology for CDM projects and could restrict projects to those employing alternative energy technologies (and could refuse to count sinks). A firm and definite supplementarity requirement, mentioned but not defined in Article 12.3, could restrict the use of CDM by requiring a specific percentage of an Annex I nation's efforts to be conducted domestically. Both these good ideas have been fought tooth-and-nail by the 'Umbrella Group', especially the governments of the United States, Australia and Canada, and they appear for now to be politically dead, to the misfortune of future generations.

Meanwhile, poor-state elites and rich-state firms are rushing to negotiate CDM deals, and the World Bank has a 'CDM-Assist' Program. CDM is by far the most popular flexibility mechanism. I have tried to show here why it may also be the most dangerous, for the most vulnerable.

Acknowledgement

Earlier versions of this chapter benefited from comments offered at Albion College, the Philosophy Department at the University of Chicago, Cornell Law School, the Department of International Relations at the Australian National University, and an annual convention of the American Political Science Association.

Notes

1 While this particular terminology and formulation is my own, I take the fundamental idea from Grubb 1998: 2. Grubb refers to a concern with technological transitions as 'dynamic efficiency' as distinguished from 'static efficiency' (economists' usual focus). He there draws upon Grubb *et al.* 1995.
2 I do not believe that one is permitted to do an unlimited amount of harm to innocent others even to save oneself, but I do not want to pursue this more basic issue here.
3 Basically, Annex I of the *FCCC* and Annex B of *Kyoto* are the same thing: a list of rich countries. While one might have expected *Kyoto* to employ its own terminology internally, that is, to refer to 'Annex B parties', its text usually – but, *of course*, not always – designates the rich as 'Annex I parties', as in the sections quoted earlier from Article 12.

References

Abbott, P. (2000) 'Essentialism', in C. Kramarae and D. Spender (eds) *Routledge International Encyclopedia of Women. Global Issues and Women's Knowledge*, Vol. 2, London: Routledge, 615–16.

Achterberg, W. (2001) 'Environmental Justice and Global Democracy', in B. Gleeson and N. Low (eds) *Governing for the Environment: Global Problems, Ethics and Democracy*, Houndmills: Palgrave.

Ackerman, B. (1980) *Social Justice and the Liberal State*, New Haven: Yale University Press.

Alesina, Alberto and Dollar, David (2000) 'Who Gives Foreign Aid to Whom and Why?', *Journal of Economic Growth*, 5: 33–64, http://papers.nber.org/papers/w6612

Alley, Richard B. (2000) *The Two-Mile Time Machine: Ice Cores, Abrupt Climate Change, and Our Future*, Princeton: Princeton University Press.

Almond, B. (1995) 'Rights and Justice in the Environment Debate', in D. Cooper and J. Palmer (eds) *Just Environments: Intergenerational, International and Interspecies Issues*, London: Routledge.

Amnesty International (2001) *Broken Bodies, Shattered Minds: Torture and Ill-treatment of Women*, London: Amnesty International Publications.

Archibugi, D. and Held, D. (eds) (1995) *Cosmopolitan Democracy: An Agenda for a New World Order*, Cambridge: Polity Press.

Arneson, Richard J. (1989) 'Equality and Equal Opportunity for Welfare', *Philosophical Studies*, 56: 77–93.

Arneson, Richard J. (1993) 'Equality', in Philip Pettit and Robert E. Goodin (eds) *A Companion to Contemporary Political Philosophy*, Oxford: Blackwell, 489–507.

Arneson, Richard J. (1999) 'What, if Anything, Renders All Humans Morally Equal?', in D. Jamieson (ed.) *Singer and His Critics*, Oxford: Blackwell, 103–28.

Association for Progressive Communication, http://www.apc.org

Atkinson, A. B. (1993) 'Participation Income', *Citizen's Income Research Group Bulletin*, 16, July: 7–10.

Australian Bureau of Statistics (2000) 'Household Use of Information Technology', Australia. Cat. No. 8146.0.

Australian Council of Social Service (ACOSS) (2001) *Breaching the Safety Net: The Harsh Impact of Social Security Penalties*, Sydney: ACOSS.

Australian Council of Social Service (ACOSS) (2002) 'ACOSS Urges Support for AWT Amendments', *Impact*, December, 3.

Baldwin, P. (1990) *The Politics of Social Solidarity, Class Bases of the European Welfare State, 1875–1975*, Cambridge: Cambridge University Press.

Barbalet, J. (1988) *Citizenship*, Milton Keynes: Open University Press.

Barber, B. (1995) *Jihad vs. McWorld*, New York: Random House.

Barry, Brian (1989) *Theories of Justice*, Hemel Hempstead: Harvester Wheatsheaf.

Barry, Brian (1991) 'The Ethics of Resource Depletion', in *Liberty and Justice: Essays in Political Theory*, Vol. 2, Oxford: Oxford University Press, 259–73.

Barry, Brian (1992) 'Equality', in Lawrence C. Becker and Charlotte B. Becker (eds) *Encylopedia of Ethics*, 1st edn, Vol. I, Chicago: St James Press, 322–9.

Barry, Brian and Matravers, Matt (1998) 'Justice, International', in *The Routledge Encyclopedia of Philosophy*, Vol. 5, London: Routledge, 153–7.

Bauer, P. T. (1981) *Equality, the Third World, and Economic Delusion*, Cambridge, MA: Harvard University Press.

Beck, U. (1992) *Risk Society: Towards a New Modernity*, London: Sage Publications.

Beitz, Charles R. (1998) 'International Relations, Philosophy of', in *The Routledge Encyclopedia of Philosophy*, Vol. 4, London: Routledge, 827–33.

Bentham, J. (1960) *The Principles of Morals and Legislation*, Oxford: Blackwell.

Berlin, Isaiah (1969) *Four Essays on Liberty*, Oxford: Clarendon Press.

Biemann, U. (1999) *Performing the Border*, Video. 42 minutes.

Bondi, L. (1994) 'Gentrification, Work and Gender Identity', in A. Kobayashi (ed.) *Women Work and Place*, Montreal: McGill-Queen's University Press, 182–200.

Bosanquet, Bernard (1923) *The Philosophical Theory of the State*, 4th edn, London: Macmillan.

Bosselmann, K. (2001) 'Human Rights and the Environment: Redefining Fundamental Principles', in B. Gleeson and N. Low (eds) *Governing for the Environment: Global Problems, Ethics and Democracy*, Houndmills: Palgrave.

Boutros-Ghali, Boutros (1996) *An Agenda for Democratization*, New York: United Nations.

Bradley, F. H. (1927) *Ethical Studies*, 2nd edn, Oxford: Clarendon Press.

Braithwaite, J. and Drahos, P. (2000) *Global Business Regulation*, Cambridge: Cambridge University Press.

Brecher, Jeremy and Costello, Tim (1998) *Global Village or Global Pillage: Economic Reconstruction from the Bottom Up*, 2nd edn, Cambridge, MA: South End Press.

Brown, Chris (1993) 'International Affairs', in Robert E. Goodin and Philip Pettit (eds) *A Companion to Contemporary Political Philosophy*, Oxford: Blackwell, 515–26.

Bryson, L. (1983) 'Women as Welfare Recipients: Women, Poverty and the State', in C. V. Baldock and B. Cass (eds) *Women, Social Welfare and the State in Australia*, Sydney: Allen and Unwin, 130–45.

Bullard, R. (1990) *Dumping in Dixie: Race, Class and Environmental Quality*, Boulder, CO: Westview Press.

Bullard, R. (ed.) (1993) *Confronting Environmental Racism: Voices from the Grassroots*, Boston: South End Press.

Bullard, R. (1997) 'Environmental Justice: Challenges at Home and Abroad', paper presented at the Environmental Justice: Global Ethics for the 21st century Conference, 1–3 October, Melbourne, Australia.

Callicott, J. Baird, (1982) 'Traditional American Indian and Western European Attitudes towards Nature: An Overview', *Environmental Ethics*, 4: 293–318.

Callicott, J. Baird, (1985) 'Intrinsic Value, Quantam Theory and Environmental Ethics', *Environmental Ethics*, 7: 257–75.

Calvert, Peter and Calvert, Susan (2001) *Politics and Society in the Third World*, 2nd edn, Harlow: Longman.

Campbell, Tom (2001) *Justice*, 2nd edn, London: Macmillan.

Cappo, D. and Cass, B. (1994) 'Reworking Citizenship and Social Protection: Australia in the 1990s', paper presented to the 26th World Congress of the International Council on Social Work, July 3–7, Tampere, Finland.

Cass, B. (1988) *Income Support for the Unemployed in Australia: Towards a More Active System*, Issues Paper No. 4, Social Security Review, Canberra: Department of Social Security.

Castles, F. G. (1985) *The Working Class and Welfare*, Sydney: Allen and Unwin.

Castles, F. G. (1996) 'Needs-based Strategies of Social Protection in Australia and New Zealand', in G. Esping-Andersen (ed.) *Welfare States in Transition, National Adaptations in Global Economies*, London: Sage Publications, 88–115.

Cerny, P. (2003) 'What Next for the State?', in E. Kofman and G. Youngs (eds) *Globalization: Theory and Practice*, 2nd edn, London: Continuum, 207–21.

Chang, K. A. and Ling, L. H. M. (2000) 'Globalization and its Intimate Other: Filipina Domestic Workers in Hong Kong', in M. H. Marchand and A. S. Runyan (eds) *Gender and Global Restructuring: Sightings, Sites and Resistances*, London: Routledge, 27–43.

Chen, Shaohua and Ravallion, Martin (2001) 'How Did the World's Poorest Fare in the 1990s?', *Review of Income and Wealth*, 47: 283–300.

Cohen, G. A. (1989) 'On the Currency of Egalitarian Justice', *Ethics*, 99: 906–44.

Cohen, G. A. (1993) 'Equality of What? On Welfare, Goods, and Capabilities', in Martha Nussbaum and Amartya Sen (eds) *The Quality of Life*, Oxford: Clarendon Press, 9–29.

Cohen, G. A. (1997) 'Where the Action Is: On the Site of Distributive Justice', *Philosophy and Public Affairs*, 26: 3–30.

Commonwealth of Australia (1994) *Working Nation: Policies and Programs*, Canberra: AGPS.

Cullity, Garrett, (1994) 'International Aid and the Scope of Kindness', *Ethics*, 105: 99–127.

Culpitt, Ian (1992) *Welfare and Citizenship; Beyond the Crisis of the Welfare State?*, London: Macmillan.

Curran, G. (1997) 'Contesting Consent: Contemporary Democracy and Ecological Crisis', *Policy, Organisation and Society*, No. 13, Summer: 149–66.

Cvekovich, A. and Kellner, D. (eds) (1997) *Articulating the Global and the Local*, Boulder, CO: Westview Press.

Diamond, Jared (1999) *Guns, Germs, and Steel: The Fates of Human Societies*, New York: Norton.

Dryzek, J. (1987) *Rational Ecology: Environment and Political Economy*, Oxford: Basil Blackwell.

Dryzek, J. (1994) 'Ecology and Discursive Democracy: Beyond Liberal Capitalism and the Administrative State', in M. O'Connor (ed.) *Is Capitalism Sustainable? Political Economy and the Politics of Ecology*, New York: Guilford Press.

Dryzek, J. (1997) *The Politics of the Earth: Environmental Discourses*, Oxford: Oxford University Press.

Dryzek, J. (1999) 'Global Ecological Democracy', in N. Low (ed.) *Global Ethics and Environment*, London: Routledge.

Dworkin, Ronald (1981a) 'What is Equality? Part 1: Equality of Welfare', *Philosophy and Public Affairs*, 10: 185–246.

Dworkin, Ronald (1981b) 'What is Equality? Part 2: Equality of Welfare', *Philosophy and Public Affairs*, 10: 283–345.

Dworkin, Ronald (2000) *Sovereign Virtue: The Theory and Practice of Equality*, Cambridge, MA: Harvard University Press.

Dziadul, C. (1993) 'Ready for Primetime', *Television Business International*, May: 52ff.

Eardley, T., Saunders, P. and Evans, C. (2000) *Community Attitudes Towards Unemployment, Activity Testing and Mutual Obligation*, SPRC Discussion Paper No. 107, Social Policy Research Centre, Sydney: University of New South Wales.

Elkins, S. (1989–90) 'The Politics of Mystical Ecology', *Telos*, 82, Winter: 52–70.

Enloe, C. (1990) *Bananas, Beaches and Bases: Making Feminist Sense of International Politics*, Berkeley, CA: University of California Press.

Esping-Andersen, G. (1990) *The Three Worlds of Welfare Capitalism*, Cambridge: Polity Press.

Esping-Andersen, G. (1996a) 'After the Golden Age? Welfare State Dilemmas in a Global Economy', in G. Esping-Andersen (ed.) *Welfare States in Transition, National Adaptations in Global Economies*, London: Sage Publications, 1–31.

Esping-Andersen, G. (1996b) 'Positive-sum Solutions in a World of Trade-offs?', in G. Esping-Andersen (ed.) *Welfare States in Transition, National Adaptations in Global Economies*, London: Sage Publications, 256–67.

Esping-Andersen, G. (ed.) (1996c) *Welfare States in Transition, National Adaptations in Global Economies*, London: Sage Publications.

Esping-Andersen, G. (1999) *Social Foundations of Postindustrial Economies*, Oxford: Oxford University Press.

FAO (United Nations Food and Agriculture Organization) (1999) *The State of Food Insecurity in the World 1999*, www.fao.org/news/1999/img/sofi99-e.pdf

Fincher, R. and Saunders, P. (eds) (2001) *Creating Unequal Futures*, Crows Nest, NSW: Allen and Unwin.

Finger, J. Michael and Schuler, Philip (1999) 'Implementation of Uruguay Round Commitments: The Development Challenge', World Bank Research Working Paper 2215, http://econ.worldbank.org/docs/941.pdf

Fletcher, G. P. (1996) *Basic Concepts of Legal Thought*, Oxford: Oxford University Press.

Fox, W. (1990) *Towards a Transpersonal Ecology: Developing New Foundations for Environmentalism*, London: Shambhala.

Friedman, Thomas (1999) *The Lexus and the Olive Tree*, London: Harper Collins.

Gewirth, A. (1978) *Reason and Morality*, Chicago: Chicago University Press.

Giddens, A. (1990) *The Consequences of Modernity*, Cambridge: Polity Press.

Giddens, A. (1998) *The Third Way: The Renewal of Social Democracy*, Cambridge: Polity Press.

Giddens, A. (2000) *The Third Way and its Critics*, Cambridge: Polity Press.

Ginn, J., Street, D. and Arber, S. (2001) *Women, Work and Pensions: International Issues and Prospects*, Buckingham: Open University Press.

Goddard, F. (1993) 'Gatt Real', *Television Business International*, November–December.

Goodin, R. (1992) *Green Political Theory*, Cambridge: Polity Press.

Goodin, R. E. (2001) 'Structures of Mutual Obligation', paper presented to Academy of the Social Sciences in Australia workshop on Mutual Obligation and Welfare States in Transition, 23–24 February, University of Sydney, Sydney.

Gould, Stephen Jay (1998) *Leonardo's Mountain of Clams and the Diet of Worms*, London: Jonathan Cape.

Green, T. H. (1907) *Prolegomena to Ethics*, 5th edn, Oxford: Clarendon Press.

Grubb, Michael (1998) 'Corrupting the Climate? Economic Theory and the Politics of Kyoto', Valedictory Lecture, London: Royal Institute of International Affairs, http://www.riia.org

Grubb, Michael, Chapuis, Thierry and Duong, Minh Ha (1995) 'The Economics of Changing Course: Implications of Adaptability and Inertia for Optimal Climate Policy', *Energy Policy*, 23: 417–32.

Grubb, Michael, with Christiaan Vrolijk and Duncan Brack (1999) *The Kyoto Protocol: A Guide and Assessment*, London: Royal Institute of International Affairs.

Hamilton, C. (1999) 'Justice, the Market and Climate Change', in N. Low (ed.) *Global Ethics and Environment*, London: Routledge.

Harcourt, W. (ed.) (1999) *Women@Internet*, London: Zed.

Harding, S. (1998) *Is Science Multicultural? Postcolonialisms, Feminisms, and Epistemologies*, Bloomington, IN: Indiana University Press.

Harris, P. (2000) 'Participation and the New Welfare', *Australian Journal of Social Issues*, 35(4): 279–300.

Harrison, Lawrence E. and Huntington, Samuel P. (eds) (2001) *Culture Matters: How Values Shape Human Progress*, New York: Basic Books.

Held, D. (1995a) 'Democracy and the International Order', in D. Archibugi and D. Held (eds) *Cosmopolitan Democracy: An Agenda for a New World Order*, Cambridge: Polity Press.

Held, D. (1995b) *Democracy and the Global Order*, Stanford: Stanford University Press.

Held, D. (1996) *Models of Democracy*, Cambridge: Polity Press.

Held, D., Anthony McGrew, David Goldblatt and Jonathan Perraton (eds) (1999) *Global Transformations: Politics, Economics and Culture*, Cambridge: Polity.

Hertel, Thomas W. and Martin, Will (1999) 'Would Developing Countries Gain from Inclusion of Manufactures in the WTO Negotiations?', www.gtap.agecon.purdue.edu/resources/download/42.pdf

Hettne, B. (ed.) (1995) *International Political Economy: Understanding Global Disorder*, London: Zed.

Hightower, Jim (1999) *The WTO and Globaloney*, Economic Reform Australia e-mail network, 26 December 1999.

Hirschmann, N. J. (2000) 'Equality', in C. Kramarae and D. Spender (eds) *Routledge International Encyclopedia of Women. Global Issues and Women's Knowledge*, Vol. 2, London: Routledge, 611–14.

Hohfeld, W. N. (1919) *Fundamental Legal Conceptions*, New Haven: Yale University Press.

hooks, b. (2000) *Feminist Theory: From Margin to Center*, 2nd edn, London: Pluto.

Houghton, J. T., Ding, Y., *et al.* (eds) (2001) *Climate Change 2001: The Scientific Basis*, Contribution of Working Group I to the Third Assessment Report of the Intergovernmental Panel on Climate Change, Cambridge: Cambridge University Press, http://www.ipcc.ch

Huber, E. and Stephens, J. D. (2001) *Development and Crisis of the Welfare State: Parties and Policies in Global Markets*, Chicago, IL: Chicago University Press.

Ignatieff Michael (2000) *The Rights Revolution*, CBC Massey Lecture Series, Toronto, Canada: House of Anansi Press.

ILO (International Labour Organisation) (2002) *A Future Without Child Labour*, www.ilo.org/public/english/standards/decl/publ/reports/report3.htm

International Telecommunication Union, World Summit on the Information Society, http://www.itu.int/wsis

Jamrozik, Adam (2001) *Social Policy in the Post-welfare State: Australians on the Threshold of the 21st Century*, French's Forest: Pearson Education.

Jamrozik, Adam and Nocella, Luisa (1998) *The Sociology of Social Problems: Theoretical Perspectives and Methods of Intervention*, Cambridge: Cambridge University Press.

Janoski, T. (1998) *Citizenship and Civil Society*, Cambridge: Cambridge University Press.

Kalisch, D. (1991) 'The Active Society', *Social Security Journal*, August: 3–9.

Kant, Immanuel [1795] (1957) *Perpetual Peace*, Edited with Introduction by Lewis White Beck, New York: Liberal Arts Press.

Kasting, James F. (1998) 'The Carbon Cycle, Climate, and the Long-Term Effects of Fossil Fuel Burning', *Consequences: The Nature & Implications of Environmental Change*, 4: 15–27, http://www.gcrio.org/CONSEQUENCES/vol4no1/carboncycle.html

Kerr, Duncan (2001) *Elect the Ambassador! Building Democracy in a Globalised World*, Annandale: Pluto Press.

Kofman, E. and Youngs, G. (eds) (2003) *Globalization: Theory and Practice*, 2nd edn, London: Continuum.

Korpi, W. (1983) *The Democratic Class Struggle*, London: Routledge and Kegan Paul.

Kymlica, W. (1989) *Contemporary Political Philosophy*, Oxford: Oxford University Press.

Lam, Ricky and Wantchekon, Leonard (1999) 'Dictatorships as a Political Dutch Disease', working paper, Economic Growth Center, Yale University, Center Discussion Paper No. 795, http://econpapers.hhs.se/paper/wopyalegr

Landes, David (1998) *The Wealth and Poverty of Nations: Why Some Are So Rich and Some So Poor*, New York: Norton.

Leake, J. and Hodge, A. (2002) 'So Much Talk to Save the World', *The Australian*, 26 August: 9.

LeGrand, J. (1982) *The Strategy of Equality: Redistribution and the Social Services*, London: Allen and Unwin.

Lødemel, I. (2001) 'Discussion: Workfare in the Welfare State', in I. Lødemel and H. Trickey (eds) *'An Offer You Can't Refuse': Workfare in International Perspective*, Bristol: The Policy Press, 295–344.

Low, N. and Gleeson, B. (1998) *Justice, Society and Nature: An Exploration of Political Ecology*, London: Routledge.

Luke, T. (1988) 'The Dreams of Deep Ecology', *Telos*, 76: 65–92.

McCarthy, James J., Canziani, Osvaldo F., *et al.* (eds) (2001) *Climate Change 2001: Impacts, Adaptation, and Vulnerability*, Contribution of Working Group II to the Third Assessment Report of the Intergovernmental Panel on Climate Change, Cambridge: Cambridge University Press, http://www.ipcc.ch

McDonald, M. (1947) 'Natural Rights', *Proceedings of the Aristotelian Society*, 47: 35–55.

MacIntyre, Alasdair (1985) *After Virtue: A Study in Moral Theory*, 2nd edn, London: Duckworth.

McKerlie, Dennis (1996) 'Equality', *Ethics*, 106: 274–96.

Mahlman, Jerry D. (2001) *The Timing of Climate Change Policies: The Long Time Scales of Human-Caused Climate Warming – Further Challenges for the Global Policy Process*, Arlington, Virginia: Pew Center on Global Climate Change, http://www.pewclimate.org

Marchand, M. H. and Runyan, A. S. (2000) *Gender and Global Restructuring: Sightings Sites and Resistances*, London: Routledge.

Marshall, T. H. (1963) 'Citizenship and Social Class', in T. H. Marshall (ed.) *Sociology at the Crossroads*, London: Heinemann, 67–127.

Marshall T. H. (1964) *Class: Citizenship and Social Class*, Chicago: University of Chicago Press.

Martin, J. P. (2000/1) 'What Works Among Active Labour Market Policies: Evidence from OECD Countries' Experiences', *OECD Economic Studies* 30: 79–113.

Mason, K. T. (2000) 'Environmental Health and Sustainability', in Redclift, M. (ed.) *Sustainability: Life Chances and Livelihoods*, London: Routledge.

Mathews, F. (1991) *The Ecological Self*, London: Routledge.

Mathews, F. (1995) 'Community and the Ecological Self', *Environmental Politics: Ecology and Democracy (Special Edition)*, 4, Winter: 66–100.

Mead, L. (ed.) (1997). *The New Paternalism: Supervisory Approaches to Poverty*, Washington, DC: Brookings Institute Press.

Mead, L. (2000) 'Welfare Reform and the Family: Lessons from America', in P. Saunders (ed.) *Reforming the Australian Welfare State*, Melbourne: Australian Institute of Family Studies.

Milanovic, Branko (2002) 'True World Income Distribution, 1988 and 1993: First Calculation Based on Household Surveys Alone', *The Economic Journal*, 112: 51–92, www.blackwellpublishers.co.uk/specialarticles/ecoj50673.pdf

Miller, D. (1993) *On Nationalism*, Oxford: Clarendon Press.

Miller, David (1999) 'Justice and Global Inequality', in Andrew Hurrell and Ngaire Woods (eds) *Inequality, Globalisation and World Politics*, Oxford: Oxford University Press.

Miller, David (2000) 'National Self-Determination and Global Justice', in *Citizenship and National Identity*, Cambridge: Polity Press.

Miller, David (2002) 'Two Ways to Think about Justice', *Politics, Philosophy, and Economics*, 1: 5–28.

Miller, David (2004) 'National Responsibility and International Justice', in Deen Chatterjee (ed.) *The Ethics of Assistance: Morality and the Distant Needy*, Cambridge: Cambridge University Press.

Mishra, R. (1999) *Globalization and the Welfare State*, Cheltenham: Edward Elgar.

Mitchell, D. (1991) *'Income Transfers in Ten Welfare States'*, Aldershot: Avebury.

Montgomery, B. (2002) 'Killer Cloud over Asia', *The Australian*, 16, August: 11.

Moses, J. and Sharples, I. (2000) 'Breaching – History, Trends and Issues', paper presented to 7th National Conference on Unemployment: Unemployment and Labour Market Policies, November, University of Western Sydney.

Murphy, Liam (1999) 'Institutions and the Demands of Justice', *Philosophy and Public Affairs*, 27: 251–91.

Murray, Charles (1984) *Losing Ground: American Social Policy 1950–1980*, New York: Basic Books.

Myles, J. (1989) *Old Age in the Welfare State: The Political Economy of Public Pensions*, rev. edn, Lawrence, KA: The University Press of Kansas.

Myles, J. and Quadagno, J. (1997) 'Recent Trends in Public Pension Reform: A Comparative View', in K. Banting and R. Boadway (eds) *Reform of Retirement Income Policy: Comparative and Canadian Perspectives*, Kingston, ON: School of Policy Studies, Queens University.

Nagel, Thomas (1979) 'Equality', in *Mortal Questions*, Cambridge: Cambridge University Press: 106–27.

Nagel, Thomas (1991) *Equality and Partiality*, New York: Oxford University Press.

Naples, N. A. and Desai, M. (eds) (2002) *Women's Activism and Globalization: Linking Local Struggles and Transnational Politics*, London: Routledge.

Negus, K. (1996) *Popular Music in Theory*, Cambridge: Polity Press.

Nielsen, Kai (1988a) 'World Government, Security, and Global Justice', in Steven Luper-Foy (ed.) *Problems of International Justice*, Boulder, CO: Westview.

Nielson, Kai (1988b) 'On Not Needing to Justify Equality', *International Studies in Philosophy*, 20: 55–77.

Nozick, Robert (1974) *Anarchy, State, and Utopia*, New York: Basic Books.

O'Connor, James (1973) *The Fiscal Crisis of the State*, London: St James Press.

OECD (1998a) *Open Markets Matter: The Benefits of Trade and Investment Liberalisation*, Paris: OECD.

OECD (1998b) *Income Distribution and Poverty in Selected OECD Countries*, Paris: OECD.

Offe, C. (1996) 'Democracy Against the Welfare State?', in C. Offe *Modernity and the State: East, West*, Cambridge, MA: The MIT Press.

O'Neill, Onora (1988) 'Ethical Reasoning and Ideological Pluralism', *Ethics*, 98: 705–22.

O'Neill, Onora (1992) 'International Justice: Distribution', in Lawrence C. Becker and Charlotte B. Becker (eds) *Encylopedia of Ethics*, 1st edn, Vol. 1, Chicago, IL: St James Press, 624–8.

Parekh, Bhikhu (2000) *Rethinking Multiculturalism*, London: Palgrave.

Parfit, Derek (1984) *Reasons and Persons*, Oxford: Clarendon Press.

Parfit, Derek (1991) 'Equality or Priority?', in *The Lindley Lecture*, Lawrence: University of Kansas.

Parfit, Derek (1996) 'Equality or Priority?', *Ratio*, 9: 202–21.

Parpart, J. L. (2002) 'Rethinking Participatory Empowerment, Gender and Development: The PRA Approach', in J. L. Parpart, S. M. Rai and K. Staudt (eds) *Rethinking Empowerment. Gender and Development in a Global/Local World*. London: Routledge, 166–81.

Parpart, J. L., Rai, S. M. and Staudt, K. (eds) (2002) 'Introduction', in *Rethinking Empowerment. Gender and Development in a Global/Local World*, London: Routledge, 3–21.

Pateman, C. (1980) 'Women and Consent', *Political Theory*, 8: 149–68.

Paterson, M. (2001) 'Principles of Justice in the Context of Global Climate Change', in U. Luterbacher and D. Sprinz (eds) *International Relations and Global Climate Change*, Cambridge: MIT Press.

Pearson, N. (2000) *Our Right to Take Responsibility*, Cairns: Noel Pearson and Associates.

Pearson, V. and Leung, B. K. P. (1995a) 'Introduction: Perspectives on Women's Issues in Hong Kong', in V. Pearson and B. K. P. Leung (eds) *Women in Hong Kong*, Hong Kong: Oxford University Press, 1–21.

Pearson, V. and Leung, B. K. P. (eds) (1995b) *Women in Hong Kong*, Hong Kong: Oxford University Press.

Peterson, V. S. (1992a) *Gendered States: (Re)Visions of International Relations Theory*, Boulder, CO: Lynne Rienner.

Peterson, V. S. (1992b) 'Transgressing Boundaries: Theories of Knowledge, Gender and International Relations', *Millennium: Journal of International Studies*, 21: 183–206.

Peterson, V. S. and Runyan, A. S. (1999) *Global Gender Issues*, 2nd edn, Boulder, CO: Westview Press.

Pettman, J. J. (1996) *Worlding Women: A Feminist International Politics*, London: Routledge.

Pierson, P. (1994) *Dismantling the Welfare State*, Cambridge: Cambridge University Press.

Pieterse, J. N. (1995) 'Globalisation as Hybridisation', in M. Featherstone, S. Lash and R. Robertson (eds) *Global Modernities*, London: Sage Publications.

Pietilä, H. (2002) *Engendering the Global Agenda: The Story of Women and the United Nations*, Geneva: UN Non-Governmental Liaison Service.

Plumwood, V. (1993) 'Globalisation, Democracy and Survival', in B. Jolly and I. Holland (eds) *Proceedings of the Ecopolitics VII Conference*, Brisbane: Griffith University.

Pogge, Thomas W. (1989) *Realizing Rawls*, Ithaca: Cornell University Press.

Pogge, Thomas W. (1994) 'An Egalitarian Law of Peoples', *Philosophy and Public Affairs*, 23: 195–224.

Pogge, Thomas W. (1998) 'A Global Resources Dividend', in David A. Crocker and Toby Linden (eds) *Ethics of Consumption: The Good Life, Justice, and Global Stewardship*, Lanham, MD: Rowman and Littlefield.

Pogge, Thomas W. (2000) 'On the Site of Distributive Justice: Reflections on Cohen and Murphy', *Philosophy and Public Affairs*, 29: 137–69.

Pogge, Thomas W. (2001a) 'Rawls on International Justice', *Philosophical Quarterly*, 51: 246–53.

Pogge, Thomas W. (2001b) 'Achieving Democracy', *Ethics and International Affairs*, 15: 77–91.

Pogge, Thomas W. (2002) *World Poverty and Human Rights*, Cambridge: Polity Press.

Pojman, L. (1995) *Ethical Theory*, Belmont, CA: Wadsworth.

Pusey, Michael (1991) *Economic Rationalism in Canberra: A Nation Building State Changes its Mind*, Cambridge: Cambridge University Press.

Rawls, John (1993) *Political Liberalism*, New York: Columbia University Press.

Rawls, John (1999a) *A Theory of Justice*, Cambridge, MA: Harvard University Press [1971].

Rawls, John (1999b) *The Law of Peoples*, Cambridge, MA: Harvard University Press.

Raymond, J. (1987) *Bringing Up Children Alone: Policies for Sole Parents*, Issues Paper No. 3, Social Security Review, Canberra: Department of Social Security.

Raz, Joseph (1986) 'Equality', in *The Morality of Freedom*, Oxford: Clarendon Press, 217–44.

Reddy, Sanjay, and Pogge, Thomas W. (2002) 'How *Not* to Count the Poor', unpublished working paper, www.socialanalysis.org

Reference Group on Welfare Reform (2000a) *Participation Support for a More Equitable Society, The Interim Report of the Reference Group on Welfare Reform*, March.

Reference Group on Welfare Reform (2000b) *Participation Support for a More Equitable Society, Final Report of the Reference Group on Welfare Reform*, July.

Ritzer, G. (1996) *The McDonaldization of Society*, Thousand Oaks, CA: Pine Forge Press.

Roberts, J. M. (1999) *The Penguin History of the World*, London: Penguin.

Rodrik, D. (1997) 'Sense and Nonsense in the Globalisation Debate', *Foreign Policy*, 107: 19–37.

Rome Declaration on World Food Security (1996) www.fao.org/wfs

Runyan, A. S. (2003) 'The Places of Women in Trading Places Revisited. Gendered Global/Regional Regimes and Inter-Nationalized Feminist Resistance', in E. Kofman and G. Youngs (eds) *Globalization: Theory and Practice*, 2nd edn, London: Continuum, 139–56.

Sassen, S. (1996) *Losing Control? Sovereignty in an Age of Globalization*, New York: Columbia University Press.

Saunders, P. (1994) *Welfare and Inequality*, Cambridge: Cambridge University Press.

Saunders, P. (ed.) (2000) *Reforming the Australian Welfare State*, Melbourne: Australian Institute of Family Studies.

Scanlon, T. M. (1975) 'Preference and Urgency', *Journal of Philosophy*, 72: 655–69.

Scanlon, T. M. (1986) 'Equality of Resources and Equality of Welfare: A Forced Marriage?', *Ethics*, 97: 111–18.

Scanlon, T. M. (1996) 'The Diversity of Objections to Inequality', *The Lindley Lecture*, Lawrence: University of Kansas.

Semmens, A. (2001) 'Maximising Justice for Environmental Refugees: a Transnational Institution on Behalf of the Deterritorialised', in B. Gleeson and N. Low (eds) *Governing for the Environment: Global Problems, Ethics and Democracy*, Houndmills: Palgrave.

Sen, Amartya (1980) 'Equality of What?', in *Tanner Lectures on Human Values*, Vol. I: 195–220.

Sen, Amartya (1992) *Inequality Reexamined*, Cambridge, MA: Harvard University Press.

Sen, Amartya (1999a) *Development as Freedom*, Oxford: Clarendon Press.

Sen, Amartya (1999b) 'Global Justice: Beyond International Equity', in Inge Kaul *et al.* (eds) *Global Public Goods: International Cooperation in the 21st Century*, New York: Oxford University Press.

Shaver, S. (1983) 'Sex and Money in the Welfare State', in C. V. Baldock and B. Cass (eds) *Women, Social Welfare and the State in Australia*, Sydney: Allen and Unwin, 146–65.

Shaver, S. (1991) ' "Considerations of mere logic": the Australian Age Pension and the Politics of Means Testing', in J. Myles and J. Quadagno (eds) *States, Labor Markets and the Future of Old Age Policy*, Philadelphia, PA: Temple University Press, 105–26.

Shaver, S. (1995) 'Women, Employment and Social Security', in A. Edwards and S. Magarey (eds) *Women in a Restructuring Australia*, Sydney: Allen and Unwin, 141–57.

Shaver, S. (1997) *Universality and Selectivity in Income Support, An Assessment of the Issues*, Aldershot: Ashgate.

Shimazu, Naoko (1998) *Japan, Race and Equality: The Racial Equality Proposal of 1919*, London: Routledge.

Shiva, V. (1999) 'Ecological Balance in an era of Globalisation', in N. Low (ed.) *Global Ethics and Environment*, London: Routledge.

Shue, H. (1992) 'The Unavoidability of Justice', in A. Hurrell and B. Kingsbury (eds) *The International Politics of the Environment*, Oxford: Clarendon Press.

Shue, H. (1996) *Basic Rights*, 2nd edn, Princeton, NJ: Princeton University Press.

Shue, H. (1999) 'Global Environment and International Inequality', *International Affairs*, 75: 531–45.

Shue, Henry (2003) 'Global Accountability: Transnational Duties toward Economic Rights', in Jean-Marc Coicaud and Michael Doyle (eds) *The Globalization of Human Rights*, Tokyo: United Nations University Press.

Siim, B. (2000) *Gender and Citizenship, Politics and Agency in France, Britain and Denmark*, Cambridge: Cambridge University Press.

Singer, Peter (1972a) *Animal Liberation: A New Ethics for our Treatment of Animals*, New York: Avon.

Singer, Peter (1972b) 'Famine, Affluence and Morality', *Philosophy and Public Affairs*, 1: 229–43.

Singer, Peter (1990) *Animal Liberation*, 2nd edn, New York: Random House.

Skocpol, T. (1992) *Protecting Mothers and Soldiers*, Cambridge, MA: Harvard University Press.

Sreberny, A. (1998) 'Feminist Internationalism: Imagining and Building Global Civil Society', in D. K. Thussu (ed.) *Electronic Empires: Global Media and Local Resistance*, London: Arnold, 208–22.

Stiglitz, Joseph (2002) *Globalisation and its Discontents*, London: Penguin.

Strange, S. (1997) 'The Erosion of the State', *Current History*, 96(613): 365–9.

Talbot, S. (1997) 'Globalisation and Diplomacy: A Practitioner's Perspective', *Foreign Policy*, 108: 69–83.

Tawney, R. H. (1964) *Equality*, London: Unwin Books (first published 1931).

Temkin, L. (2000) 'Equality, Priority, and the Levelling Down Objection', in M. Clayton and A. Williams (eds) *The Ideal of Equality*, Houndmills: Macmillan.

Thompson, J. (2001) 'Planetary Citizenship: the Definition and Defence of an Ideal', in B. Gleeson and N. Low (eds) *Governing for the Environment: Global Problems, Ethics and Democracy*, Houndmills: Palgrave.

Thucydides (1986) *The History of the Peloponnesian War*, Harmondsworth: Penguin.

Tickner, J. A. (1997) 'You Just Don't Understand: Troubled Engagements between Feminists and IR Theorists', *International Studies Quarterly*, 41(4): 611–32.

Titmuss, Richard M. (1968) *Commitment to Welfare*, London, Allen and Unwin.

Tokar, B. (1990) Eco-Apocalyptics. *New Internationalist*, August, 14–15.

Tomlinson, John (1997) 'Internationalism, Globalisation and Cultural Imperialism', in Kenneth Thompson (ed.) *Media and Cultural Regulation*, London: Sage Publications.

Tournabouni, L. (1995), 'European cinema is dying', *The Guardian*, March 2.

Trickey, H. (2001) 'Comparing Workfare Programmes – Features and Implications', in I. Lødemel and H. Trickey (eds) *'An Offer You Can't Refuse': Workfare in International Perspective*, Bristol: The Policy Press, 249–94.

Turner, B. (1992) 'Outline of a Theory of Citizenship', in C. Mouffe (ed.) *Dimensions of Radical Democracy: Pluralism, Citizenship and Community*, London: Verso, 33–62.

UDHR (Universal Declaration of Human Rights) (1992) in *Twenty-Four Human Rights Documents*, New York: Columbia University Center for the Study of Human Rights.

UNCTAD (United Nations Conference on Trade and Development) (1999) *Trade and Development Report 1999*, New York: UN Publications.

UNDP (United Nations Development Programme) (1995) *Human Development Report 1995*, New York: Oxford University Press.

UNDP (United Nations Development Programme) (1996) *Human Development Report 1996*, New York: Oxford University Press.

UNDP (United Nations Development Programme) (1997) *Human Development Report 1997*, New York: Oxford University Press.

UNDP (United Nations Development Programme) (1998) *Human Development Report 1998*, New York: Oxford University Press.

UNDP (United Nations Development Programme) (1999) *Human Development Report 1999*, New York: Oxford University Press.

UNDP (United Nations Development Programme) (2000) *Human Development Report 2000*, New York: Oxford University Press, www.undp.org/hdr2000/english/HDR2000.html

UNDP (United Nations Development Programme) (2001) *Human Development Report 2001*, New York: Oxford University Press, www.undp.org/hdr2001

UNDP (United Nations Development Programme) (2002) *Human Development Report 2002: Deepening Democracy in a Fragmented World*, New York: Oxford University Press.

UNICEF (United Nations Children's Fund) (2002) *The State of the World's Children 2002*, New York: UNICEF, www.unicef.org/sowc02/pdf/sowc2002-eng-full.pdf

United Nations Development Fund for Women (UNIFEM), http://www.unifem.org

USDA (United States Department of Agriculture) (1999) *U.S. Action Plan on Food Security*, www.fas.usda.gov/icd/summit/pressdoc.html

Vanstone, A. and Abbott. T. (2001) *Australians Working Together, Helping People to Move Forward*, Joint ministerial statement, May.

Victor, David G. (2001) *The Collapse of the Kyoto Protocol and the Struggle to Slow Global Warming*, Council on Foreign Relations Book, Princeton and Oxford: Princeton University Press.

Vlastos, G. (1962) 'Justice and Equality', in R. B. Brandt (ed.) *Social Justice*, Englewood Cliffs: Prentice Hall, 31–72.

Walby, S. (1997) *Gender Transformations*, London: Routledge.

Walzer, Michael (1980) 'The Moral Standing of States', *Philosophy and Public Affairs*, 9: 209–29.

Walzer, Michael (1983) *Spheres of Justice: A Defence of Pluralism and Equality*, Oxford: Martin Robertson.

Walzer, Michael (1985a) 'The Rights of Political Communities', in Charles R. Beitz *et al.* (eds) *International Ethics*, Princeton, NJ: Princeton University Press.

Walzer, Michael (1985b) 'The Moral Standing of States', in Charles R. Beitz *et al.* (eds) *International Ethics*, Princeton, NJ: Princeton University Press.

Wantchekon, Leonard (1999) 'Why do Resource Dependent Countries Have Authoritarian Governments?', working paper, Yale University, 12 December 1999, www.yale.edu/leitner/pdf/1999-11.pdf

Ward, Peter M. (ed.) (1989) *Corruption, Development and Inequality*, London: Routledge.

Weale, Albert (1998) 'Equality', in *The Routledge Encyclopedia of Philosophy*, Vol. 5, London: Routledge: 393–6.

Whitlam, E. G. (1985) *The Whitlam Government 1972–1975*, Ringwood: Viking Penguin.

WHO (World Health Organization) (2001) *The World Health Report 2001*, Geneva: WHO Publications, www.who.int/whr/2001

Wilensky, H. (1975) *The Welfare State and Equality*, Berkeley, CA: University of California Press.

Williams, Bernard (1962) 'The Idea of Equality', in Peter Laslett and W. G. Runciman (eds) *Philosophy, Politics and Society*, Oxford: Blackwell: 110–31; repr. in his *Problems of the Self*, Cambridge: Cambridge University Press, 1973.

Wolfensohn, James. (1999) 'The World Bank Group, News Release' (28 September) No. 2000/057/S, 1999, World Bank.

Wollstonecraft, M. (1985) (First published 1792) *Vindication of the Rights of Woman*, London: Penguin.

World Bank (1994) *Averting the Old Age Crisis*, Oxford: Oxford University Press.

World Bank (2001) *World Development Report 2000/2001*, New York: Oxford University Press, www.worldbank.org/poverty/wdrpoverty/report/index.htm

World Bank (2003) *World Development Report 2003*, New York: Oxford University Press.

Yamin, Farhana (1998) 'Operational and Institutional Challenges', in *Issues & Options: The Clean Development Mechanism*, New York: United Nations Development Program, 53–79.

Yeatman, A. (1999) 'Mutual Obligation: What Kind of Contract is This?', in S. Shaver and P. Saunders (eds) *Social Policy for the 21st Century: Justice and Responsibility*, Vol. 1. SPRC Reports and Proceedings No. 141, University of New South Wales, Sydney.

Youngs, G. (1996) 'Dangers of Discourse: The Case of Globalization', in E. Kofman and G. Youngs (eds) *Globalization: Theory and Practice*, 1st edn, London: Pinter, 58–71.

Youngs, G. (1999a) *International Relations in a Global Age: A Conceptual Challenge*, Cambridge: Polity Press.

Youngs, G. (1999b) 'Virtual Voices: Real Lives', in W. Harcourt (ed.) *Women@Internet*, London: Zed, 55–68.

Youngs, G. (2000a) 'Breaking Patriarchal Bonds: Demythologizing the Public/Private', in M. H. Marchand and A. S. Runyan (eds) (2000) *Gender and Global Restructuring: Sightings, Sites and Resistances*, London: Routledge, 44–58.

Youngs, G. (2000b) 'Embodied Political Economy or an Escape from Disembodied Knowledge', in G. Youngs (ed.) *Political Economy Power and the Body: Global Perspectives*, London: Macmillan, 11–30.

Youngs, G. (ed.) (2000c) *Political Economy Power and the Body: Global Perspectives*, London: Macmillan.

Youngs, G. (2002) 'Closing the Gaps: Women, Communications and Technology', *Development*, 45(4): 23–8.

Youngs, G. (2003) 'Private Pain/Public Peace: Women's Rights as Human Rights and Amnesty International's Report on Violence Against Women', *Signs: Journal of Women in Culture and Society*, 28(4): 1209–29.

Index

Abacha, Sani 67
Abbott, P. 118
accountability 90–1, 158
Achterberg, W. 159
'active society' concept 102
agency 122–3, 126, 128
aid programmes 65, 143–4
AIDS 83
Almond, B. 155, 158, 160
Amnesty International 119–20
animal rights 155
Aquinas, Thomas 34
Archibugi, D. 159
Aristotle and Aristotelianism 14, 34, 37, 41
Asian tigers 69
asylum seekers 152
Australia 4, 79–89 passim, 96, 99–111, 134, 151, 153, 173, 178
autonomy 34, 39–40, 43–4, 159

Bangladesh 120
Barbados 121
Barry, Brian 171
Beck, U. 148, 150–1
Beijing Conference on Women (1995) 119
Bentham, Jeremy 33–4, 37–8, 155
Blair, Tony 78, 111
Bondi, L. 117
Bosselmann, K. 160
Boutros-Ghali, Boutros 79
Brazil 56–7, 134
Britain see United Kingdom
'brute inequality' 9–10, 18–20
Buddha 37
Bullard, R. 150
Burkina Faso 82–3
Business Roundtable 79

Callicott, J. Baird 156
callousness 9, 18
Canada 85, 99–100, 140, 178
Canberra workshop (2001) 3
capabilities, equality of 41
capitalism 124, 138
Cappo, D. 103
carbon sequestration 168
Cass, B. 103
Castles, F.G. 100
CFCs 172
Chang, Kimberly 124–5
children, care of 104, 109
citizenship (including social citizenship) 4, 37, 77–8, 81, 86–91 passim, 95–8, 101–4, 107–12, 157; see also planetary citizenship
civil society 43
Clean Development Mechanism (CDM) 5, 164, 172–8
climate change 5, 146–54, 164–77
Clinton, Bill 111
Cohen, G. 6, 59–60
Confucius 37
consent, notions of 157–8
contextualism 57–62
Convention on the Elimination of All Forms of Discrimination Against Women (CEDAW) 119
corruption 13, 65–8
cosmopolitan equality 24–7, 32–3, 37–9, 43–6; see also democracy: cosmopolitan
coups d'etat 66–8
creativity 35
Culpitt, Ian 86
cultural diversity 142–4, 148
cultural impact of globalisation 132–7
'currency' of equality 28
Cyprus 120

date of technological transition 169–70, 174, 177
'decent' societies 61–2
deep ecology 155–6
democracy 3–6, 30, 37, 65, 81–2, 89–95, 148, 157–9; cosmopolitan 159–62; ecological 162–3; and environmental equality 154–63; *see also* social democracy
democratic deficit 91
deontic egalitarianism 30
descriptive equality 25–7, 31–5, 40–5; *see also* foundational descriptive equality
deserts 10, 39–40
difference principle 16, 60–3
digital divide 121
discrimination 33, 35, 50
Disraeli, Benjamin 81
distributive justice 3, 11–16, 26, 28, 39, 153–4, 164, 170–1
dominance in relationships 8–9, 17–18
double standards 62–6, 70
Dryzek, J. 162
Dutch disease 67
Dworkin, Ronald 40, 45

ecocentrism 155–6
ecological rights 160–3
economic justice 51–2, 56, 60–3
economic rationalism 77, 87
education 80–2
egalitarianism 13, 15, 19, 27–9, 36–46
egality 40
Egypt 120
elites 64–8
emissions trading 173–4
empowerment 126, 128
Enlightenment thought 116
environmentalism and globalisation 146–9
environmental justice 146, 150, 152–63
environmental risk 150–4, 157, 162–3
equal treatment 29–31
equal worth theory and Equal Worth Project 24–5, 31–9, 43–5
Esping-Andersen, G. 109
European Union (EU) 69
evaluative equality 27–33, 39–41, 44
externalities 157

feminism 4, 114–28; perspectives on globalisation 121–6
feminization of labour 123–4, 127
fossil fuels 167–8, 171, 175–7

foundational descriptive equality 27–8, 33–9, 42–5
Fox, W. 155
France 139–41
free-market ideology 89
Freud, Sigmund 93
Friedman, Tom 78–80, 85

gender empowerment measure (GEM) 120–1, 124
gender-related development index 120
gender relations 114–21, 126–7
General Agreement on Tariffs and Trade (GATT) 129
Gleeson, B. 160, 163
global cities 83–4
global economic order 51–6, 61–9
global environmental problems 158
globalisability 137–8
globalism 13–16, 19, 131
global restructuring 123–4
global warming 151; *see also* climate change
'golden straightjacket' metaphor 78–80, 85, 92
Gould, Stephen Jay 93
Greece 121
greenhouse gases 149, 153, 168–76

Hamilton, C. 149
Harris, Anna 84–5
Harris, P. 108
Hawke, R.J.L. 80, 100
health services 81
Held, D. 158–9, 162
Hightower, Jim 84–5
Hirschmann, N.J. 118
Hong Kong 117, 125
hooks, b. 127
Howard, John 80, 100, 103–4
Huber, E. 98–100
human development index (HDI) 82–3, 120
Human Development Report 55, 82–3, 120
human rights 23, 43, 45, 49, 119, 160
human worth 27–9, 34–8, 42–4

idealism 12, 14
Ignatieff, Michael 77
income distribution 1, 85, 87
India 138–40
indigenous peoples 104
Indonesia 141, 147
Industrial Revolution 169

information technology 83–4
institutional order 64–6
intergenerational equity 151, 154, 164–71, 177
International Monetary Fund (IMF) 129, 144
international resource and borrowing privileges 66–9
Internet access 83–4, 128
interspecies equity 154
intragenerational equity 153–4
intuitionism 58
Iran 133, 141

Jackson, Michael 133
Jamrozik, Adam 77, 87, 90
Japan 120
Johannesburg Earth Summit (2002) 149
Jurassic Park 141
justice *see* distributive justice; economic justice; environmental justice
justificatory properties 26–7
justified equality 30

Kant, Immanuel 34, 37
Keating, P.J. 80, 100
Kerala model 69
Kyoto Protocol 5, 151, 153, 164, 172–7

League of Nations 49
least-cost-first policy 165–8, 176–7
Leung, B.K.P. 117
levelling-down policies 8–10, 29, 39
liberalism 13, 15, 61–2, 77, 96, 99, 111, 156, 159–60; *see* also neo-liberalism
life expectancy 54–7
Lincoln, Abraham 89
Ling, Lily 124–5
Low, N. 160, 163

Madagascar 82
Madonna 133
Major, John 78
manufacturing industry 17–18
Mao Zedong 54
Marshall, T.H. 4, 90, 97–112 *passim*
Mathews, F. 156
Mauritius 82
Mead, Lawrence 104
means testing 101, 105, 108
Mexico 134
military power 52
military rule 67
Mill, John Stuart 34

Miller, David 58–9
Mishra, Ramesh 86
Mohammed 37
monism 59
monopoly 90
moral equality 7–10, 17, 32
'moral hazard' concept 86, 111
moral universalism 4, 49–52, 57–63, 70; and contextualism 57–9; and Rawls's conception 59–62
multiculturalism 4, 133–8
multinational corporations 148–9
Murphy, Liam 59–60
Muslim societies 138–9

national cultures 138–40
nation states 23, 43–6, 98, 112, 164
natural disasters 54–5
naturalism 34–6
neo-liberalism 77–82, 86–7, 104, 110
New International Economic Order 175
New Zealand 99–100, 107, 120
Nigeria 66–7
NIMBYism 163
Nocella, Luisa 90
non-governmental organisations 126
Norway 82, 107
Nussbaum, Martha 41

Obasanjo, Olusegun 67
O'Connor, James 85
Offe, C. 112
oil producing countries 66–7
opportunity, equality of 31, 40–2
Organisation for Economic Cooperation and Development (OECD) 79, 82, 85, 102
ownership rights 66
ozone depletion 172

Parfit, Derek 39
Parpart, Jane 126
participation 103, 107
Pateman, C. 157
paternalism 110–11
patriarchy 116–19, 124–7
Pearson, Noel 104
Pearson, V. 117
person-neutrality 32, 39
Pettman, Jan Jindy 125
Philippines, the 125
Pietilä, H. 119
planetary citizenship 160–3
Plumwood, V. 162

pluralisation of society 135
Poland 82
political communities 11–15, 37
political equality 7–9, 19
pollution 147–8
poverty 49, 63–70 *passim*, 90, 144, 147;
    extent of 53–5; role of global
    institutions in persistence of 66–9;
    trends in 55–6
power relations 9, 52, 115–16, 121–3,
    148, 160
prescriptive equality 29–32, 43–4
'priority' theory 39
private sphere 115–18, 122–3
privatisation 87, 90
public opinion 46
public sphere 115–18, 121–3
Pusey, Michael 77

Rawls, John 3, 7, 12–20, 41, 58–63, 171
redistribution of income and wealth
    97, 101
refugees, environmental 152
religion 134
resources, equality of 40
rights talk 77
'risk society' concept 148, 150
Rodrik, Dani 79
role models 126
Rousseau, Jean Jacques 110
Runyan, Anne Sisson 123–4
Russia 82, 134, 139
Rwanda 54

Saudi Arabia 139
self-awareness 35
self-determination 12–16
self-interest 43–4
Semmens, A. 152
Sen, Amartya 41
sexuality 138
Shiva, V. 148
Shue, H. 152–3
Sierra Leone 82
Singer, Peter 155
social constructionism 118
social democracy 91–4, 97–100
social equality 7–11, 17
social exclusion 105, 107
social policy 95, 102
social reality 121–2
sovereignty 12, 148, 152–3, 159
Sri Lanka 120
Stalin, Joseph 54

Stephens, J.D. 98–100
Strange, Susan 91
structural adjustment programmes 144
Sweden 82

Talbot, Strobe 94
Tawney, R.H. 23–5, 35
taxation 104
technological progress 83, 166–8
Thatcher, Margaret 77–8
Thompson, J. 160–2
Tickner, J.A. 115
Tobin Tax 65
trade liberalisation 79, 91
'trickle down' doctrine 91

Uganda 133
'Umbrella Group' 178
unemployment 99–100, 107
United Kingdom 85, 97, 100, 111, 144
United Nations (UN) 129–30;
    Development Program 82, 120;
    Development Report 1
United States 53, 60–1, 69, 84–5,
    99–100, 107, 111, 151–3, 173, 178;
    cultural hegemony of 137–41
Universal Declaration of Human Rights
    (UDHR) 49
Uruguay Round 69
utilitarianism 33, 38–41, 59, 155
utopianism 161, 163

'veil of ignorance' concept 16
Victor, David 173–4
violence against women 119, 127

Walzer, Michael 11, 14
Washington consensus 4–5, 143–4
welfare dependency 103–4, 110–11
welfare reform 95, 98–9, 102–11
welfare systems 4, 24, 45, 77–9, 85–8,
    94–101, 106–8, 112
well-being properties 26–32 *passim*, 39
western influence 133, 136, 138
Whitlam, Gough 88–9
Wolfensohn, James 79
Wollstonecraft, Mary 116
women's rights 119
'workfare' programmes 107
World Bank 54, 129, 144, 178
World Trade Organisation 79, 129

Yamin, Farhana 174
Yeatman, A. 110–11

For Product Safety Concerns and Information please contact our EU
representative GPSR@taylorandfrancis.com
Taylor & Francis Verlag GmbH, Kaufingerstraße 24, 80331 München, Germany